THE STRANGER INSIDE

One month into our marriage, my husband committed horrific, violent crimes. In that instant, the life I knew was destroyed and I vowed to myself that one day I would be whole again.

This is my story.

THE STRANGER INSIDE

SHANNON MORONEY

SIMON &
SCHUSTER

London · New York · Sydney · Toronto · New Delhi

A CBS COMPANY

First published in Canada as *Through the Glass* in 2011
by Doubleday Canada

First published in Great Britain by Simon & Schuster UK Ltd, 2012
A CBS COMPANY

1 3 5 7 9 10 8 6 4 2

Simon & Schuster UK Ltd
1st Floor
222 Gray's Inn Road
London WC1X 8HB

www.simonandschuster.co.uk

Simon & Schuster Australia, Sydney
Simon & Schuster India, New Delhi

A CIP catalogue record for this book is available from the British Library.

ISBN 978-1-47110-279-0

Excerpt from *The Peterborough Examiner*, reprinted on p.96,
courtesy of QMI Agency.

Printed and bound by CPI Group (UK) Ltd, Croydon, CR0 4YY

This book is dedicated to my extraordinary parents and to my Golden Circle of family and friends for their courage, love, compassion, and willingness to walk alongside me through this dark time.

I also dedicate this book to those who have experienced the devastating effects of violent crime, those who have perpetrated violence, and those working to bring all of us and our communities together by seeking justice that restores our fundamental human right to live in trust, safety, peace, and toward the fulfillment of our highest potential.

Several names and identifying details of people portrayed in this book have been changed or omitted.

In preparation to write this book, I organized years of newspaper clippings, court transcripts, psychiatric reports, cards and letters. When I found that I was missing documentation or was concerned that my memory blurred time, facts and emotions, I sought information from court transcripts, medical records, and by checking my recall of events with other witnesses. It was impossible for me to keep a journal, especially in the earliest days, because of the extraordinary stress and demands that were placed on my time and energy. I recorded my emotional experiences through artwork, and letters to others that I copied and kept for myself as well. Somehow, I knew I would need them later.

This is my own story, one that very much reflects my own experiences and perspective on what took place. It's a story I tell with reverence and respect for the fact that there are many other people who have their own stories to tell about how their lives were impacted by the tragic crimes recounted in these pages. Not one day goes by when I do not hope and pray for the safety and healing of everyone affected.

Shannon Moroney
June 2011

PART I

THE SHATTERING

CHAPTER ONE

A KNOCK AT THE DOOR

I was happily writing a thank-you card for a wedding gift when I heard the knock at my hotel room door. It was November 8, 2005, I was thirty years old, and my life was about to change forever.

I was away from home, attending a school guidance counsellors' conference. When I opened the door I expected to see my colleagues at the threshold, inviting me to breakfast. But instead, I saw what no one wants to see: the silhouette of a police uniform filling the frame. A colleague was standing behind him. My heart instantly filled with dread. Whatever news the officer was delivering, it was going to be bad.

"Are you Shannon Moroney?" he asked.

I nodded, fear blocking my throat.

I was in Toronto, 150 kilometres away from my home in Peterborough. I thought of my dad and my brother first. As salesmen who worked in and around Toronto, they both drove a lot, and I pictured a car accident. Had one of them been hurt? Were they going to be okay?

Seeming to read my mind, the officer said, "I'm not here

because someone has died or been in an accident. I'm here about your husband. Are you Jason Staples' wife?"

His question flustered me at first. Today was my one-month wedding anniversary and I wasn't used to my title of "wife" yet. During the last few weeks, Jason had been meeting me at the front door when I got home from work, saying, "Hello, *my wife*." Batting my eyelashes theatrically and pretending to blush, I would reply, "Hello, *my husband*." Then we would giggle and hug, and I'd step inside.

I nodded again to the police officer, still unable to speak. *Yes, I am Jason Staples' wife.*

He was holding a newspaper. Confused, I glanced down at it and tried to read the headlines, but it was upside down so I couldn't make out anything. I glanced back up at the officer. My colleague looked at me from over the officer's shoulder, his face full of concern.

"Do you want me to stay, Shannon?" he asked gently.

I shook my head. He was kind, but I didn't know him well. I didn't want to involve him in whatever I was about to find out. The officer stepped into my hotel room. The door closed behind him.

He stood in front of me, still holding out the newspaper. I reached for it, again trying to scan the headlines.

"Oh," he said. "There's nothing in this paper. I just picked it up from in front of your door." He put the newspaper on a nearby table.

"I'm here about your husband, Jason. He was arrested last night, charged with sexual assault."

I felt my body go numb. My mind began to race with questions: *What does he mean? There must be some mistake!* My mind clouded with confusion.

The officer continued. "I understand that your husband called the police himself." So there was no mistake.

"What happened? Who did he . . . assault?" I asked.

The officer was from Toronto, not Peterborough, so he didn't know the details. He handed me a slip of paper with the phone number of the police station and said I should call right away and ask for Sergeant DiClemente. Then, quietly, he said, "I think you better expect that it was 'full rape.'"

My stomach flipped. I felt like I was going to be sick. How was this possible? Desperation now pushed into my chest making it hard to breathe. I had to stay calm. *This can't be happening*. I turned away from the officer, walked over to the desk by the window and put my hand on the phone's receiver, terrified at the thought of what I would hear when I dialed that number.

Less than two hours earlier, I had been lying in bed with day just breaking outside the hotel window. I was so happy—a newly-wed filled with satisfaction and eager anticipation. I closed my eyes and an image of a shiny silver bowl came to my mind, filled with all the people and experiences of my recent past—my thirtieth birthday, our beautiful wedding on Thanksgiving weekend, and then a brief honeymoon at a cottage where Jason and I had lain in a hammock and daydreamed of our future and children. Everything had come together.

Under the blankets, I reached my hands down and rested them on my belly. I imagined cells splitting and multiplying inside me. The night before, in our "talk at ten" ritual that we followed when one of us was away, I had told Jason I thought I might be pregnant. "That would be great," he said. "We'll take a test when you get home."

I promised him that though I was tempted to take the test immediately, I'd wait until I was back so we could share the moment. The night before, I'd also spoken with my friend Rachael who lived in Colorado. We'd been close for years, ever since we lived in Ecuador as development workers in our early twenties. "I think this is it," I had said to her. "I think I'm pregnant!" Lying in bed at daybreak, I focused on what it would mean to become a mother.

When I was small, my mum explained to my siblings and me how we'd started off as "one speck," then become "two specks, then four, then eight" and so on, until her mental multiplication skills ran out. Delighted, we could always ask her how many specks we were at any given moment in our development: "Mummy, just before I was born, how many specks was I?" She would pause, ponder for a moment, and then say something like, "Let me see . . . I guess you were eight-hundred and ninety-seven thousand, four-hundred and thirty-two specks."

We loved it. I loved it. I loved that she knew me when I was just one speck of life, and that she had loved me even then. Now, as a grown woman, picturing those beautiful little specks inside of me, I was already loving them with all of my heart. I wanted to be the same kind of mother as my own: caring, dedicated, strong.

At seven o'clock, I got out of bed, took a shower and dressed for the final day of the conference. Then I packed my bags so that I could check out of the hotel at lunch, put everything in the car, and leave immediately after the last workshop. I was eager to get home. Jason would be there, and we had planned a simple, celebratory dinner to mark our first month as husband and wife.

At 8:00 a.m., I still had half an hour to spare before breakfast. I pulled out a package of cards and got to work writing thank-you notes for wedding gifts I'd received from colleagues at the conference. The phone rang. It was a co-worker from the board of directors, calling from the lobby.

"Shannon," he said. "There is someone who wants to see you. Can you wait in your room? I'm going to bring this person up."

"Of course," I replied, puzzled. Maybe it was a guidance counsellor from my old high school who wanted to say a surprise hello. But why wouldn't the person want me to come down? I had only a minute to wonder before I heard the fateful knock at my door.

My heart was pounding. In my hand I held the number of the sergeant in Peterborough. The officer remained in my hotel room, still standing by the door and looking at me solemnly. I dialed the number and waited.

"DiClemente speaking." The voice was loud and authoritative.

"Sergeant DiClemente, this is Shannon Moroney. I'm Jason Staples' wife."

"Oh, Shannon, yes . . ." His voice softened. "We've been waiting for your call. We need you to come back to Peterborough right away. We need to ask you some questions about your husband."

"Yes, yes, of course . . . but I don't understand. Can you tell me what happened? The officer here, he doesn't know . . ." I was stammering, my questions toppling one over the next as I tried to make sense of the incomprehensible.

"I'm not able to tell you very much right now except that yesterday afternoon, at about four-thirty, Jason assaulted two women at the store where he works. After some time, he took them to your home." I couldn't believe what I was hearing. It was as though he were talking about someone else—someone I didn't know, not my husband. The sergeant continued, "Shannon, you need to prepare yourself. This is very serious. Your husband is facing many charges."

My mind was racing. "Were the victims the two women who worked there?" I asked.

"No, they were customers. We don't think he knew them."

"Where are the victims? Are they all right?"

"They are at the hospital being treated and they are expected to recover fully. I can't really tell you anything else until you get here."

Oh my God.

"But how could he take them to our house? He rides his bike to work and—"

"He rented a van around six or seven o'clock. A clerk from the rental agency picked him up at the store, took him back across town to the car lot to sign the lease, and then Jason drove back to the store to pick up the women and take them to your house. He called 9-1-1 from a pay phone down the street to ask for help at 10:50 last night, and we were able to apprehend him there."

"Where is he now?"

"Here, downstairs in a cell. We'll tell you more when you get here. You need to come directly to the station. You can't go home, Shannon. Your house . . . your house is going to be searched. Will you be all right to drive? We could send a squad car to Toronto if necessary."

"I'm going to call my parents and I'm sure they will come with me."

"We'll be here, waiting."

I hung up the phone and stood for a moment, the sick feeling growing in my stomach. How was it possible? How could this be true? I needed to consider the facts. I'd just been told that the assaults had taken place around 4:30 in the afternoon, and Jason had called 9-1-1 at 10:50 at night. But I had spoken to him just before that, around 10:20. I had dialed our home number and after a few rings, the answering machine picked up. I figured Jason was taking out the recycling, so I called again a couple of minutes later. The second time, he answered.

"Hi!" I said. "Sorry I'm calling a little late. How are you?"

"I'm okay . . . how are you?"

I ignored his question. There was something in his tone that was a little off. He sounded tired.

"Jase," I said, "are you okay?"

"I'm just . . . not feeling that well."

"What's wrong?"

"I just have an upset stomach, nothing to worry about. I'll be fine," he reassured me.

"Have you been eating junk food while I've been gone?" I teased. He was generally a healthy eater and enjoyed exercise, though recently he'd put on weight and had shown a penchant for eating candy late at night. Like mine, his weight fluctuated easily. A week before, he had bought an inexpensive MP3 player to help motivate him to get out running. He told me he wanted to be one of those fit dads pushing a jogging stroller on the local trails. The image had brought a smile to my face; I could see it perfectly.

"I'm just not feeling that well, but please don't worry."

"Okay . . . if you're sure."

"I'm sure."

I continued chatting, telling him about a keynote speaker I'd heard that morning. The man was a thalidomide victim, born without arms. He'd overcome monumental challenges, becoming a musician, an author and a motivational speaker. I told Jason that the man reminded me of him: someone who had overcome obstacles and was making a good life for himself.

"Thanks," Jason replied softly. "That means so much to me right now. I love you, but I can't really talk."

I assumed he said "right now" because he'd been working on his portfolio all weekend, striving to launch a career as an illustrator. I figured he was struggling with the project, or trying to finish up a painting.

"Okay . . . but I have one more thing to tell you." I paused, savouring the moment. That's when I told him I thought I might be pregnant, and he said we should take a test when I got home. Then he said he loved me, and we hung up.

I winced as I recalled our conversation, now painfully juxtaposed with what I had just been told. The two women must have been there in our house while we were speaking.

No. No. No. My stomach churned again as I tried to imagine their agony. Then I thought of Jason, our life, and those who knew us. The images were pristine: Jason greeting me at the door after work each day with a smile, a hug and a smoothie to tide me over until dinner; racing our bikes up the big hill in front of our house; trips to visit my parents; nights out camping under the stars. I realized that the future I'd dreamed of was falling away with each new detail I was learning. I felt weak. I sat down on the bed where I had been writing the thank-you cards minutes earlier. The officer was still standing near the doorway. I turned to him and said that I was going to call my parents.

I dialed their number. What was I going to say? My phone call would be as shocking to them as the police officer's arrival at my door.

My mum answered cheerfully. "How's the conference going, Shan?"

"Has Dad left for work?" Thankfully, he had not. I wanted them to be together when I told them the news. Trying to remain calm, I said slowly, "Mum . . . Jason has been arrested."

"What! Oh my God, what happened?"

"I don't know . . . I don't know what happened. Mum, he's charged with sexual assault. It is very serious."

The immediate panic in her voice ignited mine. My voice wavered but I didn't want to cry. I knew that once I started, I wouldn't be able to stop. I could hear my dad's voice in the background asking what was going on, Mum trying to answer his questions and talk to me at the same time.

"Mum, I have to go back home, to the police station in Peterborough. Can you come and get me?"

"Of course, we'll leave right away. Where are you? Is anyone with you?"

I glanced over at the officer. He was looking down, attempting to give me privacy. I told her he was with me and then I gave her the name and address of the hotel. It was still well before nine and morning traffic would be heavy. It would take them at least forty-five minutes to drive here from their home in Burlington.

I stared out the window, past the full Park'N Fly lot to the busy highway. Beyond were the airport runways, and I could see planes taking off and landing. The sun was rising steadily over the concrete landscape; the outside world carried on in fast-motion, oblivious, while my world was coming to a terrifying halt.

—

When I got off the phone, I told the officer that my parents were on their way.

"Do you want me to wait with you until they get here?"

I looked at him now as though for the first time. He appeared to be in his forties, tall and slender, concern etched in his features. So far, we had barely spoken. On the one hand, it would be awkward to wait in this small space with a man I didn't know; on the other, it would be better for me to be with a stranger than to be alone. I had dealt with a fair number of crises in my role as a school guidance counsellor. I knew that I needed some support now, but I didn't want to call a colleague from downstairs and disclose this horrific information. The professional me tried to put her arms around the terrified me.

I said to the officer, "Yes, I'd appreciate if you would stay. Thank you." We stood there for a moment. Everything seemed suddenly and intensely fragile. "Would you like to sit down?" I asked, offering him one of the two armchairs by the window.

"Yes, thank you." He crossed the room and sat, the weight of his uniform and accessories making him sound heavier than he was.

In what felt like slow-motion, I pulled some warmer and more comfortable clothes from my suitcase and took them into the bathroom. I changed out of my conference outfit and when I took off my skirt, I noticed I was bleeding. A feeling of tremendous loss welled up inside. Were these the cells of my baby flowing out? I couldn't think clearly. I padded my underwear and finished getting changed. I took off what little makeup I had on. I left the bathroom and reentered the room where the officer waited patiently. Neither of us seemed to know what to say. The air was pure silence. My mind was pure noise.

I decided to call Rachael. With a two-hour time difference, it was very early out in Denver but Rachael had always been a morning person. My phone call caught her in the car with her sister-in-law; they were on their way up to a trailhead for a hike with their babies.

Her voice was clear and sweet. "Shan—do you have good news?"

I knew what she was thinking: that I'd taken a pregnancy test.

How was I going to tell her? "Rach," I said. "Jason has been arrested. They say he . . . he sexually assaulted two women at work yesterday afternoon." My voice cracked as I said the words.

Rachael gasped. "Oh my God, Shan! What happened?"

I filled her in on what little I knew.

"Oh, Jason," she said, her voice breaking. "What happened to him, Shan?"

I didn't know how to answer her question: it was the same one playing over and over in my mind. I told her I would call her when I knew more, and she told me she loved me and would be right by the phone waiting for my next call. I hung up the phone.

With a facade of calm, I sat down in the armchair across from the officer and tried to make small talk. I felt sorry for him, having to deliver this news. I asked him about his family— did he have any children? He did. I asked what grades they were in. Then I didn't know what else to say. I felt absolutely outside myself. I'm sure he could see I was in a state of shock. We sat in silence, and stared out the window at the planes and the November sky.

My mind flashed back to the previous winter, when a stone had flown up and hit my windshield as I was driving along the highway. I had had just a split second to think, "Maybe the whole windshield won't crack," then watched helplessly as a deep fracture snaked its way across the entire glass. I had been as powerless then to stop the damage as I was now.

CHAPTER TWO

A GENTLE GIANT

I first met Jason on a Wednesday afternoon in February 2003, at Martha's Table, a restaurant for low-income patrons in Kingston, Ontario. At Martha's, customers paid just one dollar to be seated and served a nutritious meal with the same respect they could expect if they had paid a hundred dollars at a high-end restaurant. I arrived that afternoon as a volunteer with a group of students from the high school where I worked. The students had been going to Martha's every other Wednesday for months but this was my first time. I was new to the school and eager to involve myself in an extracurricular activity. I had heard about the restaurant and its philosophy resonated with me. I had also heard that parolees on day release from prison were sometimes sponsored to work at Martha's, but that didn't bother me. I believed it was good for people who'd taken from society to give back.

The home of Queen's University, Canada's first parliament buildings and hundreds of limestone houses, Kingston is also known for its prisons. There are several federal institutions within and just outside the city limits, over 2500 residents are employed by the Correctional Service of Canada. In the centre of the city, on the shore of Lake Ontario, loom the giant grey walls of Canada's oldest prison—maximum-security Kingston Penitentiary—which houses some of the country's most notorious criminals. Like most residents, I rarely thought about the city's connection to the Correctional Service, even though I lived just four blocks away from the penitentiary. I worked with some high school kids who were on probation in the provincial juvenile branch, but I'd never known an adult who'd been incarcerated.

I had visited a prison once, a few years earlier when I was working for a youth program north of Toronto. My group and I had been invited to tour a new medium-security penitentiary in the woods outside Gravenhurst. A few things struck me during our visit. The first was that all convicts from Nunavut served their federal sentences there—thousands of kilometres from their homes in the Arctic. I tried to imagine what it must be like to land in such a prison, finding yourself surrounded for the first time in your life by trees, in a place where English was the main language, and where your family would likely never be able to visit. I wondered why there was no facility in the north. I considered the limits to full rehabilitation this distance might create. The second thing that struck me was the inmates themselves. We spoke to several in the hobby shop, and they were friendly and polite, not what I had expected of hardened criminals. I wondered what lay beneath the surface.

As we were led into the living quarters, the guard asked my youth group participants to imagine how difficult it would be to have to share a small cell with another person—a stranger—and to earn just six dollars per day for your work. But what the guard didn't realize was that this group of youths was also in a

federally funded program, sharing rooms with three or four
others in a house of twelve and earning three dollars per day
for their full-time volunteer work. They weren't that sympathetic. I pointed out that they still had freedom whereas the
prisoners didn't; some nodded while others shook their heads.
Several inmates were rollerblading around a large outdoor track
and one of the youths expressed jealousy at their equipment and
facilities, which were way better than the broken-down second-
hand bicycles he and his friends had. One kid said it was better
to have a rusty old bike and be able to go anywhere on it than
have brand-new rollerblades and never be able to leave the track.

Later, in our debriefing session facilitated by a parole officer,
we struggled to match the images of criminals we saw on television or in films with the well-mannered men we had met in the
institution. Were they all merely con artists, as the guard had
suggested, or were their personalities and lives more complex
than that? It was something to think about, for the youth and
for me.

Before I left the school with my new group of students for
my first day of volunteering at Martha's, the teacher who had
previously accompanied them gave us a quick prep talk. She
explained that some clients were drug addicts and that if we
saw any needles or paraphernalia in the bathroom, we were not
to touch them and to let the staff know. She provided straight-
forward information and a plan, with no fear or judgment. She
told us there would be many kinds of people at Martha's,
including some who had been in prison. The rule for volunteers
was to follow the mandate of the organization and treat everyone equally. There was to be no gawking.

When we arrived at the beautiful stone church that housed
the restaurant, we were greeted by a woman who wore her silver

hair up in a bun and was dressed simply in a blouse, hand-knit cardigan, calf-length skirt and thick stockings. She looked like a storybook grandmother. Her name was Una.

Una welcomed us warmly, but there was no time to waste before getting down to work. She led us through the large hall where tables were set up, each covered with a cloth and decorated with a small bouquet of dried flowers. She then directed us to the kitchen and introduced us to Jason, the assistant co-ordinator and head cook, who briefed us on our duties. He was tall, had an easy smile, and was wearing a blue camp-hat and dark-rimmed glasses. He was taking several quiches out of the oven and rolling out pastry for the next batch. He swiftly organized us into work areas. The students and I put on aprons and got busy: serving, clearing, making coffee and so on. I was asked to ladle out the soup. Jason showed me what to do as he put aside a bowl for Una's five-year-old grandson so it wouldn't be too hot when he arrived to eat. Everyone raved about Jason's soup—he had developed quite a fan following—and it smelled particularly enticing on such a cold and snowy day.

Just before serving, Jason and the coordinator, Susan, gathered all the volunteers into the kitchen. We stood in a circle and Susan led everyone in a short, ecumenical prayer. I glanced at Jason. I was struck by how good-looking he was, even under a dusting of pastry flour, and when he removed his hat he revealed a mop of wavy dark hair. *I wonder how old he is.* I pictured him going home after work to a pretty wife and small children, then noticed he wasn't wearing a wedding ring. *Maybe he has a girlfriend?* When the prayer ended, I guiltily snapped out of my wandering thoughts. Clients were coming in the door. Jason provided us with a quick rundown of the menu and we began serving.

I was impressed with the gentle way in which Jason

commanded everyone's attention. He was thrown what seemed like twenty questions at once, and he handled them with ease and confidence while cooking a meal for two hundred people. I quickly learned that at Martha's, if you had a question about something or didn't know what to do, you'd be told, "Just ask Jason." Everyone liked and respected him and he played an integral role in making Martha's a good space for patron and volunteer alike.

When my job of soup-ladling was finished and things were wrapping up, Jason and I struck up a conversation that began with him asking, "So . . . are you a senior student?"

I had to laugh. "I'm actually the guidance counsellor," I said. He apologized swiftly. I reassured him that I was flattered. "My days of being mistaken for a high school student are numbered—I'm twenty-seven," I said. Then we both laughed.

I wanted him to keep talking so I could size him up. I asked him if he could help me understand how the restaurant had come into being. This proved to be a good topic. Jason spent several minutes filling me in, during which time I took note of his articulate and well-educated manner of speaking. At one point he removed his glasses to clean them and I caught a glimpse of his dark, blue eyes. There was a depth to them that drew my interest. There was something special about him. For a moment, I felt as though there were no one else in the room. He told me later how he remembered looking down into my own eyes at that moment and feeling a connection. From that first meeting there had been a spark of attraction—something each of us thought was invisible to the other and certainly undetectable to anyone around us.

The shift went by quickly and soon we had finished the cleanup. Jason and I exchanged a friendly goodbye and I left to drive the students home. The last one in the car was a mature and outgoing grade-nine girl, who, as it turned out, was also very perceptive.

"So, Ms. Moroney, it seems like you and Jason really like each other. I saw you talking to him for a while."

I brushed her comment aside, but I could feel a flush of pink spreading across my cheeks.

Two weeks later, it was time to volunteer again. That Wednesday, when I got to the kitchen, Jason greeted me with a warm smile. He was putting the finishing touches on chicken à la king, a meal that he had created using donated fried chicken from a fast-food chain. As we put on our aprons and Jason organized us, he assigned me to soup duty again. This kept me near him and allowed us to chat while we worked.

After the first rush of customers, there was a lull in the activity. One of the volunteers fixed Jason a plate of food and demanded he take a break.

"Would you like to join me for dinner?" he asked, already preparing me a plate.

"Is it really okay?" I felt a little embarrassed about eating food that I thought was for the clients. Jason assured me that volunteers were always more than welcome to share the meal too. I looked around and saw some of my students sitting among the clients, chatting and eating with them. I accepted Jason's offer.

The only quiet, free spot we could find to eat in was a cramped stairwell adjacent to the kitchen. We sat on the stairs with our plates in our laps and talked about movies and our hobbies. I was quite into pottery at the time and told him a bit about the pieces I was making. I had noticed Jason drawing caricatures and cartoon figures on the menu board. I asked him to what extent drawing was part of his life.

"I've been drawing for as long as I can remember. My mum could barely get the groceries out of the brown paper bags before I was doodling on them," he explained.

"Have you ever considered art as a career path?" I asked.

"For my whole life, people have encouraged me to go to art school for graphic design or illustration, but I was never sure I wanted it to be more than a hobby. I've got a pretty good portfolio together. I may apply to an art college this year. For now, I'm happy here at Martha's."

I had many more questions, but Jason changed the subject to ask me about my work and education, and how I liked being back in the city after a semester in a remote school up north. We could have talked for hours—it was so easy—but the next wave of customers was arriving. As we put our dishes in the sink, Jason was called out of the kitchen. He returned a few minutes later and out of the corner of my eye I saw him bend over the counter to scribble something on a little card. He turned to me then, handed me the card, and said, "I'm sorry, I have to go . . . there's a situation at the front door." Then he dashed out of the kitchen and was gone.

There I stood, soup ladle in one hand and this little card in the other. Jason had drawn a caricature of himself in blue pen and next to it written his name, phone number, e-mail address and the words, *Available for pottery viewing, tea and chatting*. A smile broke over my face and I felt a tingly sensation in my stomach. With a new spring in my step, I refocused on serving the soup, participating in cleanup, and later driving my students home, but the tingly feeling stayed with me for the rest of the afternoon.

After Martha's, I went home briefly to freshen up and then returned to school for a parent information night. I found myself with a few minutes to spare before the parents were to arrive at seven. I slipped into my office and pulled Jason's card out of my pocket. Best to strike while the iron was hot, and before I lost my nerve. I dialed his number and he picked up right away.

"Hi, Jason—it's Shannon. Thanks for the card. It's a very good likeness of you." I was trying to sound nonchalant. "I'd love to take you up on your offer."

"I was hoping you'd call," he said. "Is tonight too soon for a cup of tea?"

I explained that I could meet him later, if that worked. He readily agreed and suggested his favourite café, a favourite of mine as well. I was excited, and I could hear in his voice that he was too. After saying goodbye and hanging up, I headed into the auditorium.

At eight o'clock I rushed to the staff room where I brushed my hair and put on some lip gloss. Then I drove downtown to the café. Jason arrived at the same time. He was well put-together, handsome in his leather gloves and grey wool coat over dark jeans and a sweater. We greeted each other and I tried not to show the nervous excitement I felt. We ordered tea and chose a table by the front window. It had started to snow hard outside, but inside it was warm and cozy.

We had made small talk for less than five minutes before Jason said, "There is something that I need to tell you before we get to know each other more."

I couldn't imagine what it was he had to say. My initial surprise soon turned to shock.

"Shannon, you need to know that I was in prison for ten years. I'm on parole with a life sentence. Five years ago, I began working at Martha's Table on a day-pass program from the minimum-security institution just outside the city."

The noise of other patrons in the room suddenly seemed muffled as Jason's words hit me. I couldn't believe what I was hearing. This kind and gentle young man had been in prison for *ten years*? I was dumbfounded. Questions flooded my mind, but I didn't quite know where to begin, nor what was appropriate to ask. The most obvious question was "What did you do?"—but I didn't ask that right away. It somehow seemed crass or lurid, and I could tell that it wouldn't be easy for Jason to talk about it. His eyes had darkened and there was a sadness in them that was tangible. He must have murdered someone to have been given a life sentence. Who had it been? What were the circumstances? I took a deep breath. In my shock, the only thing I managed to say was, "Oh."

I sat there looking at the man sitting across from me. I couldn't match him to the image of a killer that rose in my mind. He wasn't scary, he didn't look mean, and he wasn't covered with gang tattoos like the prisoners you see on television. He was kind and gentle—still boyish in his looks. He must have been very young at the time to have served ten years in jail already and been back in the community for five. I voiced this last thought. And that's when Jason told me his story.

"I committed the crime a few months after my eighteenth birthday, in January of 1988. I was sent to a detention centre first and then I served the rest of my time at a medium-security prison. I was moved to minimum-security 'camp,' and began coming out to the community in 1998. Now I have very few restrictions, though I still have to spend four nights per week in a halfway house, from eleven at night until seven in the morning. The rest of the time I'm working or I'm in my apartment over on Lower Union Street."

My mind was going in many directions. Part of me wanted to ask him where the halfway house was, what it meant to be on parole, but most of all, what had happened to put him in prison in the first place. Another part of me didn't want to know anything. I didn't want what he was telling me to be true. I tried to picture him at eighteen, the same age as many of my current students. Like them, he would have been an adult under the law but still a kid in so many ways.

"I'm sorry to have to tell you this," Jason continued soberly, "but you have a right to know before you develop any kind of attachment to me, even as just a friend. I'm developing a big crush on you, but us getting to know each other—in any way—is your decision. I'll never be able to change my past, though I wish I could."

I found myself feeling sad. I appreciated Jason's honesty, and his remorse was palpable. He gave me the option to stand up and walk away from him then, but I chose not to, just yet. I tried to imagine how it would feel to disclose my own worst secrets to a stranger, and I decided that at the very least I could give him a moment more of my time.

"So," I said slowly, lowering my voice, "it was murder?" I felt suddenly aware that we were in public. I glanced around the café, the buzz of conversation at other tables slowly coming back into my range of hearing.

"Yes, it was murder."

Oh my God.

He continued. "I was convicted of second-degree murder. I killed my roommate—a woman."

I was afraid to know, but I asked, "What happened?"

Jason explained further: He had lived with his mother and her boyfriend in an apartment in Ottawa for a couple of years—until 1987 when they left Jason behind to move to a house across the border in Quebec. As a high school student with part-time employment, Jason could not afford the rent on his own, so his mother found a roommate for him—a friend of a friend. The roommate was a thirty-eight-year-old woman. She and Jason developed a sexual relationship, which Jason described as being rooted in ego for him. I watched Jason as he carefully chose his words, shifting uncomfortably in his seat from time to time but not breaking eye contact with me. He apologized for having to tell me these things, and for it being so hard to talk about. As a guidance counsellor, I always felt grateful when a student shared his or her troubles with me, but this—what Jason was telling me—was very different. He was not my student, not a teenager, not my responsibility. But I stayed at the table out of respect for his honesty.

He described his adolescence as characterized by multiple moves and school changes. As he neared the end of high school, his plans for the future were vague at best. He said he had never been in trouble at school and that he'd managed to stay "under the radar" of administration by neither excelling at his studies—which he was intellectually capable of doing—nor failing at them. His easy-going nature and artistic talents gained him acceptance in the eyes of his teachers and peers and reinforced the image that he projected as a kid no one need be too concerned about.

At eighteen years of age, Jason was intrigued by the concept of an older woman. He said that they had an agreement about casual sex, that one could invite the other or that there would be a sign such as an open bedroom door late at night. Despite that, he described their living situation as stressful and disharmonious. I had a hard time imagining a mother leaving her teenage son, not even out of high school, to live with an older, single woman he didn't know.

As Jason approached graduation without goals for the future, his grades began to slip. By Christmas of 1987, after living with the female roommate for a couple of months, he had all but dropped out of school. He phoned his mom in early January to ask if he could come and live with her and her boyfriend because things with the roommate weren't going well. Jason's mom said the move would not be possible. Trapped in his living situation and without enough money to move out on his own, Jason began to spend more time at his maternal grandmother's farm, seeking refuge in their close relationship. "My grandmother was the most loving person in my life," he said.

On the day of the murder in January of 1988, Jason had been visiting his grandmother for a couple of days but needed to go home to take a shower before meeting up with friends later that night—there was only a bucket bath at the rustic farm. Out in the country without a car, he decided to jog all the way back to Ottawa that evening. He told me that he would lose all track of time and place when he was running; it was an escape. The farm was many kilometres away from his apartment, and the run home that night took close to three hours.

When he got back home, his roommate turned down his sexual advances and they got into an argument. Wanting to end the conflict, Jason went into the bathroom to have a shower. His roommate followed, yelling, "I'm going to tell your mother what's really going on here!"

Jason struggled for the right words to explain to me his overwhelming need to gain control over the situation. "I only remember wanting her to stop screaming at me, struggling to the ground, and striking her head against the bathroom floor until she stopped." He said that he wasn't aware of what he was doing until it was over.

I realized that I was holding my breath. Jason looked down and shook his head. When he looked up, his face wore a baffled expression. It was as though he still couldn't believe it, or as though he were talking about someone else.

"What happened next?" I asked quietly.

"I laid her body in the bathtub and turned on a cold shower. It sounds absurd, but I thought it would wake her up. Then I got dressed and walked out to the balcony and looked over the edge, but I couldn't bring myself to jump. Someone in the building had heard the screaming and called the police, but when they arrived at the door, I told them the screaming was from another apartment, that I didn't know anything. I thought they would actually shoot me on the spot if they saw what I had done. I was so scared."

Hearing these appalling details, my disbelief intensified. A voice in my head kept saying, *What are you doing here?* Again I glanced around the café. Everyone else's conversation seemed normal. But for me, it now seemed like a different place. I felt far older than I'd been fifteen minutes ago.

He continued. "I left the apartment, and I called the police from a pay phone, telling them a lie: that an intruder had killed my roommate. A simplistic, ridiculous plan made up on the spot, out of fear and panic. I gave the lie up later at the police station. They wouldn't have any of it—my guilt was obvious. I only asked them not to call my mother, but of course they did. Other family members found out about it on the news. At that point I had already started to shut down—to close up under the weight of what I had done. I spent the next six months between the detention centre and the psychiatric assessment unit at the Royal Ottawa Hospital."

I had listened to every word he'd said. I was horrified, but I still couldn't put the man in front of me with the story he was telling.

"What were the results of your assessment?" I wanted to know: did Jason suffer from a mental illness? There was nothing in his behaviour that suggested it.

"I was found criminally responsible, which of course I completely agreed with, but that was the only finding."

"Had you ever been violent before?" I asked.

"No, never. I don't know how I was capable of it. I've never been able to explain it; I only know that I'll never do it again." He said this with conviction, through what seemed like a cloud of confusion and sadness.

"How do you know that?" It was a direct, forceful question, but given everything I'd just heard, I had to know the answer.

"Because I never want to hurt anyone again. I'm now aware that at one moment in my life I lost control. I took her life, and I live with this awareness every day. She had two sisters." He looked down again for a moment. There was agony in his face. "They were at my sentencing and gave victim impact statements, but they expressed no blame, just pain and sadness for the fear their sister must have felt before she died. I know what I did and I wish I could change the past. But I can't. Instead, I keep my daily life and emotions balanced, and I'm surrounded by good people who support me. I've been given a second chance, and I never want to go back to prison."

I was surprised to find my heart going out to him, even as I was repulsed by what he had done, by the damage and loss he'd caused. What I was hearing was horrible, but I respected that he wasn't trying to minimize or divert responsibility about what he had done. I pictured some of my eighteen-year-old students and their varying levels of insecurity and vastly diverse home lives. I couldn't yet visualize Jason's upbringing, nor could I grasp the contrast between our lives in 1988. I would have been twelve when he'd committed this crime. I was living happily in the comfortable safety of the suburbs with my supportive, loving family.

There was so much to say. I had many questions, many concerns. "Do the people at Martha's know about your past?" I asked.

"Yes, some of them do. Una, Susan, and some other volunteers—Dan and Shirley—know everything. They've become like family. At one time, there were many of us ex-cons working there. I was hired formally about two and a half years ago. It's good to be there on my own merit, rather than through connection to Corrections, though my parole team is encouraging me to move on to something else soon."

Since he brought up his parole, I decided to ask more about that. I had only a vague idea of how parole worked. He explained that life sentences in Canada carry up to a maximum of twenty-five years in prison, the last three of which normally involve a staged parole process, moving an inmate down institutional security levels, out on escorted work release, out on day parole to a halfway house, and then, over time and with good behaviour, to full parole. His sentence, however, wasn't Life-25. It was Life-10. The judge had made note of his youth and the fact that he had no prior offences and believed he could be reformed. Jason explained that when he'd reached his full parole eligibility date after ten years in a medium-security penitentiary, he had been moved to a minimum-security facility, where after a year he earned day passes for "escorted temporary absences," also known as "work release." That's when he started working at Martha's Table. As trust was built, he'd been released on day parole—first to a halfway house for two years, then later he was hired as assistant coordinator of Martha's and rented his own apartment, where he stayed three nights a week (the rest at the halfway house). He was hoping to achieve full-parole status in the near future, which would mean the freedom to live completely on his own. Such an achievement would depend on his furthering his education and continuing to develop community supports.

"What about your mother and grandmother?" I asked. Until then, it had never occurred to me to think of what happens to the family of a convict.

Jason paused, looked down, took a breath and then looked back up at me. "My grandmother was devastated. She tried to keep in touch with me during the first few years I was inside. I was so ashamed of myself and of what I had put her and everyone else through. I pushed a lot of friends and family away. My grandmother died about five years into my sentence. And my mom, well, she has always denied my guilt."

"Your mom denies your guilt?" It didn't make sense. He had pleaded guilty in court and was sitting in front of me taking responsibility.

"During my trial and after, she made up stories about what really happened and even claimed that I was framed. Eventually, it got so hard we had to cut back on our visits."

I could barely comprehend this—a mother denying the truth about her son, even as the son himself acknowledged it. I asked Jason more about his mother. He said that she currently lived on a disability pension and suffered from severe bipolar disorder.

She did not manage her medication well and had serious side effects in addition to symptoms of the disease.

As Jason spoke, he made no complaints about his upbringing. "She did the best she could," he said of his mother. His father had died when he was six.

I asked him about his earlier childhood, before all of this. He insisted he remembered almost nothing of his early years.

The café closed at 10:00 p.m. but our conversation had not quite reached a natural conclusion, so we decided to go for a walk and keep talking for a bit longer. I'd never in my life experienced a conversation like this.

The snow was piling up, a fresh blanket over already significant banks. The snowfall muffled the sound of cars as they drove by. Bundled up with scarves, hats and mittens, we walked the city streets down to the waterfront. There I stood next to him, looking out at the frozen waters of Lake Ontario. I thought to myself, *Shouldn't I be afraid? This man is a convicted murderer!* I tuned in to my body and searched for any signs of visceral fear, but there were none. I looked at him trying to find signs of danger, but there were none. I simply wasn't afraid.

Half an hour later, we walked back to the closed café where I'd parked my car. It was nearly eleven o'clock; Jason had to check in at the halfway house and I had to get home. It was a school night, and I knew I would have trouble falling asleep after all he'd told me. We walked to my car and turned toward each other to say goodnight, or maybe goodbye. I didn't yet know if I would see him again outside Martha's Table. He leaned down and gave me a quick hug. He was shy about it. I put myself in his shoes and imagined how vulnerable I'd feel after opening up to someone like he just had.

"Thank you for being so honest with me, Jason," I said. "I have a lot to think about, but what you shared is safe with me."

"Thank you for listening. I've never told anyone all that right away. You made it a lot easier." We smiled at each other.

I turned and took a step away, then found myself turning back to look up at him: a gentle giant standing in the lamplight with snowflakes on his head and shoulders. I put my arms up and around him and hugged him again. We later coined the term "the come-back hug" to describe that moment, and Jason would tell me that it was in that moment that he fell in love with me. I didn't know it yet, but I already loved him too.

I believe there are many, many kinds of love, and this was the kind of love that felt as though it had begun long before. It was a deep-hearted compassion that took root in our view of one another as worthy human beings. I had the feeling that it was an old love, already familiar and comfortable, but wrapped in a layer of newness, romance and attraction. Had Jason not made his disclosure, I would have found myself enjoying a full-fledged crush, looking forward to a real first date. But there was nothing carefree in learning about Jason's past, and I could not return to the freedom and anticipation I'd felt just a few hours earlier when I was innocent of the facts. In fact, the more I thought about it, the more burdensome the knowledge felt. I had to face it, gather more information, and contemplate whether I could come to terms with his unalterable, shocking truth.

CHAPTER THREE

ACCEPTANCE

My job as a high school guidance counsellor was very busy; it was the beginning of a new semester and I was seeing upwards of twenty students a day for career, academic and personal counselling. I didn't have any time during work hours to think about Jason, but as soon as I'd get in my car to go home, my thought-train jumped to his track. I was overwhelmed by all he had told me and I needed to talk to someone, so I decided to confide in my roommate. She was as shocked as I was, but listened carefully. I was able to sound out some of my thoughts and questions and it was helpful. After much soul-searching, I decided I wanted to see Jason again, so we arranged a second date for dinner.

We talked for a long time that night—about his past, but about many other subjects too. We shared a similar sense of humour, political views, and a love of art. We had compatible taste in movies, but Jason was far more open-minded than I was, and a better critic. We both enjoyed reading, though Jason said he had read so many books while in prison that it was nice to have other options now for his free time. Jason loved running whereas I loved cycling, and we both belonged to the same gym.

I was struck by how *normal* Jason seemed. There was no way that I would have known he'd been institutionalized for a decade, save for the fact that his music knowledge seemed to skip the nineties, and he had a terrible sense of direction. He attributed the latter to staying in one place for ten years and then being driven around rather than driving himself. I felt secure enough with him to share parts of my own life, and with big chunks of my late teens and early twenties spent living as a student in Indonesia, Ecuador and northern British Columbia, I too lacked many pop-culture references from the same era.

Near the end of our second evening together, Jason said that if we were to keep seeing each other he needed me to meet his parole officer and psychologist. I was glad he had brought it up before I had to ask. I needed to make an informed choice about the level to which I would let him into my life, and Jason clearly understood and respected that. I thanked him but he brushed off my appreciation, explaining that one of his parole obligations was to disclose his past to anyone with whom he became intimately involved. While in no way was either of us considering physical intimacy at this point, the type of relationship his parole obligation referenced, our quickly growing emotional proximity had prompted Jason to be transparent from the beginning. I didn't know if I would have made myself so vulnerable to him, had our roles been reversed.

I asked about his other parole obligations, and he listed them for me: he had to keep his parole officer informed of his whereabouts, apprise anyone whose residence he lodged at overnight that he was a parolee, see a Corrections psychologist on a regular basis, and abstain from alcohol or drug use. I had noticed during dinner that he refused a glass of wine. Now I knew why.

"Do you have a problem with alcohol or drugs?"

"No, I don't," he said. He then explained that because he'd had a drink the night of the murder, even though he was far from intoxicated, the alcohol may have played a slight role in his actions. "Alcohol is a non-inhibitor. It can affect judgment and impulse control." His team considered that any factor that could impede his safe return to the community—however remotely connected—was worth controlling, and Jason was in complete agreement.

"But don't ever feel you can't enjoy a drink when I'm around. I can still toast with juice in a wineglass."

Jason gave me the phone numbers for his parole officer and psychologist and I called them the next day to make appointments. In doing so, I realized that I was considering more than just a friendship with him. Still, I was conflicted. It was a pleasure to be around him, and I couldn't deny that I felt a strong attraction, physically and emotionally, but nor could I deny the burden I felt every time I thought about the fact that he had a life sentence and the reason why. I believed that Jason deserved a second chance and that he was a good person who had committed a terrible act, one that could never be denied or minimized. Yet, I had reservations about whether I should—or could—cope with the many complications this brutal truth brought with it. Seeking more information became my plan.

My first call was to Jason's parole officer. He confirmed everything Jason had told me.

"What was wrong with Jason? How could he commit such a crime?" I asked.

"No one really knows," he began, "but the offence is considered a one-time incident and we are not concerned that he will ever reoffend. He was a model inmate, and has made an excellent re-entry to the community. We support him in every way. We just want to make sure that he has told you everything and that you know we are available to you should you decide to pursue your relationship. We would all like to see him with someone who motivates him to keep going forward. He's our best guy."

In a face-to-face meeting with Jason's psychologist a few days later, he asked me to recount what I knew about Jason's crime. Repeating everything out loud forced me to accept the truth even more deeply. If our relationship developed, was I prepared to make this disclosure to my loved ones as well? I knew I would never be able to hide it from the people closest to me.

When I finished, the psychologist said, "I'm satisfied that Jason has been very up-front with you, and I can understand why. You seem like a smart and understanding young woman. Do you have any other questions for me?"

Of course I did. I wanted to ask him why Jason had killed his roommate.

"It remains somewhat of a mystery, though in a pre-release report five or six years ago, the assessing psychologist labelled the offence as a reaction of 'adolescent rage resulting from narcissistic injury.'" He showed me the report.

I didn't fully understand the terms, so I went home and did some research. I knew that someone who is narcissistic has an exceptional interest in, or admiration of, him or herself. I learned that "injury" happens by an assault or rejection of that self-concept by another person. The responses to injury vary, but in some cases it is spontaneous violence. As I read, I tried to apply the clinical explanation to the scene at the apartment that Jason had described. I remembered Narcissus from Greek mythology who fell in love with his reflection in a pool. When he tried to touch his reflection, he fell into the water and drowned.

I went to see Jason's psychologist a second time.

"So, are you saying that when Jason's roommate declined his advances and she threatened to tell his mother about 'what he was really like,' Jason's ego was injured?"

"Yes, exactly that—and it triggered something."

I began imagining something deeper inside Jason that had been hurt. Where had that hurt come from? I wondered.

The psychiatrist said, "Jason may open up to us one day if he figures anything out—like past trauma—but in the meantime, the fact that he has never been violent again in fifteen years, has had healthy relationships while back in the community, is forthcoming about his responsibility for the murder, is free from addictions, and is now in his thirties are all the reasons that we believe he is rehabilitated and doesn't pose a threat to society."

I needed to hear it plainly. "So you don't consider Jason to be dangerous *at all*?"

"No, we don't."

On an intellectual level, I could grasp everything the doctor was saying, but the murder remained a senseless act of violence that was impossible to imagine occurring at the hands of the man I was getting to know. By Jason's own account, and according to his case-management team, he was a responsible and remorseful thirty-three-year-old who was making the most of his second chance at life. The question was: How much a part of that second chance did I want to be? How much could I be?

I continued to meet and talk with Jason's parole officer and psychologist while also spending time with Jason. Jason made me laugh, listen, think, and I could tell him anything that was on my mind and he would understand. We got together for dinner, movies, hikes at a local conservation area, and worked in tandem at Martha's Table. I loved being with him. Over time, I began to feel that I could move toward accepting Jason as he was now, including his past—but could I take on the burden of his life sentence? I wanted it to go away, so I could share the joy of getting to know him now with my parents, siblings and close friends, but I couldn't do that authentically without also divulging the difficult reality of his past and current parole status. And I knew I couldn't handle their questions until I had first come to terms with everything myself.

I struggled with our relationship, even as I was growing to care for him more deeply. Could I live out my dreams of travel and international work with a partner who was unlikely ever to be able to leave the country? Would Jason be able to develop a viable career beyond Martha's when so many options were closed off to people with criminal records? What would it mean for children to have a father who had murdered someone, even if it was thirty years in the past by the time they learned it?

I struggled so much that after several weeks of dating, I told Jason that I wanted to take a break to go out with another man, someone I had dated previously, someone I hoped would be as amazing as Jason was but without a painful past. Jason took a big breath, then paused.

"Shannon, I'm in love with you but I understand that this is something you need to do. The only thing I ask is that you not be in touch with me until you know what you want. It will be too difficult for me if you waver back and forth. I will wait. Take all the time you need."

It didn't take me long to realize that I was happiest with Jason—happier than I'd been in any other relationship in my life. He instilled in me an ease of being, as if I had known him my whole life. He had an extraordinary ability to read me and to ask just the right questions that guided me to better understand myself. Little things that had given rise to jealousy or competitiveness in other men were levelled by Jason's understanding, good humour and, above all, his love. I thought about what I had once heard said, that "forgiveness means letting go of all hope for a better past." Because the harm was not done to me, I didn't think it either necessary or appropriate for me to forgive Jason for his crime of murder. Yet, I did view forgiveness as a concept entwined with acceptance. This was the crux of the choice that I faced. If I wanted to fully hold the happiness I felt with Jason and love him as freely as he loved me, I'd need to let go of hope for a better past.

After much deliberation I decided that I could accept Jason's, past and present, and move forward with him into the future. I stopped seeing the other man, gathered myself together, and went to Jason's door.

I rang the bell and he opened it, stretching his arms wide the moment he saw it was me. I stepped into his arms and said, "It's you. It's you I want to be with."

He pulled me in tight and held me for a long time. I started to tell him I'd ended my relationship with the other guy but he stopped me. He put his hands on my shoulders and looked into my eyes.

"The only thing that I need to know is: are you all right?"

I nodded, we embraced again, and then we resumed our relationship. Everything in my heart, mind and body told me it was the right choice. Jason was the most special person I'd ever known—the people close to him, people of standing in the community, held him in the same high regard—and he felt the same way about me.

—

The next step was to share our commitment with the people closest to us, which, for me, began with my parents. It was very important that we seek their blessing and that they know about Jason's past. I'd invited my parents to Kingston for Mother's Day weekend and now planned to introduce them to Jason at dinner on Saturday night. "I can't wait to meet this young man!" my mum said. In his usual jovial tone, my dad said, "I'll be on my best behaviour!" But I was nervous. What parents want to find out that their daughter's boyfriend is an ex-convict on life parole for murder? And on Mother's Day? Still, before any attachment was formed between them and him, I'd tell them the truth.

My parents liked Jason immediately. We convened at a restaurant on Saturday night, and I could see it in their attitude. With his easygoing demeanour, natural conversation skills and impeccable manners, Jason fit in with my outgoing and good-natured parents. We all relaxed into a pleasant evening of getting acquainted, and I observed how he avoided questions that might provoke curiosity or digging into the past; I found myself doing the same. It was stressful to know that before the weekend was out, I would have to disclose the painful facts. I didn't fully enjoy the meal and nor did Jason, though my parents were having a great time. My mum told me later that when she went to bed that night a feeling of peace came over her as she thought to herself, *I just met the man that Shannon is going to marry and he is perfect for her.*

The next day was Mother's Day, and while I had not attended Mass for many years, I knew how much it would mean to my parents to take them to church for the occasion. Many times I had driven by a small, stone Catholic church just down the road from the imposing walls of Kingston Penitentiary. The church had an intriguing name, Church of the Good Thief, and it was built from stone quarried by inmates in the late nineteenth century. The priest that day gave a sermon that honoured mothers' ability to love their children unconditionally. As I listened, all I could think about was the conversation we were about to have in which I would break the news that the man my mum had already pictured as her son-in-law was a convicted murderer.

I looked over at my beautiful parents who had raised me to forgive others and to be compassionate. They did so under the banner of Catholicism, though the same tenet of treating others as you want to be treated is central to so many faiths. We had relied on faith to guide us through some hard times as a family. Mum coped with chronic and acute illnesses that frequently hospitalized her. Her parents and younger brother had died within a few short years, followed soon thereafter by my dad's younger sister. Though I had left the Church at sixteen, angry and unable to reconcile faith with politics and patriarchy, I held onto my belief in the existence of "something bigger" in the universe—and maintained a strong resolution that I must play a part in creating a better world.

I had learned that my upbringing had been very different from Jason's. He was adopted at three months old after being passed through three foster families. His adoptive parents separated when he was four, sharing custody of Jason. When his mother was admitted to hospital because of worsening bipolar disorder, his father wanted full custody. Sadly, he was diagnosed with terminal leukemia around the same time. Jason learned of his father's death when his teacher asked him to stand up in front of his grade-one class. The teacher told the six-year-olds to say a prayer for Jason because his daddy had died. He remembered standing perfectly still while feeling a swirl of emotions:

confusion, sadness, and even embarrassment over being centred out in front of the class. Jason had only two memories of his father. One was a vague image of a bedside visit at the hospital shortly before his dad died, and the other a clearer image of being four and in trouble over something. He ran from his house and down a little hill, while his dad called after him from the front door. His dad was upset about something. That was all Jason claimed to remember—or rather all he told me at the time.

Mother's Day 2003 was sunny and warm. My parents and I drove the short distance back to my house after Mass, where I invited them to sit at the dining room table while I made coffee. They were eager to talk about Jason, who had gone to spend the day with his own mother in Quebec.

"He seems like a wonderful man, Shannon," my mum said. "It's clear that he is in love with you, and it seems you feel the same way." My dad nodded in agreement.

I sat down in the chair across from them, my palms sweaty. "All those things are true," I began, "but there is something else you need to know about Jason." Then I told them about Jason's past the same way he had told me. The happy expressions on their faces disappeared. When I finished, my mum said, "It doesn't make sense. I can't picture the man we just met being capable of such terrible violence." Usually one to add levity to a tense moment with a joke, my dad just sighed heavily and shook his head. We spoke for well over an hour, and I explained what my journey had been over the last three months, and how, after a difficult process, I had been able to come to terms with everything.

My mum put her arm around me. Then my dad spoke up, with a confidence that surprised me.

"Well, Shan, I trust you. If he is the right person for you, then he is the right person for me."

I couldn't believe my ears.

My mum was more hesitant. "Can I talk with Jason about this myself? I have some questions I would like to ask him."

I said I'd check with him, but that I was sure he'd say yes.

Over time, and through many open-hearted discussions, my parents' fears and doubts gave way to love, forgiveness and a desire to help Jason fulfill his dreams. He assured them that he would never hurt anyone again and would never end up back in prison. They respected his honesty and sense of responsibility as I did, and they could see how happy we were with each other.

Jason moved in with me in June, four months after we'd met, and we found ourselves enjoying simple, domestic bliss—cooking together, playing Scrabble, riding bikes, and entertaining friends. We never bickered or argued. He took me to meet his mother, aunt and uncle in Quebec. As the months passed, Jason became part of our family, disclosing his past to my sister and brother, as well as to several of my close friends. The reaction was always the same: shock, sadness, disbelief, and in the end, a compassion that included accepting him for who he was now and for his desire to make a new life—one that would include me and them and would shun violence. My family, my friends and I all became part of the fabric that would form the best second chance a person could ever ask for.

Everything was in place for Jason's success at his next parole hearing, in January of 2004, almost a year after we'd first met. He was in a healthy and committed relationship; he had finally taken the advice of his case-management team on furthering his education and had been accepted to college; he had significant support around him; and he was entering his sixth year of living violence-free in the community. The Parole Board granted his application for full parole. We were all thrilled.

His case managers were excited about the possibility of seeing Jason develop his skills and talents toward a sustainable and rewarding career over the long term, and so was everyone who loved him. Jason confided in me that even though he'd always been encouraged to pursue his artistic side, what he really wanted to be was a firefighter. "I know I can never make up for the life that I took," he said, "but I have this fantasy that I'm driving along a country road and come across a burning house. I run in and save everyone, and then somehow I'm free—my own life will be justified again."

At six foot three and 220 pounds, his physical size and strength made him a great candidate for the job, but because of his criminal record, Jason was excluded from membership in the professional college of firefighters. Instead, he decided to enroll in the forest fire fighting program at Fleming College (which didn't have the same barrier)—but to do that he'd need to upgrade his math. This he could do at the Peterborough campus. We decided to move to Peterborough for this opportunity.

Since his application for full parole had been granted, he no longer had to spend any time in a halfway house and his only connection to the Correctional Service would be through a parole officer who would visit once a month. Jason was to sign in at the police station monthly and set up an initial appointment with a psychologist in town, someone whom he could see if necessary. He would no longer be required to disclose his parole status to anyone whose private home he visited over-

night. His restrictions against drugs and alcohol remained, however. "Staying stable" was the de facto goal.

My long-time friends Georgina and Mark told Jason and me
that we were welcome to stay with them at their farm outside
Peterborough until we decided on more permanent housing.
Before accepting their generous offer, we told them about Jason's
past, and they also spoke with his parole officer, who assured
them of Jason's safety. They were accepting, and Jason and I
enjoyed their good company and hospitality for six months.

In the spring, we bought a little house built just after the
Second World War and moved in at the end of the school year.
It had been well maintained, though it was almost completely
wallpapered with floral prints and the windows were covered
with sky-blue sheers. We pulled everything apart and rebuilt it,
learning how to tile, put up drywall, and install a bathtub and
toilet. We soon knew the people at our local hardware and home
renovation store by name. I painted the basement walls a bright
yellow and laid down a section of washable tile on the floor so
that Jason would have a place to do his art. All through the
summer, we worked. We got to know the neighbours, and to
know ourselves in a new light, and we built the foundation for
a life together. Almost every evening, we strolled hand-in-hand
around the neighbourhood or rode our bikes on local trails.
Sometimes our route took us by a gorgeous old school downtown, and I imagined aloud working in the guidance office there
one day. My dream job in the perfect location.

At the end of the summer, I was hired as a guidance counsellor at that very school. I was thrilled. Instead of beginning the
forestry program at the college (his math upgrade had not gone
well), Jason enrolled in the drawing and painting program at
the art school and began what was to be the most successful

and rewarding education experience of his life. When he finished his program with straight A's, he began working on his portfolio and making contacts with children's book publishers, now dreaming of being a work-at-home illustrator. I wrote a story that Jason illustrated, which he sent out. In the meantime, he got a part-time job at a health food store to help pay the bills. I loved my new job and our new community, and quickly engaged in volunteer work too.

Just after Christmas of 2004, after almost two years together, we decided to get engaged. Jason took me to the top of the hill behind our house, told me he loved me beyond words, and asked me to marry him. With the view of the city lights below and the wide-open winter sky above us, I told him I loved him just as much and said, "Of course I'll marry you!" We began 2005 by planning our wedding.

We were married in a beautiful outdoor ceremony in front of a hundred family members and friends on Thanksgiving weekend. We exchanged our vows under the autumn leaves at Georgina and Mark's farmhouse, then danced the night away at a reception in a historic downtown venue. The following day we invited the guests over to our house, where we ate leftover wedding cake, opened gifts, and listened to music performed by my friends from Ecuador, where I'd spent a year and a half as a student and then intern. We enjoyed a three-day honeymoon at my aunt and uncle's cottage—all the time I could take off from school at such a busy time of year. Then, Jason and I happily settled into our life together as husband and wife. Four weeks into our married life, right before I left for the conference in Toronto, I went out to stock up on groceries. As I put provisions into the pantry cupboard, a satisfied feeling came over me. Everything was just as it should be. I looked forward to a winter of nesting, beginning when I came back from my work weekend away.

The morning I left, I dropped Jason off for his shift at the store and kissed him goodbye.

"See you for dinner Tuesday night!" he said as he got out of the car.

"Sure thing," I called. "It'll be our one-month anniversary!" I waved and smiled, and he waved and smiled back.

CHAPTER FOUR

BREAKING NEWS

I had run out of things to say to the police officer, so we sat in an awkward silence while we waited for my parents to arrive at the hotel. I struggled to make sense of what the sergeant had told me. My life as I'd known it began to crumble around me. Forty-five minutes passed before my parents finally arrived. My mum stepped through the door first and as soon as I saw the fear in her eyes, I broke down in tears.

"What happened?" She opened her arms to me.

"Jason's broken and we can't fix him," I cried out.

My dad repeated her question, his face ashen. He put his arms around both of us.

"Didn't he know how much we loved him?" my mum asked, her voice quavering.

Her question hung unanswered in the air. How could he *not* know that we loved him? My parents still thought there must be some mistake, but as I recounted what the sergeant had told me, whatever thread of hope they had fell away.

My mum sat down with me on the bed while my dad spoke quietly to the officer, who had risen from his chair and was now back by the door. My dad and the officer took my luggage downstairs. When they returned, we thanked the officer. He suggested we leave separately so that no further attention would be drawn to us by the sight of a uniformed escort. My mum and dad led me to the elevator, down to the lobby and out past all the conference attendees to the parking lot. I don't know what the officer did next: whether he went to tell my colleagues I wouldn't be coming back to the conference, or if he just discreetly slipped out.

In the car, I began making phone calls. The first was to Jason's parole officer. I was very fond of him and trusted him. I wanted to meet him in Peterborough as soon as we got there. I needed to talk with someone who knew Jason, knew the system and could explain to me what had happened and what would happen next.

I started crying immediately when I heard his voice.

"Shannon," he said, "I'm so sorry, but I'm not allowed to talk to you. Corrections has taken me off his file . . . there is going to be an investigation—an internal audit . . ."

He sounded very distressed. He knew and cared about both Jason and me. Was he going to take the heat for this? I couldn't bear the thought of it.

"I didn't know . . . I didn't know anything was wrong," I said desperately.

"I didn't either. No one knew."

"Are you okay?" I asked.

He assured me he would be fine and that he would call me as soon as he was cleared. He didn't know how long it would take—weeks or months.

I felt completely abandoned when the call ended. I could understand that he couldn't talk with Jason, but why not me?

Would there be anyone I could talk to at Corrections in the meantime? And what about Jason's parole officer—what would happen to him? It was starting to sink in just how far-reaching the effects of Jason's actions were going to be.

I phoned the friend who'd been my maid of honour. She was starting the second day of a brand-new job in Ottawa and I felt terrible calling her at her office, but I didn't want her to hear the news from anyone but me. She began repeating in a highly distressed voice, "What? What? Oh my God!" Again, I explained what I knew.

Sobbing, I dialed Jason's aunt and uncle's number in Quebec. These were Jason's closest relatives aside from his mother. His mother was in an Ottawa hospital, fighting to stay alive after a car accident months earlier. Between her ongoing mental illness and the injuries from her accident, she barely recognized Jason or me anymore. We had never even told her that we had married. Jason's uncle Dave answered the phone. I had a hard time finding the words, though I'd now said them several times. "Jason has been arrested. He sexually assaulted and then kidnapped two women." For them, this would be the second time in their lives they'd received awful news of Jason's crimes.

Dave just kept saying, "No! It can't be . . . no!"

Finally, I called my vice-principal at school. Not only was she an administrator I respected, she was also a mentor and a friend who shared my love of working with teens. The CBC was already airing reports of Jason's arrest. What should they do? she asked. I suggested telling the school staff either at lunchtime or at the end of the day. That way, everyone would be together to hear the news before they saw it on TV. I didn't know what—if anything—students should be told. I hadn't taken Jason's surname, but I didn't know how much that would protect me, if at all. As my mind raced through all this, part of me was still the professional caregiver, wanting everyone in my school community to have support when they found out. The rest of me was terrified and in total shock, needing to support myself.

"Is there anyone you want me to call?" my vice-principal asked.

I thought of Erin, a fellow teacher. We had worked together at an emergency youth shelter the year before when I'd been asked by my principal to set up an alternative school program for homeless youth. Erin and I bonded quickly and became fast friends, soon bringing our partners into the equation to make four. Erin's six-year-old daughter, Sarah, made five. She had a particular affection for Jason, as many kids did. She was enchanted by his drawings and he by her pixie ways. Sarah was the "flower fairy" at our wedding, leading us down the aisle wearing wings and a white dress. Juxtaposing such a sweet memory against what was happening now, I could only imagine Erin's dismay at the news of what Jason had done. How would we tell a six-year-old that her big teddy-bear-like friend was going to jail?

"Anyone else?" my vice-principal asked.

I mentioned another teacher on staff, someone I had been getting to know well. She and her husband lived within walking distance of Jason and me, and we were becoming friends as couples, taking turns hosting Thursday-night dinners. We had not yet told them about Jason's past. Now they would find out everything.

The rest of the drive up to Peterborough was a blur of tears and painful realizations. My mum drove me in her car while my dad followed in my rental car. We would have to return it, on our way into town, to the same agency where Jason had rented the van yesterday. I suddenly felt like I was going to be sick and asked my mum to stop the car. She pulled over and I got out, but nothing would come up. I was empty inside. My dad pulled up behind us and suggested that we stop for some food. A few more kilometres up the road, we stopped, and he bought me tea and a plain toasted bagel, but I couldn't eat.

We drove on and I remember crying out, "Who will I have my babies with?" My mum did not have the answer.

As we neared the police station, with my hopes and dreams for a life with Jason falling down around me, I was filled with fear. What would I encounter? Would there be reporters waiting there? Would I be identified? And my house? What was happening at my house?

CHAPTER FIVE

RIVER OF TEARS

We finally arrived at the police station, where, thankfully, we did not see any reporters. We parked on the street, walked through the front doors and gave our names to the officer at reception. I had been to the police station before—once accompanying a student who was preparing to appear in court as a victim, and a couple of times to obtain clearance letters for volunteer jobs. Now I was here for a reason beyond my worst nightmare.

After a few minutes in the main waiting room, a constable led me and my parents down a corridor. We passed my school's liaison officer, who was on his way out, his face solemn. I wondered if he was heading to the school to provide support or information. I didn't have a chance to ask. We were shown into a small interview room and asked to wait. The window of the room looked out onto the street, and through it I could see the back of city hall; beyond that, my school—a beautiful, historic three-storey red-limestone building. *Why am I here and not there?*

I sat down with my mum in front of a table. My dad stood behind us, protective. A few moments later, a man in a suit jacket came in and introduced himself as Walter, the sergeant I had spoken to on the phone from the hotel room. He was a big, burly-but-friendly plainclothes cop. He greeted us kindly and then sat down across from me and my mum.

"I'm sorry for the events that have brought you here," the sergeant began. "I can only imagine how distressing this must be." We all nodded. "Let me begin by reviewing what I told you on the phone. Jason is charged with several serious offences, including sexual assault, aggravated sexual assault and kidnapping. The attacks happened yesterday afternoon and we became aware of them when a 9-1-1 dispatcher called us late last night." He spoke slowly and repeated only the facts we already knew. It was as if he were holding back—waiting for something. We were waiting too, but we didn't know for what. Later I would learn he was stalling because an investigation team was being organized and they were preparing for a formal interview. They didn't want me to know too much before they questioned me.

What he did explain was that a customer had entered the store where Jason worked. "Jason took her at knifepoint to a backroom where he bound her with duct tape and then sexually assaulted her." When Sergeant DiClemente said those words, I started to cry in horror and humiliation. So did my parents. In soft voices, we kept repeating, "Jason . . . oh God, Jason! How could you?"

Sergeant DiClemente continued, saying that the assault involved Jason forcing the first woman onto her knees to perform fellatio and later involved penetration of some sort. He was vague. Another customer came in the store then and Jason held her at knifepoint as well. She struggled until he overpowered her by choking her to unconsciousness. At some point she was also sexually assaulted. Then Jason rented the van, returned to the store, and brought the women to our house. Waves of revulsion hit me as I struggled to mentally process images of Jason committing these disgusting acts. I imagined the victims, their pain and terror. What had happened to them was my own worst nightmare as a woman. My parents and I listened in stunned silence, afraid to move. One of us finally formed the question we were all thinking:

"How are the women?"

The sergeant took a breath. "They are alive," he said. "They are being treated at the hospital and are expected to be released into the care of their families in a few hours."

They were alive? Did that mean they had come close to death? I began sobbing inconsolably again and couldn't stop. *Oh my God . . . oh my God!* I could feel my mum trembling beside me and my dad shaking his head and wiping tears from his face.

Sergeant DiClemente continued. "The women were very brave. It could easily have become a double-homicide . . . My understanding is that they talked with Jason during the assault and tried to reason with him when they were at your house. He was talking about killing himself."

"Sergeant DiClemente," I managed to say, "I—"

"Please call me Walter."

"Walter . . . I spoke with Jason last night. I spoke with him on the phone."

"You did?" He sounded taken aback. "When?"

"About 10:20. I called because . . . because we always talk at ten when I'm away." I shared the details of our conversation: how Jason had said he wasn't feeling well; how I revealed I might be pregnant. I explained about the keynote speaker at the conference who'd reminded me of Jason, and how Jason had thanked me for encouraging him, how he'd said, "That means so much to me right now." I remembered the slight, almost undetectable emphasis on his words *right now*. The significance was now so painfully obvious.

Walter was listening intently. When I finished, he leaned back in his chair. Then another officer came to the door and called him out into the hall. They had a brief conversation and Walter returned to tell us that Jason was going to be arraigned in court at two o'clock. If we wanted to be there, we should go right away; it was now quarter to two. The court was just down the hill and on a normal day it was close enough to walk. This was no normal day. We drove quickly.

More than once I had gone to the courthouse to support students or gather information on their behalf. Now, as I passed professionals I knew, flanked by my parents, I walked through the crowded halls in disbelief. *This time, I'm here because of my husband*. We read the list of charges on the docket: two counts each of sexual assault, aggravated sexual assault, forcible confinement, assault, aggravated assault, assault with a weapon, kidnapping, and one count of choking, one count of weapons dangerous, and one count of "overcoming resistance to commit an indictable offence," a charge I didn't understand. It all came to me in a fog.

In the courtroom, we struggled to retain our composure. The police told us that Jason had refused his right to counsel, but we thought he should have representation. The lawyer on duty counsel agreed, and explained that the court would never let him stand trial without a lawyer anyway, since the charges were so serious. He warned that it could be months before someone was assigned, so we might want to take on the task of finding a lawyer ourselves. He imagined we would need legal aid. We nodded, overwhelmed. We were negotiating our way through a foreign land, but we would do whatever the court asked.

There was no time to ask for clarification; Jason was being brought in. He was led into the prisoner's box in the courtroom, almost unrecognizable—a dead body standing, handcuffed, wearing an orange jumpsuit. The sight was devastating. He would not look at us. It made me want to scream, but I just cried and held my parents' hands. The judge read in the charges and the duty counsel said Jason's family had agreed to find a lawyer for him, nodding in our direction as he spoke. I felt all eyes in the crowded courtroom turn to look at us. The judge looked at me and my parents, then at Jason and asked if he was amenable to the plan. Jason flinched and nodded, never looking up. The judge scribbled something on a piece of paper before remanding him to Central East Correctional Centre, a maximum-security provincial jail in Lindsay, forty-five minutes west of Peterborough. A return court date was set for two weeks later. Jason hung his head while the guards shuffled him back out through the door.

His appearance had lasted no more than five minutes, and then he was gone. Who was he? What was going to happen? Would I ever again see the Jason I knew?

My parents drove me back to the police station. We were met by a female officer named Nora who took us into an interview room. She said that she needed to ask me some questions and then she would tell me everything that had happened the night before. She asked if I wanted my parents present. I said no. I had faint notions of wanting privacy, independence. I also wanted to protect them. My parents waited while I was taken across the hall.

Nora asked me to get as comfortable as possible, and pointed to a small couch, where I sat down. She sat in a chair opposite me and explained that my interview would be videotaped. She asked me how I had met Jason, what our life together had been like, and what I knew about his past. Then she asked me to explain in detail the sexual life Jason and I shared, which I did. There had never even been a trace of force or violence. I felt detached, pouring out personal details, grateful that my mum and dad weren't there.

The interview continued for well over an hour. Then Nora told me that Jason had confessed to surreptitiously filming people, including me, going to the bathroom in our home on several occasions over an unknown period of time. *Voyeurism.* It was another heartbreaking revelation. For reasons yet to be understood, Jason had put the videotapes in the van before calling the police, so now they were in evidence. How could he have done this? How could he have hurt me like this? The police had not yet watched the videos and the search of our house was still pending, so Nora couldn't tell me very many details about how he'd done this or who the other people videotaped were. Soon they would need me to come into the police station to watch the videos and identify the victims. What would I see on those tapes? Who would I see?

I didn't express outright any feelings of rage or hatred toward Jason during the interview—I could only cry in agony and fear. When I wasn't crying, I was overcome by numbness. I didn't have the energy that anger requires, and what I was hearing about was so overwhelming that developing an anger to match it would have consumed me completely. Nora seemed troubled by this, as though she wanted to see me raging mad.

After she finished asking me questions, she left the room,

saying that when she returned she would tell me about every-thing that had happened. I needed to lie down. It was now close to five in the afternoon and I hadn't eaten anything since the night before. I was also still bleeding, though no one knew about that but me. I asked Nora if it was okay to put my head on the arm of the couch for a while and she said it was fine. I leaned over and stared sideways blankly, feeling nothing.

Several minutes later, Nora returned and I sat up. She began to recount, in graphic detail, what had happened the afternoon and evening before.

At about 4:15, a forty-six-year-old woman had walked into the health food store where Jason worked. He held her at knife-point, threatening her life. He dragged her into a backroom where he tied her with duct tape, made her perform fellatio, and then sodomized her violently. The attack was so vicious that the woman had to be treated with several stitches. I was disgusted. My mind involuntarily created images of such an attack—an anal rape by a stranger—but because I couldn't pic-ture the victim, I pictured it happening to me. It was dirty, depraved and grotesque. What sickness could make someone do this? Another wave of nausea hit me and I felt dizzy.

I tried to concentrate on what Nora was telling me. Jason had not locked the door to the store, so when another woman came in, he held her too at knifepoint and threatened her, fear-ing she had heard the first assault. The second victim was twenty-six years old, the same age as my younger sister. She fought with Jason, grabbing his hand that held the knife. In the struggle, Jason's knife cut her deeply across her palm. I nodded silently at Nora but I was in deep shock. Now I understood what the charge of "overcoming resistance to commit an indict-able offence was": the second woman had fought back. Unable to restrain her as he had the first woman, Jason choked the second victim to unconsciousness. Then he carried her into the basement where he bound her with tape and rope. When she regained consciousness moments later, Jason sexually assaulted her too. He grabbed and pulled her breasts and twisted her nipples until she was in pain. Nora told me that he "digitally penetrated" her, a term that confused me until she put two of her fingers together and made a shoving motion, demonstrating that Jason had pushed his fingers into the young woman's vagina. I cringed.

Following these brutal assaults, Jason called the car rental company and requested a cargo van. When he came back with the rental van approximately an hour later, he wrapped the women in garbage bags, poked breathing holes in them, and carried them up the stairs and out the back door of the store to where the van was parked. He loaded them inside. No one saw him. It was dark by this time, and cold. He drove them to our house, less than two kilometres away.

When he arrived, Jason carried the women to our basement, where he ripped the garbage bags open. The women's eyes were taped, and so were their hands and feet, but they still tried to talk to Jason, to re-humanize him and bring him down from his psychotic ledge. He removed the tape from their eyes and the first victim noticed Jason's paintings and photos of us on the walls. She used them to make conversation with him. At some point, Jason left our house to go back to the store for a ladder and some rope because he was formulating a suicide plan. When he returned, the women continued to talk with him. When Jason told them about his plan to take his own life, even as their own lives were in his hands, they tried to convince him not to end things this way.

As Nora told me how the women had acted, I was overcome with emotion. I was in awe of their bravery, their presence of mind. I was also devastated by the violence they had endured. I kept picturing them in my home. I hoped, likely in vain, that something of mine—anything—would have offered some comfort or distraction during their terrifying ordeal. More than anything, I felt utterly helpless.

At about 10:45, Jason left the house and drove to a pay phone at the end of our street where he called 9-1-1 and asked to be connected to the police. He told them who he was, what he had done, and he asked them to rescue the women from our home. Then he drove to an adjacent street to watch our house and wait for the police to arrive. Almost half an hour passed but the police did not come. They later explained that they were unsure of what to do, wondering if this was a prank or if they were being drawn purposefully into a dangerous situation. No one on duty had ever heard of a Jason Staples, though he had signed in at the station once a month for the first nine or ten months we'd lived in Peterborough, until the parole office decided it wasn't necessary. They searched their parolee files but found nothing. They later blamed Corrections for not forwarding his file, and Corrections blamed the police for being disorganized.

When the police failed to arrive, Jason returned to the pay phone and called 9-1-1 again, repeating his request for the police to rescue the women. By this time they had traced the call to the pay phone and had several cruisers assembled at a park just up the road. As Jason was getting back into the van after making the second call, the police cars surrounded him. They performed a high-risk takedown, meaning that the officers' guns were drawn, though Jason was unarmed and was arrested without resistance.

I told Nora then that I'd spoken to Jason on the phone at 10:20. She seemed surprised to hear this. Later, she and several other officers, including Sergeant DiClemente, would insist that it was my phone call that prompted him to get help for the women, but I was never sure about that. I believed it was only part of the reason. The women themselves played a huge role in re-humanizing him—this could not be downplayed. Maybe our house, too, played a part. There, Jason was surrounded by our life: photos, grocery lists, the walls we had painted together. There must have been some reason why he chose to go home instead of anywhere else.

At one point during the interview, Nora paused and looked at my hand. "Do you and Jason have matching wedding rings?"

I nodded, caught off guard by her observation. What did it matter?

"He wasn't wearing his ring yesterday, you know," she said. Her tone seemed smug, almost defiant.

I didn't know how to respond. Was she thinking he'd taken off his wedding ring yesterday because he planned to go out and rape two women? Jason always took his ring off in the shower, and that is where I later found it. Still, I felt a sharp, stinging sensation. Was the officer insinuating that I was a fool, naively playing my new role as bride while my husband lurked in the filth of sexual deviancy, a pervert looking for his prey? Worse, did she think I had known something in advance—or had even been a part of Jason's deviant life?

Nora's questioning didn't stop there. "Do you know that the average cycle of a sex offender is seven years?" I shook my head blankly while she continued. "Jason has been out in the community for seven years." Her tone seemed to insinuate that I should have seen his violence coming.

Should I have known this? No one had ever mentioned anything like this to me—not Jason's parole officers in Kingston or Peterborough, nor his psychologists in both places. And why would they? Until last night, Jason had never been considered a sex offender. And there was nothing in our personal lives together that I could think of that suggested Jason could be anything other than a caring, kind, and fully reformed human being. Still, I thought I could hear blame in Nora's voice, as though I, too, had done something wrong. Nothing prepared me for finding myself the target of these suspicions. How could Jason have done this to me? How could he have betrayed our vows and left me here to be scrutinized?

Nora went on to tell me that there was already talk in the police station about Jason being a likely candidate to receive the "dangerous offender" designation once convicted. I recognized the term only from the worst and most heinous offender in Canadian history—Paul Bernardo. He and his accomplice-wife, Karla Homolka, were charged with the abduction and sex slayings of two teenage girls in the town of St. Catharines, Ontario, many years before. Homolka also twice gave drugs to her younger sister, Tammy, a girl just fifteen years old, so that Bernardo could rape her. The teenager choked on her own vomit and died after the second assault, two days before Christmas in 1990. I was fifteen that year, too. I remembered the case well and was haunted by it.

Following a long and drawn-out trial, Bernardo was convicted of numerous counts of sexual assault, two counts of first-degree murder and, in addition to the automatic sentence of life imprisonment without parole eligibility for twenty-five years, was declared a dangerous offender and sentenced to an indeterminate period of incarceration, Canada's highest penalty. He was placed at Kingston Penitentiary in protective custody—solitary confinement—with the bare minimum of human contact, deemed a psychopath. His wife was convicted of the lesser charge of manslaughter after a much-criticized plea bargain, and sentenced to twelve years. She was scheduled for release in a week.

When I heard the label "dangerous offender" attributed to Jason, my devastation deepened. My thoughts became protests: *No, no . . . not my Jason! He is not a Paul Bernardo. Are they thinking he is? Are they thinking I am his Karla Homolka?*

The last thing Nora said was that at the end of Jason's statement, he had told the detective he never wanted to see his wife again. She said he had written me a note, and also posted a message on the website he had been designing to market himself as an illustrator.

"What does the note say?" I asked Nora, desperate for any clue about Jason's state of mind.

"I don't know—it's still at your house. It will be taken into evidence during the search, and I can tell you then, if you want."

I nodded. Then I asked her about the website message and she suggested I look it up online; it would take the police a couple of days to get an order for the hosting company to shut the site down. I nodded, crushed. Just as I could not imagine anything else that had happened in the last twenty-four hours, I could not imagine Jason saying that he never wanted to see me again.

The Jason who had been presented to me over the last several hours was not a man I had ever met. He wasn't even the eighteen-year-old I'd tried to envision so many times, and whom I'd come to accept, as so many others had before me, as the correctional system's "best guy," someone who would never again pose a threat of violence. He was now a rapist. He embodied my own worst fears. I'd loved him like I'd never loved anyone else. And now I was bound to him through marriage. I felt my heart split right down the middle.

It was close to six by the time I saw my parents again—they were waiting in the lobby of the police station. While I was with Nora, they had made a number of phone calls, including one to my friends Georgina and Mark, who invited us to their farm. My parents had also called my brother and sister in Toronto, and they were on their way up to meet us there, along with my vice-principal, my doctor, and a few close friends. As we headed toward the farm, I thought of asking my dad to drive by my house, but I was afraid of what I would see. Would there be camera crews and reporters? Police? Neighbours? We drove straight on to Georgina and Mark's. The last time I'd made this drive with my parents, exactly a month earlier, I was wearing my wedding dress.

Arriving at the farm was like arriving at a wake—Jason's wake, as if he'd been killed in a sudden accident. My siblings came in right after us, their faces pale. Then my doctor arrived, followed by my vice-principal, who said that she was working on getting me approval for an emergency leave-of-absence. Everyone hugged me and each other, and Georgina sat me on the couch in the living room while Mark made tea. I was shaky and cold. Mark came back in with the tea, but I couldn't drink. My friends and family formed a circle around me. We huddled together in disbelief. I recounted everything that the police had told me.

When I finished, my dad responded in a broken voice, "I just know something must have happened to Jason when he was a little boy . . . I love him like my own son."

We all nodded solemnly. Sue, our doctor, spoke next.

"He was wounded inside and he wasn't brave enough to tell us."

Yes. This was probably true.

The couple Jason and I had recently become friends with arrived then and I stood up to greet them, our eyes flooding with tears as we put our arms around each other. They knew the charges but they hadn't been told any of the details, so I recounted everything yet again. They looked totally shocked.

"But we . . . we saw Jason last night," the man said.

"What? Where?"

"Outside the store, around seven or seven-thirty," his wife replied. "We were on our regular walk when we noticed him standing by the roadside, so we stopped to talk."

"What did he say?"

"He said that he was waiting for a rental car company to pick him up. He'd rented a van and was going to look at a blacksmithing forge that was for sale, thinking he would probably buy it. He seemed kind of . . . nervous . . . or hyper. He is usually so calm that it struck us as odd, but it wouldn't have been that noticeable to anyone who didn't know him. We didn't feel worried or anything."

No, of course not. Why would Jason's friends suspect that he was waiting for a rental van he planned to use to kidnap two women he had just sexually assaulted? It was unbelievable. The blacksmithing forge story seemed completely random at first, until I recalled that Jason had mentioned returning to art college to take a blacksmith course—he had spoken of it a few times. Was he angry with me for making him wait until we could afford it? Was this related to what was wrong with him? If it was, why didn't he tell me?

Everyone in the room was bewildered. Who was this Jason? How could this be? A month ago we'd all been in this same place, under sunshine and trees, celebrating our wedding. I had an overwhelming urge to go outside and lie down on the frosty ground of the hollow below the cedar trees, in the exact spot where we had exchanged vows. I didn't care about the cold or the damp, I just wanted to lie down on the earth and stay there until my world stopped shaking. I wanted to weep into the fallen leaves, let the soil below absorb my tears and take their salt to the tree roots far, far underground.

But I couldn't get away. I knew that people would come looking for me if I tried. Everyone wanted to keep me close, especially my mum. Georgina called everyone to the dining room table, where she'd put out some dinner. I managed to slip away then, saying I had to use the washroom, leaving my plate of food untouched. I went upstairs to the sloped-ceiling second floor of the century-old farmhouse and found my way into the bathroom, where I looked at the tub and remembered how, when we stayed with Georgina and Mark before we bought our own house, Jason had drawn me a warm bath to soak in when I was sick. He sat on the edge of the tub holding my hand, and though I looked awful, he told me I was beautiful. We shared a big bedroom down the hall as well as a little alcove at the top of a secret staircase. That winter, Jason helped Mark with the maple sugaring, while I marked assignments and told stories around the dinner table of the funny things that happened at school. At night, Jason and I snuggled under heavy blankets and I laughed as he formulated a hilarious commentary about the dopey clusterflies swarming around the window casings and dive-bombing us in bed. Those times seemed pristine, sepia-toned, against the horror of what had just taken place.

Georgina and Mark's home was alive with memories for me. The weight of the destruction that I was facing now, standing in the same place I'd been so happy a month ago, was unbearable. I crumpled to a heap on the floor in the hall. Georgina came upstairs then. I expected her to coax me back to standing, but instead she got down on the floor beside me and smoothed my forehead and hair with her hands.

"My dear," she said, "you are going to cry a river of tears. You are going to cry for a long, long time, and we're going to be here."

CHAPTER SIX

THROUGH THE GLASS

Later that night, my parents took me back to their home. I was not allowed to return to my house; it was now a crime scene. Officers would be combing through it for evidence.

Using my mum's computer, I logged on to the Internet and typed in the URL for Jason's website. I clicked on the link to his artist statement and read the message he had written:

> Hi everyone. I'm not sure who'll be reading this: police, loved ones, family, friends, my victims. Whomever you may be, I just wanted to apologize to everyone that I've hurt. I have no right to expect forgiveness and unfortunately I don't have any answers to give you either. Please know that there is nothing any of you could have done to change me. Some of us are just this way. Take care and appreciate life.
> *Jason.*

It was clearly a suicide note. I stared at the screen, my body numb at first. As I read his note over again, fury began to rise.

This is it? This is all we get? "Some of us are just this way." *What was that supposed to mean? Born to be killers and rapists?* It was a helpless and pathetic excuse. I deserved a better explanation than that; we all did.

I thought hard. If Jason's plan hadn't been intercepted by the police—if he had killed himself instead of being arrested—then there would have been no possibility for answers. But Jason was still alive. I wanted to talk to him. Didn't I deserve that opportunity after what he had just done to my life?

Next, I called my own phone. The first message was a man's urgent voice: "Jason! Jason buddy! Pick up the phone. Jason buddy, just pick up the phone . . ." It must have been a police officer in response to Jason's first 9-1-1 call. He had given our address to the dispatcher, so he or she must have thought he was calling from home, not from a pay phone. I saved the message and then listened to the next one. It was Una, Jason's grandmotherly friend from Martha's Table. She spoke slowly and calmly, but I could hear distress in her voice too.

"Shannon—we've heard on the radio. We've heard the allegations about Jason . . . Are they true?"

I imagined Una listening to the radio in her tranquil little stone cottage and hearing the horrible news.

"Call us as soon as you can. We love you and we are holding you in the light." She repeated it again, slower this time. "We are holding you and Jason in the light."

At midnight, I tried to allow Una's words to permeate as I lay down in my parents' guest bedroom, my sister beside me, rubbing my back to help me fall asleep.

"I love you, Shanny. Wake me up if you need to talk, okay?"

"Thanks, I will. I love you too." But I let her go to sleep while I lay awake, the events of the last two days playing out in my mind, over and over, bringing only questions and pain. Eventually, I fell into a fitful sleep.

The next morning, Wednesday, I took a pregnancy test as soon as I got up. I had almost stopped bleeding but I didn't know what that meant. I felt desperate and conflicted: if the results were positive, there would be new life amid all this devastation—something to hold onto from my brief happiness with Jason. But then, how could I have a baby during this ordeal? And how would I raise a child whose father was in prison for rape? I had come to terms with one day telling our children that Jason had murdered someone long, long ago. Now, everything had changed. Now, Jason would be a convict, not an ex-convict, and he carried the additional, devastating label of sex offender. How could I bring a child into this world to face such stigma?

I watched and waited anxiously as the test stick stayed white. Negative. If I had been pregnant, I wasn't anymore. Waves of relief and sadness washed over me. I crawled back into bed and tried to lie still. I had so much information to try to make sense of and it was all so painful. My mum brought me some yogourt but I couldn't eat it. She returned to the kitchen and began typing on the computer. The sound of the keyboard clicking seemed as loud as thunder. The ringing phone was almost unbearable. After a little while, I got out of bed to check my e-mail and found my inbox overwhelmed with messages. Some people had driven by our house, had seen the police tape, and became extremely worried when they couldn't get hold of Jason or me. Had we been robbed? Had there been a death? Others had heard the reports on the radio and television, or read them in the local newspapers. I began to feel responsible for letting people know that I was okay.

My body quickly developed a cycle to cope with the shock: thirty minutes of really hard-wrenched crying, easing off into numbness for an hour or so during which I couldn't really move but my mind would start to turn and gain momentum. Then I would begin talking to a family member or friend, trying to figure things out—until this search for answers reached an almost manic state. I racked my brain for a way to understand, sifting through the details I knew and searching for clues I might have missed leading up to Jason's explosion. I found nothing. I felt like an animal. When the manic process wore off I would sink back down to begin the cycle again: devastation, grief, sobbing, then silence and numbness, then the slow climb back up to make sense of the senseless.

In the early afternoon, my friend Lisa came over. She brought her bouncy and gurgly baby boy and the presence of this perfect little being gave all of us distraction and a little relief. Lisa brought me a bag she had thoughtfully filled with things she imagined I would need: a package of tea, her favourite wool sweater, and a few music CDs. I put the sweater on right away and wore it for days—I still had only the business clothes I'd worn from the conference. I couldn't listen to the music because of my extreme sensitivity to noise, but I remember what the CDs were: Ani DiFranco, the Indigo Girls, Edie Brickell, and Sinead O'Connor, all of whom we worshipped in our university days. Lisa's gift acknowledged that I was still me, our friendship was still ours, and we were going to make it through this. Two more friends came later in the afternoon, followed by Lisa's husband, Peter. He'd been one of my housemates at university. He asked me if I'd like to go out for a drive, and I said yes. We drove to a toy store where he wanted to buy something for his son. Entering the store, I was in a daze. The bright colours hurt my eyes. I tried not to think about my almost-baby, but I couldn't stop and began to cry. Without saying anything, Peter gently put his arm around me and led me back to the car.

That night was the same as the one before. My thoughts went in a million directions but there were no dreams or hopes to take refuge in. I thought of the future with dread and uncertainty. I thought of the past, which was agonizing. The pain of the present was so acute that it felt like a massive, blinding white light.

My mind created a film strip of all the violence and it circled continuously in my head. When I managed to fall asleep, those images became violent nightmares. I dreamt dreams I'd had since childhood, of being chased by snakes or Nazis, while other dreams were new, involving the details of Jason's assaults. I would often wake up screaming or gasping for air. I dreamt my house was on fire. I dreamt of men coming into my bedroom to attack me. I dreamt of the victims, bound and gagged in my basement. I had a nightmare in which I was looking for Jason because he had to go to jail—he was going to be arrested for the crimes he had committed. I found him on the street where he worked, locking his bike up to a lamppost next to a Canada Post mailbox. When he noticed me, he straightened up and said cheerfully, "Hi, Shanny!" I asked him why he wasn't in jail and told him he had to go there now. His face fell and I realized he had no idea what he had done. I had to tell him, and when I did, his eyes filled with tears. "I did that?" he said. "How could I have done that?" I woke up in a sweat.

The nightmares were terrifying and lasted for months; but the worst part was waking up to reality. My pyjamas were frequently soaked through with sweat or my pillow wet with tears.

I would lie in bed for a couple of hours while everything—every graphic detail of the crimes and every intimate detail of our beautiful life together—played out in my mind. Sometimes, upon first waking, I would be graced with one split second when I didn't remember, and then it would all hit me again, a crushing wave.

The next morning, I got out of bed and took another pregnancy test just to be sure. Negative. I wouldn't have to decide whether to proceed with a pregnancy—but at some point I would have to decide what to do about my marriage. The weight of that decision, and whatever legal process would be required to bring it about, overwhelmed me. I barely knew what being married was like, yet I felt like I'd been widowed. I put my head in my hands and sobbed for a few minutes, and then I got dressed. I decided that I would get up and dress every day, no matter what. As a counsellor, it was what I would recommend to someone in crisis. One had to hold onto something.

It was Thursday and the news was spreading. I had a vast network of friends, family and colleagues, and most were trying to get in touch to see how I was. Where was Jason? What state was he in? What had happened? How were the victims? I could not keep up. I was still overwhelmed from their outpouring of wedding gifts and cards. Suddenly, I was a crime reporter instead of a bride. I couldn't respond to the questions I myself had no answers for, and recounting the events was exhausting. Yet, I didn't know how to say no, nor how to set boundaries. The privacy lines around my life had been torn away. I needed a spokesperson, but everyone around me was coping with the same crisis to one degree or another. There was no time to think or plan; no chance to step back and take a breath; no room to grieve.

One of my mum's friends came over for tea in the afternoon. I didn't know her very well, but she was the kind of person you want to have around in a crisis: calm, stable, and ready to lend a hand. She took my hands in hers and said slowly and with conviction, "Jason's birthright to be loved unconditionally must have been taken away from him and that is why he did what he did—because he did not understand unconditional love."

Many people—some who knew Jason and some who didn't—took this same approach as they tried to come to terms with what had happened. They shared their feelings of shock, sadness, disbelief and concern for everyone affected: the victims, their families, me and my family, and Jason. But soon enough, others began to express anger and rejection, even judging me and my family. They seemed to think that our love for Jason meant we felt nothing for his victims. Lines were drawn.

A friend once told me that she understood pity as "I'm sorry for you," whereas compassion is "I feel your pain because I see that you could be me and I could be you." I agreed, and added that I thought compassion meant being with someone in their suffering. Though they were in my thoughts, I couldn't be with the victims directly because I didn't know them. I had to hope that their loved ones were with them, as mine were with me. When I pictured the Jason that I knew in his cell, I imagined he must be suffering, and I wanted to be with him.

Very quickly and painfully, I learned how to discern pity from compassion. I began to pick up on the subtleties of what people were saying: some would ask about Jason, some about me, and some about both of us. Many people asked me about the victims; but I knew only what the police had told me—that they had been brutally assaulted and were expected to make a full physical recovery, and that they were with their families. Other than report this information, I could do only what anyone else could: imagine what those women would be going through and hope that somehow they would find a way to cope. It was inconceivable to me that anyone who knew me and my family could conclude that showing care and concern for Jason precluded the deep care and concern we felt for the victims of his crimes.

On Thursday evening, my third night at my parents', my friend who'd been my maid of honour arrived from out of town to see me. She was a newlywed too, and leading up to our weddings we had talked with anticipation about our new married lives. Now she knelt beside me and cried with me as I lay in bed. She also demanded explanations about what had happened. What had Jason been thinking? How could he do this? I was his wife; I must know. But I didn't know. She was loyal to me and fiercely protective, but her anger seemed to take precedence over any feelings I might have had. I found this difficult to tolerate, her vehemence abrasive against my broken heart.

Sleep eluded me again that night, the film strip of violence circling relentlessly. As I realized with greater and greater depth the losses of my hopes and dreams, the torture Jason put the victims through, the destruction he had caused to his own life, and the number of other people who were affected by his actions, I started to feel as though I were falling into a deep, dark hole. I again pictured the Jason that I knew alone in a jail cell. What frame of mind was he in now? Was he in danger in there? I wanted to see him, even though he had said that he never wanted to see me again. I recalled the words of Sister Helen Prejean, whose work as a spiritual adviser to New Orleans death-row inmates was portrayed by Susan Sarandon in the film *Dead Man Walking*. Sean Penn played Matthew Poncelet, a rapist and murderer sentenced to death. As he is being strapped to a gurney, about to be executed by lethal injection, Prejean says to Matthew, "I want the last face you see in this world to be a face of love, so you look at me."

I reconsidered this radical act of compassion, and asked myself if I was capable of making the same offer to Jason. Could I show him a face of love? What would that mean? I hated what he had done and I would never condone his actions, but I knew I didn't hate the person he was. Like Sister Helen, I deplore violence. Caring about the human being behind the violent act would never change my condemnation of violence. Might I gain some understanding of what had happened if I visited Jason? Could he answer my questions? I hoped so. I hoped I would see that the Jason I had known was still there—the one who was loving and kind, the one who had come so far. I knew this Jason would be remorseful. If I didn't see the Jason I loved—if I saw a monster instead—then I would have to accept that too. Whether or not he would see me, I would go to the jail and show him my face of love.

First thing the next morning, Friday, I looked up the Lindsay jail online and called to inquire about visiting. Jason was being held in protective custody—solitary confinement. Like all inmates, he was allowed only two half-hour visits per week, between one and three in the afternoon. There were no evening visiting hours, and visits could not be booked in advance. Visitors had to take their chances that no one else would show up at the same time, that the two weekly slots were still open, and that the inmate they came to see would agree to see them. I asked if I could bring anything and was told no, nothing at all. I would have to go through security, so I should avoid

wearing large jewellery or belt buckles and make sure my pockets were empty. My coat and purse should be put in a locker
or left in the car.

My mum, my maid of honour and I drove up to the jail that
day. It was a two-hour drive northeast to the small town of
Lindsay, west of Peterborough. I was extremely anxious and
nervous during the whole trip. All of us were. No one knew
what to expect, nor what would happen. We arrived at what
looked like a huge, grey factory on the outskirts of town, surrounded by barbed wire. We parked in the big, full lot and then
went in through the main entrance to a glassed-in reception
desk. I handed over my driver's licence and a note for Jason
written on a small piece of paper: *Jason. I still love you. Please
come and see me.* The receptionist looked at it but said it
couldn't be shown to him. She was sorry, but I would just have
to wait to find out if he wanted to see me. Tears ran down my
cheeks, but the woman smiled warmly, and that gave me a split-
second of comfort.

I sat down in the waiting area with my mum and friend. We
waited in tense silence for a few minutes before the receptionist
called my name. I left them in the waiting area, and proceeded
through what felt like an airport security screening. But when
I was shown into a small steel elevator that sucked me up into
the second floor and deposited me at the entrance to a long,
tunnel-like glass bridge, I felt more like I had been teleported
to another world. My surroundings were completely foreign.
As I walked alone through the bridge leading from the reception wing to the main jail, I looked out at a small, empty yard
below and at the barred windows of what I assumed were cells.
Although there were 1,600 inmates inside, I knew, it was sad
and eerie to see no signs of life.

The glassed-in bridge opened into an even longer, empty and colourless hall. It led to a guard sitting at a table. I told the guard who I was visiting and he made a phone call. Then he told me to continue walking straight to the first door on my right. He said I should listen for a click and then pull the door open. My heart was pounding. I had learned that Jason and I would have a "closed" visit, sealed from each other and from other visitors and inmates, but I still didn't know what to expect. When I reached the door it clicked open and I entered a tiny room divided in half by a thick sheet of glass extending up from a steel counter. There was a small metal stool bolted to the floor in front of the counter.

I was still getting my bearings when Jason came through the door on the other side of the room—face down, drawn and grim. He was wearing a bright-orange jumpsuit. Was this my husband I was seeing through the glass? Jason looked up, our eyes met, and we both began crying uncontrollably. I put my hands up to the glass.

"Jason . . ."

But he couldn't hear me. He pointed to a phone receiver on the wall beside me. He picked up an identical receiver on his side.

I cried into the phone, "Jason, what happened? *What happened?*"

"I don't know . . ." He was sobbing, almost unable to speak. "I don't know. I'm sorry, I'm sorry!"

We stood there for several moments, each of us holding a phone receiver in one hand, the other hand pressed against the glass, our palms together but unable to touch. It was hard to stop crying, but I had a million questions.

First, I asked my mum's question: "Jason, didn't you know how much I loved you? How much we *all* loved you?"

He shook his head. "I'm sorry . . . I'm so sorry, I didn't *really* know."

As I looked into Jason's eyes, I recalled a school picture taken when he was six years old, the year his dad died. In it, his face was solemn and his eyes were dark with sorrow and profound loneliness. They were the exact same eyes I was looking into now, thirty years later.

"Jason," I said, "the police told me you said that you never wanted to see me again—why did you say that?"

The expression on his face changed from sorrow to confusion, and after a moment he said softly, "No, Shanny, I said, 'My wife never has to see *me* again.'"

I felt a pulse of relief. It was something to hold onto amidst the confusion.

Jason went on to confess that he had been gorging himself on pornography over the weekend while I was away, and that he had gone to see a very violent movie at the theatre. I despise pornography, and I had no idea that Jason even looked at it, let alone the extent to which it was part of his life. He said he'd stuffed himself with junk food that day until he was in pain— something he now admitted he had started doing frequently a few months before, during the night while I slept. I winced as I recalled teasing him about eating too much junk food while I was away.

"How long have these things been going on?" I asked.

He said he'd become addicted to pornography while he was in prison the first time. It was something he was ashamed of, and that's why he'd never discussed it with me before. The issues with food had come and gone to greater or lesser extents throughout his life, beginning in his early teens. The voyeurism was new in the last few months. He explained that he had always known something was wrong with him, but that he convinced himself that he was in control of whatever it was, experiencing long periods of time when he was "unplugged" from his demons, times when there was no "interference with the wires in his brain." Recently, the addictive behaviours had been building again, though he couldn't explain exactly why.

In agony, I asked him, "Why didn't you tell me?"

"I'm sorry. I was so afraid. I wanted to keep you out of it; to protect you from it. I thought it would go away." This choice was one of the biggest mistakes of his life, and he knew it. He shook his head. "I see now how wrong I was, and it's too late."

"You could have told me anything, Jason. I would have done anything to help you. We could have prevented this, if only you had the courage to tell me—or anyone—what was going on inside."

"I know. I know that now." He looked strained and without hope. We cried for several minutes, unable to speak.

It pained me to find out that Jason had let himself fall into the spiral of this degradation. Learning about his hidden habits repulsed me completely. Jason had fooled himself into thinking his addiction would go away on its own, and in so doing, he had victimized me and others. He had denied the seriousness of his compulsions and let shame and fear prevent him from getting help. Then he exploded, wreaking havoc on the lives of the two women and countless other people who were now affected. I felt helpless, and completely betrayed.

Several years before, I had lived in the Andes Mountains of Ecuador, in what is called the Valley of Volcanoes. Looking at the magnificent valley vista, it was impossible to distinguish a volcano filled with molten lava from an inert mountain. I was there in 1999 when Guagua Pichincha—"the baby"—erupted.

I remembered being struck by a feeling of total powerlessness as I watched that huge mushroom cloud burst into the clear blue sky, knowing that I wasn't going to be able to escape the aftermath no matter what I did. The same feeling overwhelmed me now, as I watched and listened to Jason. He was beautiful to look at, by all accounts a solid mountain, but something had been churning in him for some time. What had caused him to explode when he did, and where had all that malice come from?

"Jason, my dad said something the other day. He wondered if something happened to you when you were a boy." I was desperate for an explanation.

"I don't remember anything about my childhood. I'm just . . . like this." He shook his head back and forth. "I don't know what's wrong with me!" There was something in his "just like this" that was too quick, too simple. I felt he was hiding something.

"But what happened? I don't understand—what happened when the first woman came in the store?" I asked, trying to remain calm and focused.

"I don't remember—she came in the door and I just felt . . ." His brow furrowed as he seemed to search for the right word. "Panic. I felt extremely panicked, and like I had to get control over the situation."

"What do you mean, 'situation'?" I demanded.

"I don't know . . . she didn't even say anything, but I had this feeling like I was in danger." He looked even more confused now. "But that's crazy—how could she have been a danger to me?"

"She wasn't, Jason. She wasn't a danger to you—" The phone clicked off then and there was silence.

We were left looking helplessly at each other, separated by

the thick glass. My heart hurt. In anguish, I mouthed the words that came to me first, *I love you. I still love you.* Jason mouthed back, *Thank you. I love you, too.* We held our hands up to each other's for a couple more minutes and then a guard came to get Jason at his door. Before I left through mine, I mouthed, *I'll come back.* Jason nodded before he disappeared through the doorway.

I felt raw and drained as I walked back up the corridor, across the glass bridge, and into the elevator, though I also felt a trace of relief. The Jason I had known—the man who was caring, kind and good—was still alive. Now I had to figure out who the other Jason was, how they had lived in the same body, and what had happened to cause such an explosion of violence. To begin this journey, I knew what I would have to face and where I'd have to go.

CHAPTER SEVEN

GOING HOME

Back downstairs in the jail's waiting room, I had a hard time describing my visit to my mum and friend. I was distracted by a new compulsion to go home, to the house I'd shared with Jason. They were reluctant to take me there, but I couldn't be dissuaded. I said I needed some things, which was true: I was living out of the small suitcase I'd taken with me to the conference a week ago. Moreover, I needed to go home to see what still remained of my life. I also felt I had to look for clues that might help me understand what had happened. Could I ever live in my house again? I didn't know.

Nora, the police officer who had first interviewed me, had called that morning, Friday, to say the police search was over and I was now free to return home. The detectives couldn't find the pinhole video camera that Jason had told them about—the one he used to commit acts of voyeurism in our bathroom. Nora told me her team had tried not to mess up the house too much. They had taken our computer and cleaned up as much blood and hair as they could from the basement. She explained that Jason had ripped and cut hair from the women's heads as he removed the duct tape from over their eyes. The blood was from the cut on the second victim's hand. Nora advised that I might want to have the little white couch we had in the basement removed before I went home. I winced as she spoke. I was thinking about the women sitting down there . . . they had suffered in *my home*. I would have done anything to help them, but I wasn't there. Was there anything I could have done? I thought hard. There was nothing. Jason had given me no chance to stop him, no clue as to what was going on. I could be only grateful that I'd called him that night, that he'd answered, and that maybe, just maybe, our conversation played into his choice to call the police.

At the end of our phone call that morning, Nora had made a confession. She said that when she heard that Jason was married, she thought to herself, "Oh great—he has a wife," and jumped to conclusions about what I would be like. I suspect she thought I'd be a stereotype of an offender's wife: with a criminal record of my own, married to a "creep" who abused me, lacking self-esteem, delusional, drug-addicted, an alcoholic, or a co-dependent enabler. When she met me a few hours later, she realized that I was nothing like she had expected. "You didn't fit my image," she said.

When she left the interview room for a few minutes during our session at the station, she went into another room where officers were preparing to watch the closed-circuit television of our interview. She found those officers making similar assumptions about my character.

"It isn't what we thought," she told them. "She is not like what we thought."

Having recently learned that I had been videotaped secretly by my own husband in the bathroom of our home, I found it upsetting to learn a few days later that I had also been watched by a group of officers—all men—in another room while I talked with Nora about my sex life. She'd told me I was being video-taped, but I thought that was just for their records. I didn't know I was being watched live. I felt a sense of retroactive violation.

Nora then revealed she had been the lead officer on the house search. She had gone through all of my photos and all of my personal belongings. She was surprised to find out just who I was—someone who had lived and worked in other countries, a dedicated volunteer, in her words "a good person." She said she was sorry for having jumped to her initial conclusions, but her apology offered only cold comfort. As the wife of a man who had committed serious crimes, on the basis of no evidence, I had temporarily been deemed guilty by association. I hung up the phone and thought about what to do.

I remembered that a colleague, Ian, had a pickup truck. He'd already made me promise to ask him for anything I needed. I could ask him to go to my house and get rid of the couch. It was a dreadful request, but I didn't know what else to do. I started to wonder why the police hadn't taken the couch into evidence themselves, or simply taken it away. Was I, as the wife of the offender, really responsible for cleaning up the crime scene? I called Ian. Without a moment's hesitation, he said he would take care of it and take another colleague with him. I said he could pick up Jason's house keys from the police station to let himself into my house. Ian called back shortly thereafter to say that the task was completed and that he had cleaned up the rest of the hair from the basement floor before taking the little white couch to the dump. I thanked him profusely. "Don't thank me," he insisted. "Just promise you'll call again if there is anything else I can do."

Later, I would learn that Ian knew one of Jason's victims because she was the partner of his neighbour. Ian never said anything to me about that. It hurt to think about what it must have been like for him to be in my house cleaning up the hair and blood of a woman he knew who had been assaulted by my husband. Ian's response was a selfless act of kindness, and he chose to make himself useful instead of laying blame and condemnation, or running away. Beyond the practical help he provided, he—along with many others over the coming days—proved the existence of good in a world that had become so marred by violence.

Now it was Friday afternoon, and I was driving with trepidation, wondering what would be waiting for me when I arrived home. I decided to assemble a few friends to meet me there. Though I hated to bring them to the scene, I knew I couldn't do this alone. My support team was there when I pulled into the driveway. It was four-thirty and almost dark. I was seeing my house for the first time since I'd left it a week ago. The police tape was gone, and although past their prime, the pumpkins and flowers by the front door still gave a welcome feeling. I stepped up onto the porch, my friends and my mum following behind me. I unlocked the yellow front door and we entered.

Everything was stopped in time. Jason's slippers were by the door; my knitting was in a basket next to the couch. There were dishes in the sink and food out on the counter. The kitchen garbage can was filled with empty bags of the licorice, chips and other junk food Jason told me he'd gorged on. Knowing that the police had seen this messy kitchen embarrassed me. It didn't represent how Jason and I had lived. My friends set right to work washing dishes and getting things in order. Meanwhile, as I surveyed the last scenes Jason had lived in our house before he left for work on the day of his crimes, I was surrounded by evidence of how he'd unravelled. If I had only known something was wrong with him. If I had known that Jason was dangerous when he wasn't with me or others, I would never have left him alone. The police had told me that they didn't believe this ever would have happened if I had been home or if my family had been around. But I didn't know, we didn't know—only Jason knew, and he had been in denial.

I walked into the middle of our living room, where I found search warrants on the coffee table. On them were listed the names of the two women, names I didn't recognize. I had spoken with my vice-principal earlier that day. She told me that the first of Jason's victims was the stepmother of a boy at our school, but that she could not disclose his identity. Our school population was close to a thousand. I racked my brain to see if I could match the first victim's last name to any kids at school. Maybe they didn't share a surname. Whose parents were divorced or widowed? I felt concern and sorrow for the boy and his family. I respected their need for privacy but felt that if I knew their identities I would be better equipped to ensure that privacy, not to breach it. Our town was small: if I ran into them at the grocery store or on the street, I could walk away. But if I didn't know who they were, I might encounter them by accident. I didn't know how they were feeling about me or if they felt I was in some way to blame for what had happened. What if they confronted me? How was I going to go back to work knowing that a student there was related to one of Jason's victims but without knowing which one? I hoped the matter would be resolved before it was time to return to work.

With the search warrants in my hand, I read over the charges and scanned the list of what the police were to look for: duct tape, scissors, green garbage bags with holes torn in them, pornographic materials, computer and recording equipment, a note addressed to me, and the purses and identification of the two women. That this evidence of violence and degradation could be found in my home seemed unbelievable. How could the same duct tape Jason and I used to repair camping equipment have been used to confine and restrain two innocent women? How could the scissors I used to cut gift wrap or fabric for curtains have been used to cut tape from their hair?

I put the warrants back down on the coffee table and went into the dining room at the back of the house, a room we had painted green and used as an office and art space. The computer was gone and the cords lay scattered on the floor, the desk empty. It looked like we had been robbed. I went across the hall and into the bathroom, now knowing it was a crime scene. Somewhere there was a pinhole video camera that Jason had used to commit voyeurism.

I opened the back door leading to the deck outside. I saw Jason's bike chained to the railing. The police had moved it there from where Jason had locked it in front of the store when he went to work on the day of the crimes. My eyes filled with tears again. Memories flashed in my mind: Jason riding along in front of me on the streets of Kingston and Peterborough, ringing his bell to make sure I had not fallen too far behind; me ringing back to say I was still there, right behind him. Then a different series of images forced themselves into my consciousness: Jason putting the women in garbage bags, loading them into the van at the back of the store, carrying them over his shoulder, through the backyard, up the steps of the deck, through the door and down to our basement. The women must have struggled, but Jason was very strong. About two months later, he would be taken from the jail to the Lindsay hospital for surgery to repair a hernia. When I found out, I shuddered. I knew how the hernia had occurred.

I went upstairs next. Up the maple stairs that as new home-owners Jason and I had delightfully uncovered after ripping out the 1970s-era, multicoloured striped carpet. Our duvet was in a big heap in the middle of the bed—the police must have been looking under it. Drawers were opened and contents rumpled and out of place. In the guest room across the hall it was the same scene. The doors to the crawl spaces under the eaves were open, letting in a cold draft. I closed them and went back downstairs.

I could hear my mum's voice rising from the living room; she was begging me to get back in the car, pleading with me not to go into the basement, but I could not stop myself. I had to face it. I opened the door to the basement, the sound of my mum crying in the background. I trusted that somebody else would look after her. I went down the stairs and turned left at the bottom, into the room that just last summer I'd painted a cheery yellow. It looked just the way I'd left it, save for the missing couch and a streak of dirt across the carpet. I looked at our pictures on the wall, which later Jason told me the first victim had tried to engage him in talking about: *Who is she? It looks like you have a girlfriend or partner . . . She's my wife, Shannon.*

Standing there in the stillness, I thought about what *could have* happened that night—as the sergeant had said, this could have become the scene of a double homicide. And a suicide. At that moment I chose to look at my house as the place where three lives were saved instead of lost. I knew I could live there again for that reason . . . that, and because I simply could not become homeless on top of everything else. The comfort of my personal belongings and proximity to the places I needed to be—the police station, the jail, the courthouse, and my job—would be necessary until I figured out a longer-term plan.

When I came back upstairs, my mum had gone out to the street and two friends were making attempts to comfort and calm her. I tidied up a little bit more and then gathered a few items of clothing to take back to my parents'. I made some tea, and my mum came back inside, calmer. After a short time, the others left, and I got back in my mum's minivan with her and my maid of honour. I would stay at my parents' another night or two until I could figure out my next steps.

Arriving back at their home late that night, I wrote an e-mail to a group of friends and acquaintances to tell them about having seen Jason. I believed I was writing only to people who had asked me how Jason was doing, where he was, and what the conditions were like in the jail. I wrote a relatively short e-mail, describing how I found Jason to be filled with remorse, that we had cried, and that he was broken. Many had asked about the victims, but I didn't have any new information. I wrote that they were with their families.

I heard back from most recipients right away—messages of understanding, concern and hope. Some requested Jason's address so they could write to him. I didn't realize that I hadn't heard back from everyone yet—that some replies were still to come, and that they were going to wound me deeply.

PART 2

AFTERSHOCKS

CHAPTER EIGHT

NO WAY OUT BUT THROUGH

In the immediate aftermath of a disaster, survivors look for each other and then for shelter. Cleanup begins when these needs are met. By Day Five, Saturday, I knew that my immediate family was still intact, that the Jason I knew still existed in some form, that my house was still standing, that I had a job to return to, and that I had friends I could count on. I also had an innate sense that I was going to have to be my own best friend through this.

In the afternoon, I headed to Georgina and Mark's farm, where I planned to stay the night before returning home the next day. In our sombre conversation at their kitchen table, Georgina and Mark comforted me as much as they could, but of course they were troubled by what Jason had done. I later learned that they were acquainted with the first victim and were facing this complexity along with everything else. As we sat around the table trying to piece our thoughts together, I noticed a stack of newspapers by the kitchen door, ready to be taken out for recycling. I excused myself from the table, walked over to the pile and began searching. Georgina warned, "You might not want to see what's in those, Shannon." But I felt compelled to know everything, and to see what about the crimes was being reported and how. I had to arm myself with all the facts.

I found Wednesday's paper, the first day the events were reported in print. The headline on the front page read, "Murderer charged in kidnapping: two women held captive in local business, home." I read the article:

> A man on full parole from a life sentence for second-degree
> murder was back behind bars yesterday after city police
> charged him with the kidnapping and sexual assault of two
> city women. . . . Police said the man kidnapped two women,
> forcibly confined them and assaulted them in a [downtown]
> business Monday afternoon. Sergeant Smith said the 26- and
> 46-year-old women went to hospital with injuries but were
> later released. He wouldn't reveal the nature of the injuries,
> citing the sensitivity of the case and the fact that it's an
> on-going investigation. . . . Smith also wouldn't reveal how the
> police became aware of the situation.

Why didn't the article say Jason had called the police himself? Wasn't that a significant detail? It revealed some measure of responsibility. Isn't that what the public would want to know? The reporter made it seem as though Jason had just been released from prison—a murderer looking for his next victims. I feared the impact this image would have on me, making it appear that I'd married him while he was incarcerated and brought him to Peterborough.

The article went on to provide our street name, identifying our house as the one on the corner. A photo showed our little blue house with its blue roof, yellow front door and wide porch.

There was a police car parked in the driveway. Surrounding our house were metres of plastic tape, POLICE LINE: DO NOT CROSS printed in bold, black letters. My sweet little house . . . a crime scene. Tears pricked my eyes.

Neighbours had been interviewed for the article and one neighbour was quoted as saying, "You don't know who you live with. . . . They were quiet people. You wouldn't have suspected anything." The reporter asked the sergeant in our driveway about our marriage. "It's not relevant," was his reply. "She's not involved in any way."

I put the paper down, feeling somewhat relieved by the officer's words while alarmed at my neighbours'. Did they think I was Jason's accomplice? Fearfully, I began to imagine the implications this could have for me. Mark was watching me read the article from where he sat at the table. Suddenly, he got up from his seat and rushed over to put his arms around me. He began to cry as he explained how he had driven by our house on his way to work the morning after the assaults. When he saw the police car in our driveway, he thought maybe I had been hurt, or worse. As he told me, I began to cry too.

It upset me to learn what others had gone through, and I often tried to comfort them, but that proved to be an unsustainable effort. Some people grappled with the issues they had with Jason through debate with me, but I quickly realized that I could not be that sounding board. I was grieving and coping with trauma as it affected my life from inside the nucleus of the disaster. Eventually, I had to tell some friends that I could not engage in these discussions and suggested that instead they seek out each other for support or talk to a professional counsellor. Most understood. A few gave advice or divulged how they would have reacted in my place. Others told me how I should be reacting. That night at Georgina and Mark's, I received my first big dose of unsolicited advice.

The phone rang. Georgina answered and, with her hand over the mouthpiece, whispered, "It's your maid of honour's dad."

Strange. I didn't know him very well. Why would he be calling me? I took the phone from Georgina.

"Shannon—how are you?" He sounded frantic and spoke loudly.

"I'm okay. I mean, this is a difficult time, but I'm holding up."

Then he began firing. "We're sorry to hear about what happened . . . Obviously Jason is a really sick man and I hope you can just push ahead, not waste any more time, just put it all behind you. What are you going to do with the house? Have you got it on the market yet? What are you going to do with your life?"

I listened in a stunned silence. *Was my house on the market?* No, my house was not on the market. It had only been five days. *What was I going to do with my life?* How could I possibly know?

I stumbled. "Well, I—"

"I think you should move to Ottawa and live with my daughter. You know, she is suffering too, parted from her husband overseas. You two could be good company for each other. You can get a job there . . ."

I realized then that I had to get out of this conversation. I thanked him politely for his concern and said I did not yet have a plan though I was certain I would find the right way forward. Moving to Ottawa was not a reality, nor was making rash decisions.

In a matter-of-fact tone, he said, "Well, you're welcome.

I just wanted to say my piece. We're here for you."

"Thanks. I appreciate that," I heard myself say.

"Okay, Shannon, goodbye for now." He sounded satisfied.

"Goodbye."

I hung up, stunned. A short while later, I called my parents. I told them about the call. My dad was absolutely outraged. My friend's father had called my dad earlier, shared his opinion, and asked where I was so he could call me. My dad told him I'd gone up to Georgina and Mark's but asked him not to call. I needed time, he said. The man had gone ahead anyway.

Two weeks later, my maid of honour invited me to get away from everything for the weekend at her parents' home in the country. The idea of a brief respite was appealing, but I knew I wouldn't feel comfortable around her father. I explained my hesitation to my friend of ten years. Her response was curt. "Well—he's right. You need to move on."

It was clear that she believed in the "cut-and-run" route, too, which might work for some people; however, I knew that wouldn't work for me. I knew if I did that—attempted to escape without facing the trauma and working through it—everything would come back to haunt me in the future. All the intense emotions would hold their power and threaten my long-term well-being. Escape was a seduction, one that I wouldn't give in to. There was no way out but through.

I turned down the invitation. My friend said that was fine—to call her when I was moving on. I figured that meant when I'd forgotten all about Jason and didn't need to talk about what happened anymore. Maybe I was supposed to be married again before I contacted her—she wasn't specific. I felt abandoned, a decade of memories sealed off and a future thrown away.

The cliché about finding out who your friends are in a crisis became real for me as I tried desperately to navigate the aftermath of Jason's crimes. The friendship with my maid of honour was the first to be lost, but it wouldn't be the last. I felt rushes of both anger and sadness, but there was no time to work through these feelings. Instead, I clung to the comfort I found in friendships that were strengthening and growing, hoping with everything I had that they would be enough to sustain me until some better time came, until sometime in the future when I would feel happiness again.

CHAPTER NINE

WELCOME TO THE TRAUMA CLUB

Several years ago, my mum had open-heart surgery. She said that for weeks she would wake up every morning in pain. Her chest had been broken in two and her heart taken out and opened up, and afterwards, all she could do was lie in bed and say to herself, "If I don't move, maybe it won't hurt so much." Now I felt exactly the same way.

When I woke up on Sunday morning at Georgina and Mark's farmhouse, the flood of confused memories and emotions broke over me again, as it did every morning. I was exhausted from tossing and turning most of the night. I stayed in bed for a long time—perfectly still and silent—but in my mind everything was crashing in on me. How long would the court process last? What would Jason's sentence be? How were the victims doing? Could I stay married to him? *Should* I stay married? What was the matter with Jason—and could it ever be fixed? What would happen to our house? When would I go back to work? There were no clear or easy answers. Everything hurt. All I wanted to do was stay still until the pain had subsided.

When I finally got up and got dressed, I called my friend and

former teaching partner Erin, to take her up on an offer to drive
me to the jail that day. I had told Jason I would return and I
felt compelled to continue the conversation we had started on
Friday. She'd offered to meet at a café for coffee first, but I was
afraid to go out in town. Already, the few times I'd driven
through the streets I'd found myself imagining every woman I
saw as one of the two victims. I didn't know what to say to
anyone I might run into. I then called my cousin Tamara. She
was more like a younger sister than a cousin, and I had been
so pleased when she chose to come to Peterborough to study
International Development at Trent University like I did. Now
I was worried about her. I had heard that the second of the two
victims was a Trent student. What if Tamara knew her? What
if someone at the school linked her to Jason?

We had a serious talk on the phone, and Tamara assured me
that she was fine. Her concern was for me, and she wanted to
offer her support. I felt proud of her maturity, but devastated by
what she and all my other young cousins were now exposed to.
They loved and trusted Jason—now they faced a loss of innocence
too. Tamara offered to accompany Erin and me on the drive to
the jail. As her older cousin, I didn't want her to have to take
care of me, but I thought it was a good idea for Erin to have
someone to wait with while I visited Jason. There was strength
in numbers. We picked her up on our way to the jail in Lindsay.

My second visit with Jason was as filled with tears and questions as the first. He looked the same, though I noticed that he
was already starting to lose weight. His eyes stayed focused on
mine, though I sensed dark clouds behind them and he frequently furrowed his brow as he tried to remember—and put
into words—what had happened the previous Monday and

anything that led up to the assaults. I had written down my questions so I wouldn't forget in our time-constrained visit. I kept the little piece of paper in my pocket and hoped the guard wouldn't notice. The questions ranged from "How could you have done this?" to "What were you wearing?" I had to know everything. I had to fit the jagged pieces together.

Some questions had definitive answers—"I was wearing jeans and my black corduroy shirt"—while others Jason struggled with, often answering with another question.

"I don't know," he said, hanging his head, "I don't understand what came over me. I don't hate women. All the people I'm closest to are women, so it doesn't make sense." He was right about that—nothing made sense.

There were practicalities to discuss too.

"Has anyone come to see you about applying for Legal Aid and obtaining a lawyer?"

Jason shook his head. "I haven't seen anyone at all."

"No one?"

"Only the guard—once a day when I'm taken out. My food comes in through a slot."

"What do you do all day?" I asked.

"I pace," Jason said. "I pace and I think. I think about you and the women and all the lives I've ruined. When the guard comes, he takes me to a little balcony for fifteen minutes of fresh air, but I find I can hardly breathe it in."

A moment of silence passed. "I'll sign whatever papers you need me to," he said. "I will never ask you to stay with me."

We had just signed our marriage licence. I wasn't ready to sign divorce papers—the word *divorce* felt like tinfoil in my mouth, but I knew practicality would have to take precedence over sentimentality.

"I'll call a lawyer this week and find out what my options are," I said quietly.

I came out of the visit with a few more answers, a little better understanding of what happened and who the two Jasons were—and completely dehydrated from crying. Many tears had been shed on both sides of the glass. I prepared myself to return to my home to live.

Erin dropped Tamara back at her residence and took me to my house, where she offered to come in with me. We entered gingerly and began tidying a little more. The search warrants were still on the coffee table and Erin picked them up without realizing what they were. She saw the names of the victims and drew a sharp breath. "I know her! I dreamt that it was her, I don't know why."

It was a strange and terrible moment. Erin knew Jason's first victim. She put her arms around me and said, "I promise to protect you—if we go anywhere together and we see her, I will tell you so you will know who she is, and you won't have to wonder if every woman you see is her. Maybe one day we can talk with her; it might be good for both of you."

Erin didn't know the woman well at all, and she didn't know anything about her personal life, like who her family was, but in a small way her connection helped me. These women, Jason's victims, were on my mind constantly, but their hidden identities kept them abstract.

I wasn't quite ready to spend the night alone at my house, so Erin volunteered to stay over with me, but soon she would have to go and get her daughter, Sarah, from the babysitter's. We talked about what to tell six-year-old Sarah. Neither of us believed that lying to her was the right thing. That evening, when Sarah asked where Jason was, we sat down with her and told her that something very sad had happened, that Jason had made some bad mistakes and that he'd gone to jail for a while to think about them. She asked when he would be coming back and we said not until he was a lot older. She was clearly puzzled. Then she looked up at us and asked, "What did he do?"

We told her that he had hurt some people. She asked why, and the best we could come up with was, "We don't know exactly, but we think he had a place inside him that hurt a lot— and he never told us about it, so we couldn't help him. The hurt was so big it made him hurt other people. That is why we always have to talk about our problems and our pain with people we love and trust."

Sarah seemed to take all this in stride. She asked if Jason had his paints with him and we said not yet. She seemed to grow concerned. Erin asked Sarah if she would like to draw a picture for Jason, and she agreed enthusiastically. She drew a picture of herself with Jason and us. We were all four in a row, holding hands.

While Erin put Sarah to bed in the guest room, I took out the garbage and recycling. It was a job I disliked and that Jason usually looked after. This brought home to me that I was now going to be living alone and every responsibility would be mine. When I placed the bags and bins at the end of the driveway and turned to go back into the house, I saw a neighbour coming toward me. On the day we moved in, he had brought Jason and me coffee and muffins, and we'd often chatted with him or borrowed his tools. Did he now think that Jason and I were a criminal team?

"I'm sorry, I'm so sorry—" I began, but the man shook his head and interrupted. "I don't understand what happened . . . I don't understand . . . I loved having Jason as my neighbour . . .

watching you two work on your house and take care of the property . . . I don't understand what happened, but if I saw Jason today I would greet him as my neighbour." I was so grateful for those words. "Anything you need, Shannon, anything you need, I'm here."

I thanked him through tears and went back inside.

The phone rang. It was another neighbour, one who lived in a house that I could plainly see from my living room window. I didn't know her well at all; in fact, it was Jason who had recently introduced us. She was a regular customer in the health food store where Jason worked and over time they'd figured out we were neighbours. Her kids loved seeing Jason at the store, and her eldest girl, who was eight, had a particular fondness for him because she was an artist too. One time, he received a gorgeous painting of a multicoloured crocodile from this little girl with an invitation for him to come over and see her new drawing pencils.

On the phone, my neighbour said how worried she and other neighbours had been about me. When she saw the lights on, she decided to call. What she said next surprised me. "I have an illness that sometimes makes me act like a completely different person, so I can understand to some degree how Jason could have suddenly changed." Later she would explain that she had suffered from post-partum depression with psychotic delusions following the birth of two of her children. It was controlled now by medication and therapy. She wanted to pop over during the week with another neighbour who lived across the road, and to know if there was anything they could do.

Over the six months that followed, I would stay in my house and those two neighbourhood women (and, by extension, their families) would form a lifeline for me. They made sure I was up and dressed. They lent me their cars. They listened and they cried with me. One wrote to and visited Jason, and they both came to court with me. They treated me like a normal woman in abnormal circumstances. They let me say anything I was feeling. They hugged me a lot.

With Sarah tucked into bed, Erin came back downstairs. We began to make tea but were interrupted by a knock at the door. I answered with some trepidation and found a man I recognized but could not place right away. He identified himself as someone from the school board. He knew me for my work at the youth shelter program. He stepped right in and began talking really fast, about his new program for students in conflict with the law, as though nothing were out of the ordinary. I could not make sense of what he was saying. I began to wonder if he knew what had happened with Jason. I asked him and he said, "Oh yes, of course I do. That's why I'm here—to see how you are, and make sure that you won't lose your faith in the work you were doing . . . that you won't leave teaching or working with troubled youth because of this."

Leave teaching? Stop working with youth? The thoughts hadn't crossed my mind. If anything, I was sure I would feel more dedicated to my job. Every time I thought about Jason, what his life was like at eighteen, and the lack of support he'd had growing up, I became more focused on my work to help teens. Mostly, I wanted to stop the cycle of violence in any way I could. My principal had approved a short-term leave of absence, so I knew I'd be going back to work after that ended. Maybe it would be part-time, since there was so much ahead in terms of Jason's court process and I had a lot of emotional healing to go through, but I would definitely continue my work with youth. Eventually the man from the school board left, and Erin and I went to bed in the room that used to be Jason's and mine.

I was grateful for Jason's empty space to be filled up that first night. It was too much to think about all the lonely nights to come. I had to try to go one step at a time or I would lose my mind. I also had to get some sleep. I had made it through the first week on just a few broken hours.

The next day was Monday, one week after the day everything had happened. I made a list of errands I had to take care of. My list grew longer with each passing moment—so I started a notebook. As days passed, it filled with page after page of scrawled notes about decisions to be made, information to be sought, people to notify, places to ask for assistance, and thoughts about next steps. My to-do list from two weeks before the crimes read:

- Put away wedding gifts
- Rake leaves
- Buy milk

These tasks still needed to be completed—the last remnants of my old, normal life—along with the list of tasks that were my "new normal":

- Find a criminal lawyer for Jason—someone who can defend a dangerous offender application
- Find out about divorce? Or maybe annulment?
- Call Employee Assistance Plan for counselling referrals
- Call chaplains at Lindsay jail—source of support?
- Call union rep re: applying for emergency funds

- Apply for publication ban on my name
- Jason: remand in court—Tuesday 10:00 a.m.
- Ask someone at the parole office what I should do with Jason's stuff
- Call psychologists and psychiatrists about Jason
- Rent carpet cleaner for basement
- Buy a car?
- Buy yogourt, bananas and tea
- Write letters in response to sympathy cards
- Notify friends in Ecuador
- Get vacuum cleaner fixed
- Replace broken latch on shed door
- Repair fridge door to stop incessant beeping
- Buy a new kettle
- Washing machine—what is making the loud noise?

I sat back feeling completely overwhelmed. I didn't know where to start. Then the phone rang—it was a friend's mother, Pam, who had been widowed in her thirties. She asked, "Have things started breaking yet?" She explained that when you lose your spouse at least five things break right away. It was an insider tip from the trauma club. I glanced at the last five things I'd just added to my list.

I sighed heavily and then gratefully accepted Pam's offer to help me with a few widow-chores. I reviewed my list again. Where was the check-box for *grieve*? It was what I most needed to do—mourn the loss of my husband and our marriage, the life we were to have together. In my heart of hearts I knew that Jason was never coming home.

Again, I switched "on" my role as a counsellor and thought about what advice I might give someone coping with sudden loss. I would tell them not to be alone—to be with others who were grieving the same loss, to talk about it. It usually helped everyone. Members of the trauma club needed to stick together. I thought of Jason's friends in Kingston—in particular the women from Martha's Table who considered him part of the family. I would go to them. Everything else could wait a few more days.

CHAPTER TEN

MY GOLDEN CIRCLE

Arriving in Kingston, I first went to Una's house. Seeing her little green Toyota in the driveway as I pulled in, my mind flooded with memories of the many times Jason and I had done food pickups together for Martha's Table using her car. I would drive and Jason would jump out and load the donation bags in the trunk, hopping back in to sing with me to the radio between stops. Would I ever be able to listen to those songs again? My heart heavy with grief and uncertainty, I walked toward the door of Una's stone cottage. She was standing on the porch, waiting, and pulled me into her arms without saying a word. Tiny Una embraced me with the strength of a professional football player.

I sobbed into her shoulder. There were no words.

"I know, Shannon, I know . . . Come inside."

Una led me to her dining table in front of the lit fireplace. Jason's two other friends, Susan and Shirley, were already there. I recounted to them what I knew and they asked questions, but mostly we shared our shock and sadness. We tried to put pieces together, but there was still so little we could make sense of. The women had only love and praise for Jason; they'd been so proud of what he was doing with his life and how far he'd come since the days when they'd first escorted him to Martha's Table on day passes, now seven years ago. Una recalled how shy and quiet he'd been—always proper in dress and manner, often mistaken for the guard instead of the inmate. Over time, he came out of his shell and grew into a leadership role in the organization—a position of trust. Each woman took a turn reminiscing and I fixed everything they told me into my own bank of memories, getting to know wonderful things about Jason—sadly, after I'd already lost him.

Out loud, we struggled through our questions: Why did he do it? Why those women on that day? Jason worked with women every day, often alone with them in the basement of the church. He had had every opportunity to take advantage of them but he never did.

If he'd had these urges then, how had he suppressed them? We didn't know. His friends lamented that they hadn't stayed in closer contact after we moved to Peterborough.

"Why didn't he tell me something was wrong?" Susan asked, desperation in her voice. "I knew everything about his past. He was part of our family. I would have tried to get him help. I would have stayed with him."

We all felt the same way.

A few weeks later, the lead detective would interview each of these women, as well as Jason's former girlfriend, a teacher he'd dated for a couple of years before we met. He reported that none of them had anything negative to say about Jason. He shook his head. "It just doesn't fit. In twenty years of doing sex crimes investigation, I've never met anyone like Jason. He was surrounded by extraordinary people with everything going for him. It just doesn't make sense."

Later that night, I visited friends whose baby girl was just a few weeks old. Many of my friends were having babies. I held this little girl for a long time, taking in the perfection of her new life. My heart ached to hold her, and I felt a wave of emotion wash over me. It dawned on me then that I had a choice: I could either experience the birth of new babies with sadness—a reminder of the possibilities I had just lost—or I could experience births with joy and gratitude, and celebrate the hope that infants bring with them to their parents and the world. In an instant, I chose the latter. Why choose further suffering when there was already more than enough pain to go around? This proved to be a decision that would save my soul many times over.

I returned to Peterborough the next afternoon. My vice-principal dropped by to hug me and deliver a bundle of letters and cards from my fellow teachers. Some contained small gifts—tea, poems, and a smooth, silver angel amulet. A married couple on staff gave me three pairs of warm woolly socks. These were all gifts of simple comfort that I appreciated enormously.

My vice-principal updated me on the situation at school, telling me about teachers who had dropped into her office to ask how I was doing. We decided it would be good for us all to reunite, soon. I was so grateful to have a job to go back to when I was ready. The return to my place of belonging in the school community was a goal that kept me focused. My twenty sick-days plus three personal days were already rushing past and would end in the middle of December. Perhaps I could take additional leave until Christmas, and start back at school in January—a new year, a new beginning.

I asked about the students I was currently counselling. I worried they would feel abandoned, especially the ones who were having significant problems and for whom I was their only confidante. My VP said that kids had been asking for me and didn't seem to know what had happened. Our guidance secretary had told me the same thing in an e-mail. My name had not appeared in the press, and I didn't share Jason's last name. They were told that I was sick or my husband was sick. I did fear, though, that because I was a victim of his voyeurism—a crime the police had said fell into the category of mischief—once Jason was officially charged with this additional offence, the press would grab hold of those details and print my name as both victim and Jason's spouse. I figured that, as a victim, I would soon hear from a Crown attorney and could ask if there was any way to apply for a ban.

For the moment, though, it seemed that the public and my students did not associate me with Jason's crimes. My vice-principal let me know that a teacher would be assigned to cover for me while I was away, and I arranged to go to school after classes to brief the substitute and to see some of my colleagues.

My first visit to school was short and tearful. Several people embraced me warmly and asked what they could do to help. One colleague passed me on the stairs coming into the building and froze for a moment before scurrying past. I had expected these awkward interactions—they occur following death or other bad news. Some people just don't know what to say or do. It was uncomfortable when nothing was said or acknowledged, but discomfort was better than insensitivity, as I was about to learn.

At a gas station later that week, I ran into one of the school secretaries at the pumps. She asked me where I was off to. I said that I was going to Lindsay. The town is known for its jail.

"You're not going to see *him*, are you?"

I scrambled to explain that we had a lot of things to talk about, Jason and I, but she had already dropped eye contact with me. She backed away as though I were contagious and hurried to get in her car.

Just before she closed the door, she said with a seeming combination of pity and disdain, "Well, Shannon, there are other fish in the sea." Then she drove away.

I stood motionless, gas pump in hand and snow blowing from all directions. I realized that I was going to have to be a lot more careful about what I said and who I spoke to from then on.

The colleague who was assigned to cover my absence from work was a very strong woman, someone who had overcome several tragedies in her own life. She passed on some advice that she had once been given. Pressing her hand over mine, she said, "Give yourself five years to recover. It's going to take at least five years until you feel that not every decision you make is ruled by this trauma."

Five years? I thought to myself. How was I going to cope with this pain for *five years*? On the other hand, I felt that I'd just been granted permission to go through a process. Maybe she was right. Five years seemed both reasonable and realistic. Much more so than the five days my maid of honour's father had allowed me to put my house on the market and move on. In five years, I would be thirty-five . . . still young enough to become a mother.

I needed time and patience, but some people didn't have it to offer me. When I called one long-time friend whom I'd supported through the years and told her my terrible news, she

said, "I really don't have time for this right now; things are
really crazy at work."

I was stunned. What was wrong with her? I was numb when
I hung up the phone. A few weeks later, I ran into her and she
seemed really glad to see me. She put her arms around me and
said, "You feel small." She invited me to have dinner with her,
and I accepted. At dinner, she asked me to tell her the whole
story, and I did, believing she cared and just wanted another
chance to show it, realizing the abruptness of her initial reaction. When I finished, drained, she said, simply, "Well, I'm
afraid of Jason." She said she would call me, but never did.
Later I learned she'd shared her fears and opinions with everyone but me.

Around this time, I received a two-page typed letter from
another long-time friend. He wrote on his own behalf and that
of his spouse, responding to the group e-mail I'd sent after my
first visit with Jason in jail. He was deeply troubled by the compassion I was showing toward a sex offender and he was saddened to know that the women would never recover. He
demanded to know what message would be sent to Jason's victims if he were to show compassion for their assailant. What
message would he be sending his sons? What message would
he be sending to all the women in his life who have experienced
sexual assault and abuse? He informed me that he had taken
an oath at a white-ribbon breakfast that very week to speak
out against acts of violence against women. He said that my
correspondence made it sound as if Jason were the real victim
and the women minor casualties of a tortured mind. He mentioned that in our last conversation, I had expressed feelings of
anger. He said that made him glad. He admitted that he had
not spoken with me very much over the past few weeks, and

therefore was not entirely up to date on what was going on. Clearly that hadn't stopped him from sending me his opinions when I was most vulnerable and dealing with my own losses.

The letter hurt me deeply. I could not believe that two people who knew me so well could accuse me of not feeling enough for the victims. I could not believe that their interpretation of my, or anyone else's, love or support for Jason meant we were minimizing his offences. My family and I were devastated by all violence against women. I was also incensed that he and his partner had decided that the victims would never recover— didn't that only victimize them further, condemning them to victimhood forever? How could they ever hope to recover if society deemed them ruined for life? And why was I the target of anger, not Jason—the one who had betrayed everyone's trust? What had I done wrong? I was starting to see that jails, which locked dangerous people away from society, also protected those very same criminals from facing the impact their actions had on the rest of society. In the perpetrator's absence, someone—often someone close to the perpetrator but not in any way involved in their crimes—would have to bear the brunt of a community's hostility and fear. In this case, that burden was mine.

It was also becoming clear what many people now wanted of me. It was a pattern I'd see over and over in the months and years to come. They wanted—sometimes even demanded, as these friends had—for me to walk away from Jason and never look back. To them, it was simple and clear-cut: Jason was evil. Therefore, I should shun him, ostracize him, eliminate him from my life, mind and heart to prove that I *wasn't* like him and to prove that I was on their side—the side of "good." Any other action from me—any attempt to understand the nuances of his mind, the motives behind his actions and the deeper reasons that led him to commit such heinous crimes—was to these people a betrayal and made me guilty by association.

Fear is a normal and completely understandable emotion. I knew that beneath their words lay a deep-seated need for safety and security. Separating themselves from me was a way to protect themselves—to deny that what had happened to me could happen to them. The faster they could do that, the faster they'd feel safe again.

I responded to my former friends with a short e-mail in which I briefly shared the impact their letter had had on me, attempted to right their wrong impressions, and then asked that they refrain from having future contact with me.

After I received that letter, my anxiety increased dramatically. But it would increase even further when another friend contacted me. She accused me of putting her family in danger by bringing Jason into their lives, obviously forgetting that it was she who knew Jason at Martha's Table before I did. She told me that if she had known Jason was a parolee, she never would have been friends with him. It seemed to me that she felt charitable to the forsaken of our society as long as they kept their distance. She wanted everyone labelled so she could spot potential danger from a mile away. We would all like to know where danger lies, but the harsh reality is that we rarely know in advance.

All of these judgmental reactions affected me profoundly, and I began to question myself all over again. Had I done anything wrong? Many seemed to think I had. Had I been negligent in any way? Jason had never given me even the tiniest clue that anything was going wrong or that he needed help. I spent months getting to know officials and experts who said that he was not a risk, that his first offence had been a one-time event—the explosive act of a teenager. I trusted that the Parole Board of Canada had not released someone who was dangerous. I trusted the experts who said he was making a good life for himself, and saw that evidenced in Jason's work and relationships. I trusted Jason when he said he would never go back to prison and that he would never hurt anyone again. Did my trust, after all of this due diligence, really mean *I* was culpable? I knew that wasn't so.

From then on, I decided to get my sister to screen my e-mail and my neighbour to pre-read letters for me. Soon, I opened a new e-mail account and stopped checking the old one. I created a notebook where I divided a page into three columns and gave each a title: "People Who Love and Support Me (and understand that I'm grieving Jason)," "Undecided/People I'm Not Sure About," and "Unsafe People." I filled in names with each new correspondence received. I dubbed that first column in my notebook "The Golden Circle." These were the people I could trust. It was into their embrace I would fall many, many times.

CHAPTER ELEVEN

SOLITARY CONFINEMENT

When he was about seven, my brother could fall asleep only if he had a bucket of water beside his bed. We'd watched *The Wizard of Oz* a few too many times and he was terrified of the wicked witch. So was I, but it seemed to me that the only way to rid Oz of the witch was to seek her out the way Dorothy did, and face her straight on. By doing that, Dorothy set herself free.

By the end of November, I had seen Jason six times, and each time I spoke with him, I understood a bit more about what had made him commit those heinous crimes. It helped that he consistently accepted responsibility for what he'd done, and each time, what I saw before me was a repentant, broken human being, not a monster. There was no bucket of water I could throw to melt away all the evil he'd caused; trying to understand how it got there in the first place was what made me feel stronger and safer. No one else—no lawyer, no doctor, no social worker or other professional whose job it may have been—had been to see Jason yet. I found that profoundly frightening. How was he supposed to address the deeper triggers for his violence if he wasn't even properly assessed? If he was locked up like an animal for twenty-three hours and forty-five minutes a day?

Prisons perform an essential function: they keep us safe from dangerous people, at least as long as they are locked up. For some, that knowledge alone is enough to alleviate their fears. For me, the strategy of incarceration on its own left me feeling helpless, alone to wade through the damage I'd been left with, to try to recover my life as an individual and as a community member. I had to do something more to help the situation and get to the bottom of the fear. For me, that meant not turning away from the one who had caused it, the one in closest proximity to me: Jason. I had to try to help him, not just because I loved him, but because it seemed the only chance he had to approach rehabilitation and the only chance I had to mitigate the devastating harm he'd caused to me, and maybe to others. Helping him face what he had done, encouraging him to use the power of his remorse as a transformative force, I believed, was one way to bring him—and all victims of crime, myself included—closer to justice.

I would help Jason by continuing to visit him—with the aim of getting to the core of why he'd done what he'd done—but there were practical things I could do, too, like find him a lawyer. I'd promised the judge I would at Jason's arraignment, and I had to see my commitment through. Though I believed Jason needed to be incarcerated for safety reasons, I couldn't bear the idea of him sitting in solitary confinement at the provincial jail without help or human contact (save for the one hour a week he was allowed visitors), and without an end in sight. It wasn't only causing suffering for him—which many might argue he deserved—it was causing suffering for the people who loved him. I believe that the usefulness of pure punishment has a short lifespan. After that, some kind of rehabilitation should occur. What if Jason had a mental disorder that could be treated or cured? Wouldn't early intervention be optimal? What if something could be learned from his case that could prevent others from committing crimes? We were desperate for answers and some better way forward, yet we had no one to help advocate for this. We all needed a lawyer for Jason—someone to move the justice process forward, help him plead guilty as he wanted to do, and get him out of solitary and back into the federal system where the conditions were better.

Technically, Jason could be pulled back into federal custody right away rather than waiting to be convicted and sentenced for the current charges. As a "lifer," Jason was incarcerated now not only because he was awaiting trial for violent crimes, but also because he'd broken his parole. He could in fact be held for the rest of his natural life, without even being sentenced separately for the crimes he had just committed. Parole hearings would still take place, but there was no legal obligation for the Parole Board to release him by a certain date.

I still wasn't allowed to speak to Jason's parole officer, so I pieced together this information from asking whomever I could—lawyers at the court, the police, and the regional manager of parole services—some of whom were helpful, and some of whom were dismissive. Finally, the regional parole manager explained that she had already requested Jason be transferred back to a federal prison—either the one where he had served most of his first sentence or a higher-security one. "Don't worry, Shannon," she said, "he'll be back in federal in a couple of weeks, a month at the most." I was relieved. The following week a provincial Corrections staffer told me Jason wouldn't be transferred until he had a lawyer. If they let him out of the jail and into a federal prison without one, the court knew from experience that his motivation and urgency to acquire counsel would decrease as he became comfortable in the more livable conditions. The case would be delayed even further. He was in the hands of both correctional systems—provincial and federal—but sometimes there seemed to be a disturbing lack of communication between the two. Jason needed a lawyer, and soon.

As an inmate in solitary confinement, Jason was not allowed to make phone calls to unapproved numbers, including toll-free numbers. Most criminal lawyers accept collect calls from their clients in jail, the operative words being *their clients*. How could an inmate become a client if he wasn't able to make the initial calls to law firms? Frustrated by what seemed like ridiculous rules, I told Jason I would make some initial calls to lawyers. If their response showed they were equipped to take on Jason's case, I would give him their numbers to get approved so he could call for himself. While I was tackling this, Jason was making some headway applying for Legal Aid, but it was slow. He could not hire anyone without it.

Meanwhile, Jason was called to appear in court every two weeks, and each time, after a thirty-second video appearance, he would be remanded back to solitary confinement in the Lindsay jail. For most of his appearances, I went to court with either my mum or friends—I never went alone—because it was only there that we had the hope of getting any information about the process. We knew nothing then about the length of time this case would take to be tried. From our layperson's viewpoint, we saw it as clear-cut: Jason had given a full confession that matched the victims' statements. He would plead guilty without hesitation. He already had a sentence that could keep him in prison indefinitely. We were in for a sobering reality check.

I struggled to get my bearings, as I tried to navigate and understand the legal system, its many players and its complex terminology, I approached different lawyers I saw at the court-house. One told me, "If Jason had wanted to move this case along quickly, he should have taken a gun and shot himself." I stood frozen, feeling like I'd taken a bullet myself, while the lawyer shuffled papers into his briefcase and left in a hurry. Other lawyers were more sympathetic. One told me that a case like Jason's could consume an entire small practice, so there was no way I would find anyone locally to take it on; I should look in Toronto. I should try to find someone who had experience with dangerous offender applications, as they are extremely rare. I called lawyers whose names I remembered from highly publicized cases: John Rosen, Brian Greenspan, and Paul Copeland. Their clients included some of the most infamous criminals in the country. I dialed the numbers in a state of dis-belief. None of these lawyers could take on Jason's case—either their practices were full or they didn't work on Legal Aid rates—but I was kindly referred to someone else at a Toronto firm. I made an appointment to see him.

At our meeting, the lawyer and I talked at length, and I went over every detail I could think of. I clearly explained Jason's desire to plead guilty. He seemed interested, kind and support-ive. He said he was impressed—and seemed even surprised—that I was articulate and not in denial about the gravity of Jason's crimes. He accepted the case at the Legal Aid rate and told me he'd get a psychiatrist up to Lindsay to see Jason right away. He knew someone really good, an adjunct professor at the University of Toronto and a leading psychiatrist at the Centre for Addiction and Mental Health. He also ran a clinic for sexual offenders. Maybe this doctor could shed light on what was wrong with Jason and maybe even eventually treat him. The lawyer promised to do what he could and assured me we would be in communication very soon. I trusted him, and felt relieved to have found someone to take on a process that I found so daunting. I had a criminal lawyer for Jason, but now I still needed to find a lawyer for myself, to help me decide what to do about my marriage.

I checked the next item on my ever-evolving to-do list. It read: *Separation? Annulment? Divorce?* Three big question marks that made my heart heavy. I had just signed a marriage certificate and now I would have to undo it. I hadn't broken our vows—Jason had. I felt the depths of this betrayal right to my core. I didn't want to be divorced, but I knew I couldn't stay married either. I had to protect myself. I was terrified that I would be made responsible for Jason's legal costs, or even his student loan. I sifted through all of our financial documents and in them found a file Jason had hidden: credit card bills for an account I believed he had closed months ago when we met with a financial planner to consolidate our finances in preparation for married life. Now, looking at a total of over $3,500 on Jason's credit card bill, I reached a breaking point. Suddenly, I became filled with rage and disgust. All of the charges were for purchases of Internet pornography, save one, which was for my birthday gift. How could Jason have watched me work so hard to scrimp and save money for our house and wedding while he accrued debt by purchasing filth? How could he have destroyed everything we had and deceived me like this? How could he have assaulted those women? As I sat on the floor of the living room, bills spread out around me, anger pulsed through my veins with so much force I thought they would burst.

The phone rang. An operator's voice. Would I accept a collect call? Jason. I was livid—on top of everything else, now I would have to *pay* to tell him how angry I was, not just about this but about everything: how he'd hurt people, how he'd lied to me and betrayed me, how his actions had destroyed everything we'd built together. I accepted the call and laid into him. All Jason could do was apologize; he couldn't fix anything he'd broken. That was left to me.

I was in a perilous situation. I could manage mortgage payments with my salary but there wouldn't be much breathing room without Jason's income. My parents raised me to be fiscally responsible and I had never carried a credit card balance or let a bill go unpaid before and I didn't want to start now. In my notebook, I made a list of things I could sell if I needed to: Jason's bike, a set of weights, some DVDs. We didn't have any expensive electronics or jewellery. I placed some unopened wedding gifts in the car with the gift receipts taped to them so that I could return them for cash. No matter how I looked at things, the total didn't come close to balancing what was owed on Jason's debts.

I wrote to Jason demanding further accountability. He responded with a shame-filled apology, explaining that he had been living in complete denial and fantasy and that there was no excuse. Beyond that, he had no practical way to right his financial wrongs. As an inmate in a provincial jail on remand, he did not earn any wages. He could not work or participate in any programs while in protective custody. Even once he was transferred to the federal system, the highest inmate wage was $6.90 a day. He was given two stamped envelopes per week to write letters. Phone calls were collect only and were long-distance. Having the discussions I needed to have with Jason were costly any way I looked at it. Yet the cost of not being in contact would be even higher. Without those discussions, I would be left without answers, apologies or accountability. I decided I would bear the expenses for as long as I could, for as long as I found being in contact with Jason essential. How long that would be I didn't know.

I called a legal help line and spoke to three different family lawyers. No one had heard of a situation like mine and they were hard pressed to give me advice. I was given the name of a local lawyer. He explained the bases on which I had grounds for a divorce in Ontario: separation for a minimum of one year, adultery, and cruelty. The latter two would require entering a legal process for which Jason and I would each have to hire a lawyer and go to court to testify in front of a judge. I would have to prove that Jason had been cruel and/or had committed adultery, and despite his confessions, until he was convicted in a criminal court I wouldn't actually have the proof needed for a family court. I didn't think I could wait on tenterhooks through a year of separation to gain legal protection. What if Jason's creditors pursued me? The lawyer suggested that I contact the officiant who had married us, to see if an annulment was possible.

The word *annulment* pressed on my heart: a marriage that had never happened. The part of me that still loved Jason wanted to hold onto that month that we'd had, but I couldn't afford to be sentimental. I called the lay minister who'd performed our marriage ceremony. She had read about what happened in the papers—Jason had seemed like such a lovely person, she said. She was very sorry. I made an appointment to see her. When I arrived at the church office, she said we'd be meeting with the head clergy, a more experienced woman who knew about annulments. The head clergy arrived a moment later. She too said she'd read the newspaper articles, but concluded that Jason was a monster. I couldn't believe what I was hearing. The clergywoman continued: "It is presumed that your relationship was consummated in the one month you were married or in the nearly three years you were in a common-law relationship, so there is no way to get an annulment. Divorce is your only option."

Her eyes fixed on mine coldly. "I guess you'll make a better choice next time."

Anger shot through me and I leapt to my feet. "How can you call yourself a spiritual leader when you are so quick to judge? You don't know anything about me. I didn't come here to be chastised—I came for help."

I headed for the door, passing the lay minister on my way out.

I'm sorry, she mouthed weakly.

When I got into the car, I broke down in anger and frustration. I was no further ahead in dissolving my legal ties to Jason. Reluctantly, I called my sister. She had recently graduated from law school and was three months into her year of articling at a firm outside Toronto. I didn't want to impose upon her, but I felt desperate. She agreed to ask her boss for some advice. He told her that I could gain the protection I needed through a formal separation agreement made retroactive to the date of the offences (the date Jason and I had become separated), a fact none of the other lawyers had raised. After a year I could proceed with a desk-order divorce. My sister could prepare the document, her boss would check it over, and then it would have to be signed by both Jason and me in front of separate Commissioners of Oaths. I could sign in front of my sister, and we presumed there was someone at the jail who could certify

Jason's signature. The agreement would protect me from having to pay Jason's legal costs, but any debts accrued during the time of our relationship were still mine to handle.

The days went by quickly as I completed task after task in the aftermath of Jason's crimes. I was exhausted but couldn't sleep. At night, when I could no longer make phone calls to lawyers or help agencies, I searched and searched for information that would help me understand what was wrong with Jason. I read psychiatric journal articles about sexual deviance, men who murder and rape, and adult survivors of childhood abuse and neglect, still suspecting something had happened to Jason that might help explain his acts of violence. I wrote authors to ask for more information. I banished my maternity books to my nightstand cabinet: a mausoleum of lost hope. I read and reread Jason's letters, which began to arrive every few days in small, white, prison-issue envelopes—pages and pages in his neat handwriting, disclosures about what was going on inside his mind.

I don't know where to begin to apologize. I don't believe that language, as I know it, is capable of describing the depths of my regret for what I did to the victims, and to you, and to everyone connected to us. The awareness comes most vividly with the first waking moment of my day. It's then that I'm most raw and yet without the buffering distractions of shouts and clanging outside my door as the range comes to its own version of life. . . . When I was eighteen, misguided as I was, I was shielded against much of the reality that confronts me now. Back then, no matter what I told the powers that be, I had convinced myself on some operational, background level that I was not responsible for what I had done—not fully, anyway. But now I'm thirty-six and find myself without any delusional means of escaping the weight of the world that sits on my chest. Right where it belongs. . . .

How precious my life with you was. You gave me every love, every support, every solace that you could. In return, I let obsession, twisted and dark, grow like a cancer under the surface. At times I was oblivious to it myself. At times I felt myself really believing in "us" and the proof that you gave each and every day that my "second chance" wasn't just an illusion. But the darkness would always return to pull at me. And I would shut down. Rather than ask for any real help from you when I knew you would have understood, I shut down and let it grow in the cracks of my own selfish pride, fear of exposure, and (ultimately) an overestimated level of control.

After everything you had given me and all we had been through, the best I could come up with was a cryptic note on my website, a quickly scrawled note on the art pad left in the kitchen, and a last request called downstairs to two people I had just victimized horrendously: "I have no right to ask this of you," I said, "but if you see Shannon, could you please tell her I'm sorry, and that there's nothing she could have done, and that I love her." [The first victim] said she would. And then I left, thanking her.

I remember then feeling a strange sort of peace as I drove to call the police. I had apologized face-to-face with my victims, I had apologized to you in my way, and I felt like I was making the right choice. . . .

We all know what happened next. . . . I saw the cruiser lights flashing in the van's rear-view mirror. I stretched my fingers out on the steering wheel and exhaled, long and slow.

I thought to myself that this, too, was right. With a sort of resigned objectivity, I thought that justice was being done. . . .

Reading Jason's words stirred conflicting emotions. Sadness, anger, frustration, desperation and longing lay like jumbled puzzle pieces inside me. I tried to put them together, but there were still so many pieces missing. I searched our entire house for clues of any kind about what was wrong with Jason, though I didn't know what I was looking for. I reached my hand down into the pockets of every article of his clothing, hoping that I would find a note to explain everything. As I searched, I cleaned and scrubbed. I felt compelled to remove the stain of crime.

There were times when I longed for insanity. I would cry so hard that I thought I was losing my mind, and then I would think, *Good, maybe someone will come and take me away.* I often wished I could trade places with Jason—I would be protected from the outside world and be given three meals a day and a chance to think, and he would have to face the consequences of his actions and clean up the damage he'd left behind.

CHAPTER TWELVE

THE TWO JASONS

Jason told me I could find the pinhole video camera he used for the voyeurism on a shelf in the art room. It was a black cube, smaller than one inch square, and it looked like a pencil sharpener. It was no wonder neither I, nor the police, had noticed it. I put it in a Ziploc bag and took it down to the police station.

There I met Detective Jeff Morgan for the first time. He was the officer who had taken Jason's statement on the night of his arrest. He had now been assigned as the lead investigator on the case. His size was imposing but his manner was kind and gentle. The first thing he did was ask how I was doing, expressing deep sympathy for my situation. I asked him if he knew how the victims were. He said their physical wounds were healing and that the second victim was expected to regain full use of her hand once her stitches were removed. As he spoke, he opened his own hand, palm facing up, and traced a line from the bottom of his index finger to just above the wrist. That's where her scar would be. I closed my eyes. *Let her be okay.*

We spoke briefly about Jason. Detective Morgan said that in

over twenty years of working in sex crimes investigation he had never met anyone like Jason. "He just doesn't fit. We don't have guys like this phoning us not once, but twice to say what they did. We don't get confessions that match up exactly to what the victims say. It's so sad—Jason had everything going for him. He was making a great start."

"I can't make sense of it either. No one can."

We stood in silence for a moment.

Detective Morgan asked when I would be available to return to the station to identify all the voyeurism victims on the videos Jason had taken. I would be asked to determine the dates on which the crimes had taken place, if possible. This would help the investigation team decide what charges to lay, and how many counts of each. Detective Morgan told me the footage was not overly explicit or violent in any way. Some was taken in the basement, but most was taken in the bathroom. He explained what he had determined from previewing them: that the camera must have been in or near the back of the toilet, since what it caught was people undoing their pants or lifting up their skirts, and then using the toilet (though this last part could not be seen). It also showed the faces of most people as they came into the bathroom, so I would be able to make identifications right away and then, hopefully, I could turn away before I saw anything else. I did not want to invade anyone's privacy the way Jason had. I did not even want to see their faces during what they believed was a private moment. This would incriminate my husband, but I would do what I had to because the police had asked me and because it was the right thing to do. I would never protect Jason.

"I'll come whenever you need me," I said firmly.

A few days later I returned and was seated in the same

interview room where Nora had questioned me two weeks earlier. Detective Morgan carefully explained what I was to do and then pressed play on the video recorder. As I watched each victim enter the picture, I immediately felt protective of them. I flinched every time I said the name of someone I knew and loved. One of them was my mum. How could Jason have done this to her, to me, to any of us? I felt so ashamed of him. Then I became numb as I watched myself on screen coming out of the shower, completely unaware of being watched. That woman seemed years younger than I was now, and I watched her almost as if she were someone else.

I determined that the videotaping had taken place on four different occasions, beginning about four months prior to the day of the assaults, and ending a week or so before they occurred. As I watched, I recollected what else was happening on those days: here Jason and I had had dinner with friends; here we had worked in the garden; here we had watched TV snuggled up on the couch. His ability to "flip" frightened me. Jason himself appeared on tape several times. He would adjust the camera, leaning in close so that he was framed in the lens. I looked at this face but my Jason was not there. It was the same skin, features and hair, but his eyes were vacant. He was the man I had seen in court that first day—a dead body standing.

The police decided to lay a single charge of mischief for all of the voyeurism. They said that in cases where a camera has been recording indiscriminately, typically in public places like a shopping mall washroom, identifying victims is impossible so they are never notified. But in this case, since the filming had been indiscriminate but victims could be identified, they weren't sure what to do. They deferred the decision about notification to me and my parents.

It was an enormous burden to be handed, but at the time we were partly grateful. This meant that we could mitigate harm by informing victims in a compassionate and personal way. The people we knew wouldn't hear about it from a police officer or someone at the Crown Attorneys' Offices—they would hear it from us. We began by telling anyone who had thus far chosen to maintain a relationship with Jason. We felt they needed to know they had been directly victimized in order to make an informed choice about continuing or abandoning their relationship with him. One by one, we went through the list. Victims handled the news with grace, and several chose to confront their offender directly through letters or visits. Jason expressed his remorse, apologized, and was offered forgiveness by some. He was a lucky, lucky man.

I was exhausted by the process, left with no energy to really consider my own experience as a victim of voyeurism. In the wake of what had happened to the two women, it felt to me a far lesser form of violence. When I started seeing a social worker a few months later, I mentioned the impact Jason's actions had had on other victims of voyeurism. She stopped me and said, "What does all this mean for *you*, Shannon?" I could not come up with a response. I didn't know. I had been so caught up in gathering information, providing support to others and answering questions posed by officials, I hadn't been able to stop and consider what it meant for me.

I had now been given official victim status in the legal process, but the charge of "mischief" carried no protection for victims' identities. That meant my name could still appear in the press. I shuddered at the thought of my students or their parents knowing that my husband had filmed me naked in the bathroom, and others, too, during private moments. Never in my life had I felt so anxious and powerless. I couldn't make sense of the law: Why would the public ever need to know the names of victims? Didn't we have enough privacy taken from us by the offender without having to fear everyone in town would know what happened to us? These were big questions, but for the time being, I had to put them aside. I still hadn't heard from the Crown's office, but was sure I would imminently. In the interim, I had to get ready to return to work.

December was approaching and my leave of absence was rapidly coming to an end. I filled out forms for emergency funds and was awarded the maximum amount by my union: twenty-five hundred dollars. This would buy me some more time, maybe a month.

My union rep called to make sure I had received the cheque. He said that we should get together to talk about my return to work, indicating that there were some concerns on the part of the school board. This did not surprise me as I had concerns too. My principal had already called to invite me to a "re-entry meeting" with her and the superintendent the following week. On the phone, she had sounded nervous and uncomfortable. Prior to Jason's crimes, we had always enjoyed an easy and very personable relationship. My union rep said he would help me prepare for that meeting, so we met at my house and had a good discussion. I made a list of ideas for the smoothest return possible, one that was sensitive to the victim's stepson and the larger school community. We were certain that a plan could be developed to best fit everyone's needs.

That night, I borrowed a friend's car and went to Toronto to meet Rachael at the airport. She was coming from Colorado to stay the weekend, bringing her ten-week-old daughter with her. It was wonderful to be together and to have the baby with us—a tiny sign of hope. Rachael had decided, as I had, that she needed to talk with Jason herself. She wanted the chance to see him, to express her devastation over his actions, and to offer the friendship and love she still felt. We drove to the jail the next day. I waited with the baby while Rachael went in. After the half-hour visit, a tearful Rachael returned to me.

"Shan," she said softly after a few minutes, "he looked like a little boy."

"I know, Rach. I know."

Rachael just kept shaking her head. "Remember how he was with the baby at your wedding? I watched him button up her sleepers then listen to her so closely, counting how many breaths she took in a minute. He was . . . so gentle with her. I have that lovely photo of him having a nap with her on his chest, and I was so sure he would make a wonderful father for your kids. I was so happy for him." Rachael put her hand on mine. "I've never met the Jason who was capable of doing what he did to those women."

"Neither have I," I said.

"In that room just now, Jason said he was sorry, and I believed him. I told him that while I couldn't forgive his actions— what he did is unforgivable—I did forgive *him*, as a person."

I thought about her words—about forgiving the person, not the actions. I hadn't had the time to deeply consider overt forgiveness until now. But this concept made sense to me. It was what I felt too. I hated what Jason had done and I could not condone or accept his choice to harm, but I just couldn't write him off as a monster. I knew he was, in fact, very human—a human who had acted inhumanly. When I looked at him through the prison glass, I saw a broken man and couldn't help but feel humility. I wasn't necessarily different or better than the person in front of me. Maybe just luckier. I grew up surrounded by people who loved me, and on whom I could rely, and who guided me to make the right choices. I considered who I could have become if my life circumstances had been different, and I had to admit that—though difficult to imagine—it could have been me on the other side of the glass. In a different life course, it could have been me.

"What do you think 'forgiveness' really means?" I asked Rachael.

"I think it means that we can see ourselves in others, even at their lowest moments, and remember that we were all created as equal and precious children of God." Rachael was a devout and practising Christian and though we had quite different views on religion, I understood what she was saying in a spiritual sense, and I agreed. For both of us, forgiveness seemed to be about the choice to see someone as still possessing goodness even as they had acted out of total darkness. We admitted that we were fortunate in this situation, because Jason's remorse and confessions made it easier to see his humanity. If he had denied or minimized what he had done, or had not called the police, it would have been a lot harder. Still, I struggled with the concept. I knew I didn't condone or pardon his actions, and I never would. Did that mean that I was or I wasn't forgiving Jason? Did I have to forgive him directly, or could I just live in a forgiving way? Was love the same thing?

I had never said "I forgive you" to Jason. It hadn't occurred to me. If I found myself ready to offer forgiveness to Jason one day, the way Rachael had, would he have to accept it for it to become real? I didn't know if someone who was as ashamed and as guilty as he could do that. I doubted that I would be able to forgive myself if I were in his place.

Maybe choosing a mindset of forgiveness—encouraging the humanity behind the horror—was less a philosophical choice than a practical one. Would it help to combat the resentment and enduring, festering anger around me? Or the anger that had flooded me before and which I was sure would surface again? I wanted more than anything to hold onto my deepest self very tightly—my self that is loving, kind and compassionate—so that when I emerged from this nightmare, I would again be capable of feeling happiness. To deny that future to myself would be the ultimate victimization: the loss of my ability to love and trust. I had already been robbed of so much; I wouldn't let that be taken from me too. Maybe forgiveness meant rejecting a lifetime bond to violence and victimization. Maybe forgiveness could be as liberating for the victim as it was for the perpetrator—perhaps even more so.

Much later, I heard it said that forgiveness is the fragrance the violet sheds on the heel of the one who has crushed it. I wanted to be that violet.

Strengthened by my visit with Rachael and my new resolve, I began looking forward to returning to work. I wanted to get back to helping my students, though I wasn't sure I was ready to return full-time right away. I consulted my Golden Circle about this, and everyone agreed that getting back to the routine and purpose of a job would have a positive impact. No one was naive; we all knew that I wouldn't just walk into the school, sit down in my counselling office, and open the door for my usual rush of students as if nothing had happened. But we believed that if handled the right way—with leadership and dialogue among staff and with professionals—my return to school would be healing for all.

CHAPTER THIRTEEN

GUILTY BY ASSOCIATION

I arrived at the school board office for the re-entry meeting and ran into my principal in the parking lot. "Wow, you look great!" she said. "You've lost a lot of weight!"

It was nothing to congratulate me over. I'd lost weight because I was extremely stressed and sad all the time. "Grief diet," I answered.

We shuffled over the ice and into the building. She went to the superintendent's office while I waited for my union rep, who arrived shortly thereafter. We gathered in a small meeting room: my principal and superintendent on one side of the table: my union rep and I were on the other. The meeting began with offers of condolences, but then quickly transitioned into concerns over my return to work. My principal told me that parents had called her to say that they didn't want their children anywhere near "that Ms. Moroney" and that some colleagues were questioning how I could be a good counsellor when I had married an ex-con. She told me people were very upset to have learned that I was visiting Jason. "But they don't know the context in which I'm seeing him," I protested. "I neither deny his guilt nor condone his actions."

She brushed me off. "Well, at any rate," she said, "too many bad things have happened at our school recently, like the death of the former principal last year and two teachers sick with cancer. This is just too much for everyone."

This is too much for everyone? Too many bad things have happened? Would I have to pay the price because my tragedy came last? Was there a limit on the number of "bad things" that could befall any one school?

"I think it would help people to see me. I have a stack of letters and cards from well-wishers and—"

"Yes, Shannon," she interjected. "I'm sure your friends on staff support you, but we have to think about the whole school."

The superintendent cut in. "And we have to pay particular attention to one student, and that is the stepson of one of the victims."

"Absolutely," I responded, "but I didn't hurt him."

My principal and superintendent were expressionless.

"Will you tell me the name of the student?" I asked.

"No, we will not." The principal's tone was cold. "We are respecting the student's privacy."

"I will respect his privacy too, but it is extremely stressful for me to wonder if every young man is him." My employers remained unresponsive.

I made a suggestion that we could hold a meeting with staff before I returned and that we could invite the school liaison officer from the police department, but my words fell on deaf ears.

My principal looked me in the eye. "Shannon, you will not be returning to our school. It is just too hard for everyone. You will be relocated when your doctor says you are ready. There is a position opening up across town in February."

What? Had I heard correctly? Not going back?

The superintendent picked up where my principal had left off. "I would like to remind you that you are an employee of the school board, not the school, and we can move you around at any time based on a concept of 'best fit.'"

I looked at my union rep, incredulous. "Can they do this?"

He looked as stunned as I felt. "It is true that you are an employee of the board, but relocations are to be made in consultation with the employee . . ." His voice dropped off.

"This is the consultation," the superintendent said.

I pictured myself starting a brand-new position in a new school a few weeks later—a school where I didn't know anyone but where there was a good chance a lot of people would have heard about what happened through the press or the grapevine. How would I find the energy to start over so soon—to face a new environment and get to know all the ins and outs of a different school, staff and student body? Was I the one who had committed the crimes? Or was this my punishment for marrying Jason?

I managed to speak up. "I don't think relocation would be the best option."

"We're doing this to make it easier on you. We're even willing to pay you until the position begins, which would amount to an extra three weeks beyond your leave. We don't have to do that, you know," my superintendent explained. His message seemed to carry a degree of warning.

My principal spoke up next. Suddenly her tone seemed to be one of pity. The abrupt change confused me. "Is there anything I can do for you?" she asked.

I thought for a moment, trying to consider her question seriously as panic rose inside. I pictured teachers and parents going into her office as she had described, approaching her with anger, confusion, or allegations against my character. I asked her to encourage people to abstain from judgment for the time being.

Her response to my request was a cold and curt, "I won't do that."

Then she delivered the final blow. "And, Shannon, one more thing—don't come into the school without permission. It's too upsetting for people to see you. You represent something terrible."

I represent something terrible. The words undid me completely. I heard myself weakly thank her and the superintendent for their time. I was shown the door. I walked out of the room with my union rep, trying to keep my composure. In the hallway I turned to him and asked what the union could do. He was sorry, he said, but he didn't think there was anything he could do, other than help me fill out the forms for employment insurance. The decision was made. He would be in touch in the next few days. We said goodbye and I left.

In the car, I put my hands on the frozen steering wheel and focused my eyes forward. *This isn't right. I am a victim of crime, not the perpetrator.* Detective Morgan had told me once that I was welcome to seek the support of police victims' services and now I knew it was time to accept the offer.

From the car I called ahead to the police station to make sure someone in victims' services was available. I asked for Detective Morgan but he wasn't there. Instead, I was connected to Nora— the officer who had interviewed me on the first day—and she said she would meet me when I arrived. I knew where the victims' services office was—just a few months earlier I had accompanied one of my students from the youth shelter there, a young woman who had been sexually assaulted and needed help preparing herself to testify in court. To our surprise, my student and I found the victims' counsellor cold and businesslike. I had the feeling that she didn't fully respect my student and wondered if it was because this girl was young and homeless and had been in some trouble with the law.

At the police station, Nora greeted me and led me into the victims' services office. She introduced me to the counsellor. It was the same woman my student and I had met with months ago. I said hello.

She stood up, looked me up and down and said, "What are *you* doing here?"

Was I mishearing? Hadn't Nora told her who I was? I explained that I had been invited by Detective Morgan to seek her help. I explained that I was Jason Staples' wife and began to tell her what had just happened at the school board. Another expressionless face was looking back at me.

"You need to understand how serious Jason's actions were. You need to give everyone else time."

A wave of dizziness washed over me. What made her think I didn't understand? We had never spoken before. I looked behind me and saw a chair. I sat down, weak. Nora and the counsellor sat down as well.

I turned my gaze to Nora, my eyes searching hers for help.

"Nora—you understand, don't you?"

Nora had been in my house; she was the one who had gone through all of my belongings and photos, who had told me that she regretted her initial assumptions about me. I looked to her now for support—I needed someone to stand up for me—but she said nothing.

The counsellor then launched into a soliloquy about criminals.

She had worked for years at one of the Toronto-area jails with "guys like Jason."

"They never change," she said. She told me that she would never again work "on that side" of the justice system and she had come to "this side" because of what she had seen at the jail. I feebly tried to explain that I wasn't on the side of crime, that I wanted justice and cared a great deal about all victims of crime, but she didn't appear to be listening.

"Jason's moves were calculated. He knew exactly what he was doing. He planned this."

I didn't know on what she was basing her conclusions, or why she was sounding off at me. Then she reviewed some of the facts of the case—as if I didn't already know what had happened. I didn't know how to respond. I wasn't there about Jason; I was there about *me*. I tried to redirect her focus.

"Isn't there something you can do to stop the repercussions on me?" I asked.

"You need to give everyone time," she repeated. End of story. Dead end.

She stood up. Clearly it was time for me to leave.

I gripped the armrests of my chair and pushed myself to my feet. Before I left, I asked one more question. "Please—how are they?" I used the first names of the two women.

Nora looked at her and then back at me.

"They are strong and are doing their best," Nora said. "They are finding some support in each other."

That was good.

"They have asked about you, too," she added, softly. I felt a swell of energy. "They asked how you are doing."

"Please—please tell them that my family and I are always thinking about them. Let them know we would do anything we could to help them," I said to both of them.

The counsellor jumped in. Looking me straight in the eye, she said firmly, "We will not. The victims do not need to hear from Jason's arena."

Her words were crushing. Before leaving, I whispered to Nora, "I think you understand."

She nodded.

I never saw her again after that, but I did see the victims' services counsellor a few weeks later in court at one of Jason's biweekly remands. She was with two women who appeared to be in their twenties. As they entered the courtroom, I was filled with panic. Was one of them the younger of the two victims? They walked past me and sat in the front row, the counsellor dropping me a cold look like I was the enemy. Then I saw her lean over to whisper something to the two women with her, who both turned around to look at me. I could only imagine what she was telling them. I asked Detective Morgan, sitting in the row behind me, if either of the young women was the twenty-six-year-old victim. He told me not to worry, they were new victims' services volunteers in training. This information did nothing to reassure me. I feared their counsellor training included lessons on censure.

I went home to find my mum waiting for me. I'd called her after the meeting at the board office and she had driven the two hours to my home, thinking I might need her. I collapsed on the couch in despair and she tried to comfort me, but there was nothing she could do.

The next day, I didn't get dressed. My mum went to see Jason at the jail to tell him about what had happened at the school board and at the police station. She returned to report that Jason had stood shaking with his head in his hands and tears streaming down his face, repeating over and over, "How could I have done this to her?"

Not knowing what else to do, my mum suggested we watch some episodes of *Seinfeld*, which she had brought on DVD. I had never cared much for this show, but gave it a shot anyhow. I had a strange reaction while watching: I hadn't laughed in weeks and somehow the ridiculous scenarios and improbable lives of the characters seemed hilarious. No sooner had I started to giggle uncontrollably than I reverted to tears again. Something else funny would happen on screen and I curled up in hysterics once more. My mum said later that she'd never seen anyone do that: switch back and forth between fits of laughter and agonizing grief. At one point in this grief cycle, I cried out, "I want my life back!" It was one of my mother's most painful moments, she later told me—watching me sob so hard and call out for something I could never have.

When we woke up the next morning, my mum said, "That's it. Let's get out of here." She suggested her house. In Burlington, I could go out in public without worrying who would see me. I could spend a little time with my brother and sister in neighbouring Toronto. I decided it was a good idea. I got dressed and went outside to shovel the driveway. It had snowed quite hard during the night. After forty-five minutes of shovelling heavy packed snow, I had cleared a path. I waved to my mum, who was looking out the window, indicating we could go. I was finishing clearing the last bit when a snowplow turned the corner. It quickly ran the circle of our little cul-de-sac, starting across the road and ending up right at the foot of my driveway. I watched in dismay as the area I had just finished clearing was filled in with a mountain of snow.

I threw my shovel into the mound as hard as I could and yelled, "Fine! I give up! You win!"

I was defeated. I was angry at Jason. I was angry at my employers. I was angry at the Victims' Services Counsellor. I was angry at everything. Tears streamed down my face and caught the eye of the snowplow driver. He looked at me for a second, and then he backed up, turned around, and in a moment plowed out what he had dumped at the end of the driveway and redeposited it on the boulevard. It was an act of mercy. I gave him a small wave and he waved back.

From the road, I called my doctor and made an appointment for later in the week. Now, having experienced two character assaults, the loss of my position at school and place of belonging, a rejection from victims' services, the ending of friendships, and all of Jason's betrayals, I really wasn't well. I didn't know how much more I could take. Images of violence continued on their endless circuit in my mind. I feared going out in public. I had barely slept in a month and was plagued by nightmares. I was rattled by loud noises and my hearing remained amplified. I could barely eat and had lost almost twenty pounds. Now that I didn't have a future return to work to focus on, I feared my condition would deteriorate. As a guidance counsellor, I had learned that there are four pillars to trauma recovery: people, places, routines and rituals. Save for my family and remaining friends, many of my pillars had crumbled, and were crumbling still. I faced a sea of unknowns as I looked into the future. I needed to know what all these symptoms added up to and how I could return to good health. I needed help.

CHAPTER FOURTEEN

DIAGNOSES

My doctor, Sue, is a down-to-earth person dedicated to helping her patients through a variety of methods, from talk therapy, to coaching, to pharmaceuticals. She had already been very helpful to me over the previous weeks and had also been to visit Jason, whom she still considered to be her patient. She expressed her regret that Jason had never told her what was really going on inside him, for she believed she could have helped him herself as well as gotten him specialist care. Sue had treated many insidious diseases in her twenty-five years as a practitioner. She viewed sexual deviance as one such disease, and as treatable—lamenting its existence, not condemning the person living with it. She cleared her commitment to continue to see Jason with me first, demonstrating acute sensitivity. She also asked me to disclose the names of the victims to her. If they were her patients, she would have to consider her role with each of us very carefully.

It turned out that they were not her patients. With that clearance, Sue registered herself as a professional visitor at the jail and drove to see Jason for one hour every other week. She saw me every ten days or so, depending on when I could make it. At previous appointments, I had talked with Sue about the impact that Jason's acts of violence were having on me, along with what was happening in the community. I felt afraid, worried, anxious and sad. I was always on high alert, scanning my surroundings for danger and unable to stop intrusive thoughts or slow down the film strip constantly running in my mind.

This particular visit, however, would be different: we would talk about a formal diagnosis, something that could be typed into a letter for my school board so they would grant me a medical leave. Sue told me I was suffering from post-traumatic stress disorder (PTSD). I knew about PTSD from my work and study as a counsellor, though like many people, I first heard about it in high school history class. Soldiers returning from the trenches in the First World War experienced the array of symptoms after both surviving and perpetrating the violence of combat. Then it was called shell shock. That's what was happening to me.

Sue took her *Diagnostic and Statistical Manual of Mental Disorders* (DSM-IV) off a shelf. She read out the common symptoms: "'The person's response to the event must involve intense fear, helplessness, or horror. . . . The full symptom picture must be present for more than one month, and the disturbance must cause clinically significant distress or impairment in social, occupational, or other important areas of functioning. . . . These symptoms may include difficulty falling or staying asleep that may be due to recurrent nightmares during which the traumatic event is relived. . . . Some individuals report irritability or outbursts of anger or difficulty concentrating or completing tasks.'"

It all sounded painfully familiar. "But, Sue," I said, "I never endured direct violence."

"It doesn't matter," she said. "Listen to this: 'People who witness or learn about events causing death, injury or violence of someone or by someone closely associated to them are equally at risk of developing the disorder.'" She scanned farther down and read one more line: "'The disorder may be especially severe or long lasting when the stressor is of human design, for example torture or rape.'"

The weight of my diagnosis began to sink in. "Do people recover from this?" I asked.

"With time and help, yes. And I am going to help you." I let myself be comforted by her confidence, and I was relieved to know that at least my reactions were common given my circumstances, even if they made me feeling like a stranger to myself. She prepared a letter for the school board and I made another appointment for a few days later, so we could start tackling the PTSD.

I left Sue's office, which was located just behind the store where the assaults had taken place, but I now walked the long way to avoid passing in front of the store windows. I had gone in once, to return a book Jason had borrowed, and decided I would not go in again. The store owner was there and I started to cry when I saw him. He was a victim too. Photos of his business with crime-scene tape around had appeared in the paper. Now, instead of a quaint, small-town shop, his business was associated with danger and crime. What would happen to his livelihood? Would his patrons remain loyal to him? When he saw me that day, he was solemn.

"Hi, Shannon. How are you?"

"I'm so sorry, I'm so sorry! I didn't know . . ."

"I know, Shannon."

"How are you?" I asked him.

"I'm okay."

His face looked drawn. I handed him the book and he took it, slowly. We stood quietly for a moment until a woman's voice from over at the cash register broke the silence.

"I'd like to let you know that Jason has a tab here of $113.65. You can pay it the next time you're in."

I nodded.

"It's for the snacks he ate while he was here. And the supplements he took off the shelf."

The supplements. In a visit earlier in the week, Jason had told me that when he'd woken up on the day of the crimes he had felt incredibly sluggish and weak.

"I didn't know how I was going to get through the day," he explained. "I felt exhausted even though I'd slept for hours. I grabbed some caffeine pills off the shelf and took some, hoping they would help."

"How many?" I asked.

"I'm not sure—a few, maybe five or six. A few hours later, I took some more. I also took some ephedra tablets."

"What's ephedra?" I had never heard of it.

"It's an herbal energy-booster," he said. "I don't remember anything after I took the pills—I don't remember any customers; I don't remember the other employee being there; and I don't remember any of the work that I was doing. I only remember the moment the first woman came through the door—when I felt the panic. After I assaulted her, I felt drained again, so I took some more of the tablets—a handful of both kinds. I didn't know what to do next. Other customers came in and left, but I barely remember them. Then the younger woman came in, and for some reason I feared she had heard the woman I'd taken to the basement. I felt I had to gain control over her too. I trapped her by asking her to help me hold something I was fixing, and then I pulled the knife." Jason looked down.

I shuddered, closing my eyes as I pictured what he'd done.

Jason did not normally take drugs of any kind, not even painkillers for a headache. His regular diet was virtually caffeine-free. The only time I had known him to drink coffee was the night that we were moving from our apartment in Kingston to our friends' place where we were house-sitting for several months. I went to bed at nine-thirty that night, and Jason said he would look after the rest of the packing.

"But you're tired too. You were up early and worked all day." I tried to convince him we could do it the next day.

"It's okay. I can get it done—I'll have a cup of coffee."

I kissed him good night and headed to bed. At midnight he woke me up to say that he had packed the whole living room and was going to start on the basement. He was practically buzzing. At two, I felt a thud in the bed as Jason fell in next to me.

"It's all done," he whispered before he was out like a light. He had packed the entire house.

Many times I had recounted this little anecdote with humour. Now, trying to piece together what had happened on that fateful day in November, I wondered what role the caffeine and ephedra had played in the assaults. Nothing could ever exonerate Jason—he was responsible for the crimes and that was a fact—but I began to wonder if the supplements might have affected his behaviour control that day. Was this another piece in a very complex puzzle?

Jason had also confessed that he had been taking a libido enhancer since our honeymoon. He had a sexual dysfunction that made it difficult for him to ejaculate during intercourse. He'd had the condition since he was a teen, and being celibate in prison for ten years had not helped the matter. Once, a few years earlier, he had spoken to his psychologist in Kingston about it but felt the issue was brushed aside. Before our wedding, we spoke with Dr. Sue and she recommended a few things we could try that would help. If we didn't conceive within six months, she would find us a specialist. It sounded like a good plan, but Jason, unbeknownst to me, had taken matters into his own hands. Why?

"Because I thought it would help me perform in our efforts to conceive a baby."

"Why didn't you *tell me*?" I asked, knowing by now what the answer would be.

"I'm sorry," Jason lamented. "I just wanted things to be easy for us, and I didn't think you needed to know."

I looked at him directly. "Did I ever do anything to make you feel pressured, or think I wouldn't have listened?"

"No. You gave me everything. All the mistakes are mine."

Now, Jason needed help not from a fertility specialist but from a forensic psychiatrist with expertise in assessing and treating sexual offenders. Jason's defence attorney had hired a renowned doctor who treated sex offenders in Toronto and who was frequently called upon to provide expert testimony in cases of serious sexual offences and homicide. He'd just spent an hour interviewing Jason at the jail, mentioning that I was welcome to talk with him. Jason relayed the message and I immediately called and made an appointment to see the doctor at his office in Toronto, hoping to gain a professional's opinion about what was wrong with Jason.

"Jason is a sexual sadist," the doctor stated. "He has sadism. That means that he could never—or almost never—reach orgasm without picturing, inflicting, or enduring violence."

The facts pierced my heart. It was a devastating diagnosis. This was not a description of my husband that fit my experience with him. He was only ever gentle, thoughtful and playful in our love life. There was never a trace of violence that I could see—had it been present in his thoughts? His attacks on the women proved he was capable of both violent thoughts and actions. The fact that Jason had another side to him frightened, saddened and repulsed me.

"How does a person become a sadist? Are people born that way?" I asked. "Can it be cured?"

"There are several factors and some mysteries, and many patients are responsive to treatment programs that include therapy and sometimes medication. I suggest you do some reading on the topic."

He handed me a heavy, leather-bound medical textbook. The embossed title read *Sexual Deviance and Disorders: Sadism, Pedophilia, Transvestism, Masochism and Pornography*. I felt the weight of the book as it landed in my palm.

"You may borrow this for a while. Just bring it back whenever you can, and . . . take care of yourself, Shannon. Don't hesitate to call me again, if there is anything I can do for you."

It meant a lot to hear him say that. He had been generous with me and kind. I left with the book concealed in my bag and walked to the corner. I'd been at the downtown Toronto intersection many times in the past, to grab a hot dog from a street vendor when I was in teachers' college, or to meet friends for a coffee while on a break from classes. I had not known there was a sex offenders' clinic there, nor that there would come a time when I would step through the doors of one. I could feel my own ghost as I headed toward my parked car—a younger, happier version of myself happily going about her studies and full of hope for her future. How was I ever going to get her back?

At home, I put the textbook on my desk next to a file I'd been ignoring. It contained a partially completed application form for a master's degree program. I'd begun filling out the forms a couple of months before the crimes, after reading about a program on international development and education offered in Britain. Jason and I had two dreams for our first anniversary: having a baby or going to England. We joked that maybe we would even have a baby *in* England. We had gone so far as to speak with his parole officer about the possible move and were told that it wasn't out of the question. Someone with Jason's stability, clean parole record, and solid marriage might be able to obtain a visa. The Canadian parole board had a good relationship with the British parole board, and there was precedent for shared supervision. Now, looking down at the forms, I contemplated continuing with the plan on my own. Could I manage a year alone in a different country? Could I handle academic rigor with Jason's criminal process possibly still going on? I didn't know for sure. All I knew was that further education would open up doors, and with doors closing all around me, I was going to have to do everything I could to give myself options for the future.

A few days later, I completed my application and sent the package overseas. Then I opened up my notebook and made a few additions to my to-do list: *Apply for scholarships* and *Apply for a student loan.* I added one more item with question marks: *Put house on the market?* I didn't want to lose my home, but I had to be realistic. Without an income, I could not afford to keep it.

Two weeks later, I learned that I was approved for government employment insurance related to illness at a compensation rate of $350 per week for twelve weeks, starting in February—not enough to live on. My union rep believed he could get the board to uphold what they had offered—an extra three weeks of salary—which would take me to mid-January. There were serious gaps and shortfalls ahead. Come the end of April, I would have no income at all unless my teachers' insurance company would provide long-term disability coverage. The ground underneath me shifted again, and fear surged through me. What was I going to do?

CHAPTER FIFTEEN

UNCONDITIONAL LOVE

A few days before Christmas, a beautiful flower arrangement arrived from my school with a card that read, *Thinking of you, with love from the staff.* Instead of feeling comforted, I felt confused. Who was this from? I remembered the day I ran into the school secretary at a gas station and her disgust at the fact that I was going to visit Jason. Her words rang in my ears. *There are more fish in the sea.*

I knew that leaving my marriage and finding another relationship was an option. My sister had drawn up the separation papers and I'd signed them in front of her. I did it quickly, without dwelling—it hurt too much. Jason signed them in front of a commissioner at the jail. Our separation was legalized back to the date the crimes took place. Still, even though Jason and I had now been physically and legally separated for six weeks, I was nowhere near ready to walk away from him. Our bond was actually strengthening as we worked through this colossal crisis, and just as I could not conceive of a life in which I waited outside a prison gate for years on end, neither could I imagine moving into a new relationship. There simply wasn't space in

Lloyd Brown

Jason Staples, 1970.

Jason, age six.
A school photo taken the year
his father died.

Jason working on the Kingston Millennium Mural Project, three years before we met.

Jason and me skating on the canal in Peterborough, January 2004.

Our wedding,
October 8, 2005.

The Shattering, the
first piece of art-therapy
homework Dr. Sue
prescribed me in February
2006. I showed this
collage to the judge
during my victim impact
statement at Jason's
sentencing.

Exploding with Anger (acrylic and glass on board, November 2006). Expressing into art my rage and frustration made me realize the vital importance of finding a non-violent outlet for powerful—and potentially harmful—emotions.

Let Me Lie Down in Leaves (mixed media on illustration board, November 2006).

Meeting Grace, my roommate in England, September 2006.

My mum and Jason in the visiting room at the prison, 2008.

Jason and me in a prison visiting room, January 2008. He was sentenced five months later.

Una holds her portrait, which Jason painted for her inside prison, July 2008. She died a few weeks later.

Paul McCarthy

My family, August 2009. From left to right (front row): Me; my mother; my sister. From left to right (back row): My father; my brother.

Speaking to inmates in the Resolve to Stop the Violence Program (RSVP) at San Bruno County Jail, California, January 2009.

Me and my friend Rachael in Colorado, April 2010.

my heart yet. I was deeply conflicted.

I began calculating the years Jason would be in jail. His lawyer, the police, correctional staff and the parole office figured he'd serve ten to twelve years if he wasn't declared a dangerous offender. If he was, he wouldn't be released until he was an old man, if ever. The lesser sentence would put me at forty and Jason at forty-six. Maybe we would still have a chance—if doctors finally figured out what was wrong with him, if he were to receive extraordinary treatment and be healed. Without those prerequisites being met, I could never be with him again. My mind circled around fantasies. I began to bargain. We could live in a remote area; I could spend those years he was in jail saving to build us a house. Or, we could live in a big city where there was a lot of support and anonymity.

These were the desparate daydreams of a grieving widow. I'd hold onto them for a moment at a time—before reality fell in a heap at my feet. I didn't know if Jason would ever be well enough to return to society. And after what had happened, how could I—and society—ever be guaranteed he wasn't a risk? How could I ever trust him again? What if he hurt someone again? I could never take that chance. I couldn't bear the responsibility of being his keeper either. I needed—and deserved—companionship as well as freedom. And as for my hopes of starting a family one day? Even if there was some miracle cure for Jason and he was a wonderful father, I could not bring children into the world to live under Jason's stigma. Before these new crimes, I didn't associate Jason with the label "sex offender." I had made a choice—a difficult one—to trust he would never offend again, and had lived without fear in that decision along with everyone else who knew him. We had come to terms with the long-ago past. The situation was vastly different now, and the future held no promises. I turned my thoughts back to the present. I was still wearing my wedding ring and I was still a newlywed. It was—and would remain for a long time—very difficult to accept tht the life I'd planned for was over. I wanted to be Jason's wife—to hold onto everything that was good in our life together for just a little longer—but that too was a fantasy. I had to deal with the here-and-now, but I wasn't ready to take off that ring permanently. I moved it to my right hand.

Coping with my altered social status and the heavy burden of stigma had changed me. Where I used to be outgoing, a social butterfly, I was now fearful and introverted. Instead of saying "yes" to an invitation to a dinner party or get-together with friends or strangers, I had to ask the host a series of questions before deciding if I could attend: Who knows about what happened? What do they know? Where do they lie on the judgment spectrum? Will I become the main topic of discussion? Then, depending on the answers, if I decided to go, I would ask myself more questions: Can I talk about Jason or what happened? What should I say if asked what I do for a living? None of the answers came easily and it was both exhausting and stressful to be in this constant state of negotiation for social safety. I began to avoid gatherings and did so for months, missing weddings, birthday parties and reunions. I made a decision that I would not go to a celebration for another person until I was able to participate fully and with joy, rather than being consumed by self-consciousness. I trusted that people would understand, and that the necessity of this decision would eventually come to an end.

In the meantime, I developed a script of small talk I could use when introduced to new people. When asked questions like

"Are you married?" I'd answer, "I'm separated," or "I lost my husband," or simply, "No, I'm not married," as well as reasonable explanations for why I wasn't working. The truth was always a gamble, so I floundered my way through various levels of truth and then tried to keep track of what I'd said to whom. The process was draining. I missed my old life, when I had nothing to hide.

Then came the holidays and what would have been Jason's and my first Christmas and New Year's Eve as a married couple. The year before we had volunteered at a tree farm and brought home our first real Christmas tree for our new house. I had sewn us stockings and kept enough of the fabric to make one for a baby or two in the future: a family set to last years and years. Jason had stayed up late on Christmas Eve finishing paintings for each person in my family and one for me—a portrait of us. This year I would see him for thirty minutes through glass.

They say that Christmas is the hardest time of year for people experiencing loss. In the past, my family had always had big Christmases with tons of presents, but at age eighteen, when I started travelling the developing world, I began a fruitless rally for fewer material gifts. Ironically, this was the year I finally had the toned-down kind of Christmas I'd always wanted. My parents, siblings and I each opened one or two gifts; we ate a traditional homemade meal; we sat around talking while it snowed outside. We were gentle with each other in all our interactions, letting our words fall softly like the snow. Jason's absence was acutely palpable, and as I grieved what should have been, I struggled to keep images of violence from intruding on an otherwise peaceful scene.

My dad and I went to visit Jason on Christmas Day. Getting dressed was surreal. In a daze, I chose a red sweater and a funky red-and-white tweed skirt with scattered clear sequins—something I'd bought in a vintage store on my honeymoon. I had told Jason it would be my Christmas outfit and I would wear it every year as long as it fit, predicting that I would become plumper as the years went on. As I zipped up the back, I noticed how loose the skirt now was. It struck me again that I was spending my first Christmas as a married woman visiting my husband in jail. Nothing fit. Literally.

As we arrived at the huge, grey institution, a new feeling came over me. I felt a sudden sense of gratitude. My family was still intact, and while Jason would be spending twenty-three-and-three-quarter hours that day locked in a cell, he was fortunate to see our loving faces. That was a whole lot more than most other inmates could expect.

The reception area was almost empty. As I walked over the glass bridge leading to the cell blocks, I looked out at the rows of barred windows and hoped for peace for every person inside—the staff and the inmates—their families, and for all the victims. I started doing this every time I visited, every time I passed another institution in a city or by the highway, and whenever I heard of a new crime or arrest on the radio. I could conjure up a web of agony spinning itself from one person to another, all of these people caught in the devastating effects of crime. The ripple effect was far wider than I'd ever considered.

A friend taught me a simple Buddhist meditation that I came to repeat over and over: "May I be at peace, may I be safe, may I know I am loved." After saying it the first time for myself, I then began changing the "I" to the names of others who were in my thoughts—my loved ones, or groups of people such as prisoners, victims and people working with them. Once in a while, when I was feeling really brave, I would say the names of my enemies—the names of people who had hurt me. I taught the meditation to Jason, who started using it immediately despite the fact that his own faith was a dim and distant shadow, if it was there at all. The hardest part for him was the first line: may *I* be at peace. How could he fold his hands and ask for his own well-being when those same hands had shown such disregard for the sanctity of human life? I thought of my own guilt, of instances in my life when I'd hurt someone, even inadvertently. If I had done something that really hurt someone the way Jason had, intentionally or not, could I have carried that burden? I knew I would wish to die, to shut myself away from this world. There is an exile worse than prison, worse than punishment, and worse than being condemned by others: the exile of self-hatred. Thinking of what Jason was going to have to live with, I began to appreciate that I had never had to wonder if I am loved. I had never questioned my basic human worth. I was lucky. I was lucky not to be in prison. I was lucky that I didn't live in a prison of my own making. I was lucky that no one had stolen my birthright to unconditional love, because once gone it is very hard to get back.

When Christmas was over, I returned to Burlington with my parents to get through the next holiday—New Year's Eve—followed by the first day of 2006. I pulled myself out of bed on December 31 after another sleepless night and trudged downstairs to the kitchen. The *Toronto Star* lay on the counter and I pushed it aside to make room for a cup of coffee. I had no strength to read about all the terrors of the world, nor trust in those writing about them. My mum came into the kitchen.

"Shan," she said, "I just got off the phone with someone named Molly Wolf. Does that name ring a bell? She said she was a volunteer at Martha's Table during the years Jason was there."

The name didn't sound familiar.

"What was she calling about?"

"She was calling to say that there's an article about Jason in today's *Toronto Star*."

My heart stopped. Oh God. Jason's case had reached major newspapers. This was one of the things I'd been dreading.

Seeing the colour drain out of my face, my mum rushed on. "No—it's not what you think. It's a good article. Molly wrote it herself. She's given Jason the pseudonym 'Toby.'"

My heart started beating again as I turned to the newspaper I'd pushed aside. I opened it and found the article on page seven: "Prison ministry teaches need for giving unconditional love." The timing was uncanny. I began to read. Molly described her experiences volunteering at the prison chapel as a visitor for inmates. Then, she wrote about one prisoner in particular, a man she described as her "own personally beloved murderer— call him Toby—who was in deep trouble."

"This was a guy I'd grown to love when we worked along-side each other in the fall of 2003," she wrote, "chopping onions in a kitchen that serves meals to the poor three times a week. I wasn't the only person who loved him, by any means. We all did. Toby was very special—bright, thoughtful, infinitely patient and invariably courteous, someone who belonged more at Queen's University than in a federal prison. . . . He'd com-mitted a violent but unpremeditated murder when he was 18. I met him not long before he was finally paroled and moved away from Kingston. In his mid-30s, he was newly married to a wonderful young woman and doing well."

I swallowed a growing lump in my throat and continued reading. "But now all who loved Toby were grieving, me included. He'd blown it, offended again big-time, and fetched up back in The System, this time probably for more decades than I want to think about. I wanted to wring his neck, frankly, but I also needed to know what I could do for him. I prayed for those whom Toby had hurt, but they weren't mine to care for. Toby was; I knew that in my gut. So what did Toby need most?" She puts the question to another inmate, who answers simply, "Unconditional love."

"It's about the only thing that can turn a soul around," Molly concluded. "A person isn't defined by the stupid things he or she does and the disastrous choices that he or she makes. [Toby] needs love not in spite of what he's done, or for anything he could ever do, but simply for who he is. That's the healing, transforming thing."

I recalled my first visit with Jason. I had asked him if he knew how much we loved him. He said, "I didn't really know." When I told him I still loved him, he began facing many truths, admitting to his darkest demons. Maybe love *was* the foundation for healing and transformation, as Molly suggested. I kept reading.

"It's counterintuitive," Molly wrote. "Faced with a Paul Bernardo, we want to hurt him as badly as he's hurt others; we want to lock him up and throw away the key. . . . And Paul Bernardo will indeed spend the rest of his days behind bars. But there are those—me among them—who feel that letting someone rot in jail does not make things better; it's only another life wasted and does nothing for the victims. Revenge does not bring closure or healing."

I called Molly at the number she'd given my mum, and I thanked her for the gift of her article. Then I found the online version and copied the hyperlink into an e-mail message that I sent to my Golden Circle.

At midnight on New Year's Eve, my sister and I were soaking in my parents' outdoor hot tub, the cold winter air swirling around us. I looked up at the stars, feeling small against the universe. What would the year ahead bring? Last New Year's, Jason and I had laughed like crazy as we danced a Virginia reel in the snow at Georgina and Mark's annual party. Tears fell down my cheeks and into the warm water. My sister, not normally a person who is comfortable handling emotional moments, put her arm around me.

"You will feel better," she said.

I held onto those words as the night rolled over into a new and very uncertain year.

CHAPTER SIXTEEN

HELP WANTED

Marrying Jason had given me the strangest set of in-laws in the world: a combination of parental figures and custodians that included officials from the Parole Board of Canada, the Correctional Service of Canada, and the province's mental health care system, who also looked after my real mother-in-law. It was a lot to contend with.

Back in Peterborough at the beginning of January, I was asked to participate in a meeting with the national investigation team from the Correctional Service of Canada. Assembled from across the country, this team was leading an internal audit of Jason's case to determine if any mistakes or oversights had been made on the part of the Correctional Service or the Parole Board of Canada in handling Jason as a parolee. I willingly accepted their request with the hope that I might be able to express some of my concerns, ask questions, and tell them about what I was seeing in Jason during our visits. I also wondered if they would be in any position to help me with my own situation.

I had mixed feelings about these organizations. On one hand, I felt sympathetic: Jason had been "one of their best guys," a success story, until he reoffended, letting them down brutally. His actions would have a negative impact on individuals who'd supported him and on the justice system's reputation as a whole. On the other hand, I was angry that I had been assured he wasn't a risk and was now left alone to face the societal fallout. The disappointment of those who had worked with him and believed in him over the years was justifiably massive. So were the potential reverberations his actions would cause through the layers of their system, from tightening restrictions on other parolees to casting doubt as to whether enough was being done to protect the public. Newspaper reporters focused on Jason's having earned full parole in 2004 but gave no mention of the fact that he was released on day parole in 1998 and had steadily earned decreased restrictions over six years by working and contributing to the community. People who knew something about parole systems might be able to figure this out but anyone else reading the coverage would simply think he was a madman who had been irresponsibly unleashed on the world.

The Parole Board and Corrections were under heat to explain themselves internally, though by now the press seemed to have forgotten all about their roles. Part of me wanted a public inquiry of their processes, some demand for accountability. Without transparency, I knew that community members who hadn't known me for very long might jump to conclusions about my relationship with Jason, like that I had married him while he was still in prison. In general, society often questions people who develop relationships with reformed offenders, but people think even worse of women who choose to marry men actively serving time. I had enough judgment to face without that as well. I hadn't married a man in prison. I'd never abetted his crimes or denied his guilt. I hadn't known he was dangerous.

It was a time full of judgment, and I wasn't the only person facing it. Friends and family who visited Jason learned the hard way that it was best to keep their choices a secret. My parents were questioned by some of their friends for engaging in conversations with their ex-son-in-law. None of us liked how we were looked at by many of the prison guards, and we suspected many people around us were spreading rumours about our values, our morals and our motives.

While I sympathized with the Correctional Service and the Parole Board for the position they were in, I also wanted to hold them up to scrutiny. I now had questions as to just how much they had really known about Jason and if there was anything they had held back from me. When I decided to be part of Jason's second chance, they were encouraging and pleased, but now that he was no longer their poster boy for successful rehabilitation, they had not been in contact. More than two months had passed and I was still denied access to Jason's parole officer.

I met the team at the Correctional Service regional office in downtown Peterborough. The three officials were seated around the table as if we were on a baseball diamond and they were umpires. I was the batter at home plate. The first base umpire asked the questions; the second took notes; the third listened intently, hands folded on the table in front of him. I gave as much information as I could, detailing everything I now knew about Jason's distorted sexuality and thought patterns. They looked visibly pained as I spoke about him and about the losses I'd experienced being the one on the outside answering for Jason. I asked when they thought Jason would be transferred back into federal custody and into better conditions, since his parole had been formally revoked. The area manager for

Corrections had told me back in November that it would just be a couple of weeks, but there was no sign of any movement. This, the three men said, was outside their jurisdiction.

After about an hour, I could tell our meeting was drawing to a close. They had the information they needed and I—well, I'd turned over everything I knew. They gave me their business cards and said I should call if I remembered anything else that could be important. I could tell that nothing would come out of this meeting for me. *I* was out of their jurisdiction as well. They thanked me for my time and said they were extremely sorry for what I was going through. We all stood up.

I turned toward the door to the hallway and one of the men— third base—rushed to open it for me. Then he followed me down the corridor.

"Ms. Moroney," he said, "you're a very strong individual. Please take care of yourself."

"Thank you," I said. I entered the lobby and took an elevator out of the building. Very strong, indeed. But for how long? Take care of myself? Didn't I deserve professional support too?

I decided to visit the office of the John Howard Society, an agency that provides services for incarcerated and paroled men, and, I hoped, their families. I didn't know exactly what kind of help I was looking for, but if I showed up, perhaps the staff would guide me. When I arrived, I spoke to three staff members, all of whom looked at me blankly. They said they knew of Jason's case (who didn't?), they nodded kindly, and then stared at me.

After a long, awkward silence, one person said, "I'm sorry. We really don't have services for families."

I asked who did. No one knew.

The Attorney General's office was responsible for helping victims of crime in my province, so I called them. I'd given up waiting for them to contact me first. They had a fund to help people with counselling expenses and other support, but I was told that they compensated victims of physical harm only. I did not fit the criteria. Still, I felt relieved that both of Jason's assault victims would be able to obtain funds if they needed them.

I searched for a book to read about being the family member of an offender, but I could not find one that even remotely applied. Instead, I read a memoir by a woman whose husband had committed suicide. It was very helpful to me, much more than I could have imagined. I was surprised to read about what many people have to face when someone they love commits suicide: police investigations often view family members as murder suspects; loved ones are the first to find the body; after learning the graphic details of the act, they often return to live in the scene of trauma. The loved ones left behind sometimes endure stigma—friends or family members may refuse to go to the funeral in protest of the suicide, while others act like their loss may be contagious, or insinuate that those closest to the deceased might have played a role in a person's decision to end his or her own life. Surviving loved ones quickly become familiar with shame and exclusion, and they have to fight for their right to grieve. Many learn to cloister their grief. But grief can fester. Hidden pain doesn't go away with time. It just gets worse.

I let myself grieve in the small hours of the day, alone in my home. In my lowest moments, I wished that Jason had died. I found a website for young widows and I read the chat room postings in an attempt to ward off the isolation I felt so deeply. I could relate to almost everything I read and it comforted me to know that my emotions were normal following the loss of a spouse, especially at a young age. I longed to engage in the dialogue—to put up a posting myself—but I worried I would be rejected. I pondered the idea of making up a fake name to avoid being identified. I considered lying about how I lost my husband, but I didn't want to offend anyone or take away from the integrity of the group. I read about how widows longed for that one last embrace, one more hour or one more day, and while I had the same longings, the person I yearned for was still alive.

I related to what others wrote about coping with terminal illness, only I was coping with a terminal illness in reverse. I knew the day when I lost my husband; the day that our life together was over; and the day that his life in the outside world came to an end—but I was just starting the process of obtaining his diagnosis, providing hospice and working out how to live without him in my daily life. I knew that someday I was going to have to make the final decision whether to let him go. Would we arrive at a time when the end of our marriage wouldn't be so excruciating, or would I have to rip away the life-support? Who would I be after that—someone capable of loving again? I did not have the consolation of being able to imagine my husband in any kind of heaven. Quite the opposite. I could only picture him pacing in a prison cell, caged in by grey cement walls for every birthday, holiday and celebration for the rest of his life. Whatever decision I made, I would have to work very hard to enable myself to enjoy life again, not only for myself but for the people who loved me. Otherwise, what was the point of living?

Like other widows, I mourned what should have been. In a letter, Jason wrote, "My bloodline is a period; a full stop. I don't know anyone that had my blood before me and now no one will come after me. I will never be a father. How could I have done this?" I did not have the answer.

Another letter arrived that highlighted Jason's lost potential. He'd sent his illustrations to one of the biggest children's book publishers in Canada and received a response inviting him to make an appointment with the art director right away. It was his big break, too late.

I found a website chat room for people who had loved ones in prison in Canada, but as I read the postings, I found myself cringing at their lack of dignity and angered by an apparent disregard for the gravity of the offenders' crimes or the impact those offences had on victims. One person wrote, "When my man gets outta the joint he's gonna do me real good to make up for all he done!" Another wrote, "How am I gonna get through six months of him being in jail—that's forever!"

Nothing about these remarks resonated with me. Nonetheless, hoping for the best, I made myself a pseudonym and an e-mail account. I posted my story, half-heartedly hoping there might be someone out there who would respond. A few days later, I received an e-mail from a woman named Dawn in another province. In her message, she told me how she had been searching for two years for someone she could relate to: someone who had similar interests, lifestyle, and a professional identity before it was all traumatically altered by crime. Her life had been blown apart by the sudden, unpredictable violence of her partner, who was now serving a life sentence for the shooting deaths of his ex-wife and her boyfriend—crimes that occurred in front of his children. Like me, Dawn had had a happy life, enjoyed a loving relationship, and had been planning a future that would fulfill her dreams. Those dreams had been destroyed and she was in the process of figuring out what she could still hold onto.

She told me she kept picturing the children witnessing this violence, wondering what long-term effect it would have on them. She wondered how her partner was, where he was and what was going to happen. She thought of his family, the victims, and their families. Like me, when she heard the news, her first reaction was not of hatred but of grief.

I removed my posting from the website and Dawn and I began writing to each other. Over time, we filled in the details of our stories. I told her my real name. We talked on the phone. We shared not only our anguish, but also our hope, strength, and anything good that was happening in our lives. We wondered where everyone else like us was, for surely there were more hidden victims out there. Current statistics showed the number of men serving life or indeterminate sentences in Canada was about 4,300, plus 200 women. If each of them had ten family members and friends at the time of their crimes, that meant we were a group of 50,000. Many of those "lifers," like Dawn's partner, had killed family members, so those left behind were doubly victimized—losing more than one loved one in the crime. I thought of Dawn's partner's children, their mother murdered by their father. They had lost both parents: one dead, the other in prison for the rest of their childhoods and beyond. Now they lived with aging grandparents. Who would help them over the long-term?

Beyond those inmates serving life and indeterminate sentences, there were another 10,000 federally incarcerated men and a few hundred women in Canada, plus thousands more waiting for trials or serving sentences of less than two years at the provincial jails. All of their family members and friends add up to a sizable community. But these victims were invisible.

I could now understand why: we were no one's priority and

we were easy targets for blame. Despite my many losses, I was lucky to have a strong and loving family and supportive friends, a good education that gave me options, an ability to advocate for myself, and no inclination to use drugs, alcohol or self-harm as ways of escaping reality. I was dealing with a remorseful offender whom I was able to talk with and hold accountable. Maybe, just maybe, one day I could find others besides Dawn who were going through what I was and reach out to them.

For now, I had to focus on myself. I continued to be plagued by nightmares, insomnia, anxiety and flashbacks. The film strip ran its circuit several times a day. I worried incessantly about the victims, but was helpless to do anything for them. I was easily agitated and had no outlet for my anger when it surfaced. I couldn't find comfort or distraction in any of my old hobbies, nor could I concentrate on reading anything for enjoyment. I could no longer afford my cable bill, so there was no escape into television. I was desperately lonely for companionship, affection and intimacy, all of which I had had with Jason. I lived largely on a diet of yogourt, bananas, poached eggs and soup— my digestive system rejecting almost anything else. Shopping and other normal errands now took three times as long to complete and demanded enormous energy. Seeing people in town would elicit a warm embrace or a cold stare—many days, I couldn't take the chance.

Every day involved making a choice to move forward, and it wasn't easy with the heavy weight of all the broken pieces inside me. What would I be like in five or ten years if I didn't fully deal with everything that was happening now? I imagined a woman aged by depression, bitterness and resentment. I believed that if I suppressed or masked my painful emotions, they would come back to haunt me. I just didn't want that to happen. Talking with my doctor, friends and family was helping to release emotions, but I still needed to come to terms with things on a deeper level. How would I ever overcome post-traumatic stress disorder? How could I move from coping to actually healing while the aftershocks continued?

One January afternoon, my vice-principal called to see if she could stop by with a gift. A few teachers at school had taken up a collection for me—enough money for a mortgage payment. I was overwhelmed with gratitude, but confused like I was when I received the bouquet of flowers at Christmas from the staff. Their offering didn't mesh with what I'd been told was going on in the building—the rumours, allegations and anger toward me that, according to my principal, typified the teachers' responses.

When my VP arrived at my door, I invited her in for tea. Finally I summoned my courage and said, "What are people saying at school?"

"I haven't heard anything at all from students," she replied. "Only that they ask where you are and when you're coming back. We're still saying that your husband is sick. They don't seem to know anything else. No parents have called me. Any teachers coming into my office are coming to ask me how you're doing or to drop off a card to give you."

"I was told there were rumours. . . . Do you know I was told to not even come in the building?"

She shifted uncomfortably in her seat. "I really can't speak for the principal," she said. "And I don't know anything about what happened in the meeting at the board office. I'm really not involved in staffing decisions."

I had no real choice but to respect what she was saying. She was in an awkward position, and while I wanted to press her on the topic, I was also terrified that in so doing I might lose her support and friendship. I could not bear more loss. I decided to pose another question.

"Will you please tell me who the student is—the one who is the stepson of the first victim?" I asked. "Not knowing is causing me a lot of anxiety, and I think it would be better if I knew. As it is, I'm starting to avoid going out anywhere that I might see students, always wondering if the stepson is seeing me, or if I might be confronted. I already know the names of the victims," I added. "I just can't match them to the student."

My VP shifted in her seat again and then looked away. "I'm sorry, Shannon. I am not allowed to tell you."

"But please," I said, "I didn't hurt anyone. I'd never approach anyone. You know that."

"I know, but I am obligated to follow the instructions I have been given."

I looked away then too. I just hoped that someone would speak up before I found myself meeting the victims or their families by accident, before I or they were prepared.

My last school board paycheque came through in January and at the beginning of February I received my first employment insurance payment. The amount was frighteningly small, so I went through my clothing and took some items to a consignment shop. I loaded Jason's barbells from the basement into the car and drove them to a hock shop, where I sold them for fifty dollars. I took some CDs and DVDs to a second-hand store, and some books to a used bookshop. Not drastic measures, yet, but I was already feeling scared. I didn't own anything I could sell for a significant amount, nor did I have a car. I just had my house, which didn't hold much equity. Then I received a letter from the teachers' insurance plan telling me that my application for long-term disability insurance had been turned down because a regular family doctor's diagnosis of PTSD did not meet their requirements. I would have to obtain a specialist's diagnosis to start an appeal process.

More stressed than ever, I took the letter to my doctor. She said she'd refer me immediately, but it would be hard to find someone who could take me on short notice. Sue found the only psychiatrist in the area with an open appointment and set one up for the next week. I made the drive to the doctor's office and told him why I had come—that I needed confirmation of a diagnosis of post-traumatic stress disorder. I explained the causes and all of my enduring symptoms. I told him I needed time to recover, build a new life and become strong enough to find and face a new job or further my education.

He furrowed his brow. He had read about Jason's crimes in the newspaper. He asked me what my father did for a living and if I had ever been in any relationships with men in the past. What did it matter if I had been in one or ten relationships in the past? What difference did my socio-economic background make to my medical condition? Why did he ask only about my father and not my mother? I said that both were educated professionals, my father in sales and my mum a retired teacher, and that I had a normal relationship history for a thirty-year-old. I restated my list of symptoms and indicated that I had been victimized directly through voyeurism and by proxy through close exposure to violent events and their fallout. The psychiatrist stood up and said he would send a letter to my doctor in a few days.

When his letter arrived at Sue's office, it was littered with misinformation about my personal history. Had he listened at all to what I'd told him? It sure didn't seem that way. He neither supported nor negated Sue's diagnosis of PTSD, which was the precise reason why she had sent me to him. His letter concluded, "Because she is intelligent, healthy and psychologically normal it is curious that she would choose such a man." I was incensed. It had been not merely a wasted appointment, but a harmful one. I hadn't gone to this doctor for an assessment of my character and decisions, but for a diagnosis.

Legally, Sue had to disclose the psychiatrist's letter to my insurance company, but she put a note in with it saying she felt that his response was unprofessional in nature and that she would be sending me for a second opinion. She hoped his letter wouldn't damage my application irreparably. We were back to the drawing board. Who could I see, and soon?

I decided to approach Jason's assessing psychiatrist, whom I had met in Toronto, and ask if I could take him up on his offer to help me. Though his clinic was set up for sexual offenders, he was a psychiatrist all the same—and a reputable one. I had his card in my wallet, so I called his office and was put through to him directly. Without hesitation he said to come down and see him as soon as I could. A week later I sat down in his office for the second time, and we spoke for over an hour.

The psychiatrist wrote a letter back to my doctor corroborating her initial diagnosis and recommending that I be given support from the insurance company until I had time to follow a recovery plan that would allow me to return to work or school. He asked me to keep in touch with him and to remember that he was there for me. It was a little ironic that I could feel so much better having been diagnosed again with a major medical condition, but I did. I felt validated. Now that I could stop trying to prove how bad things were, maybe I could focus on getting better.

CHAPTER SEVENTEEN

ALL THE BROKEN PIECES

When I lived in Ecuador in my early twenties, there were wise women you could go to for advice about what ailed you. They didn't have titles—they had strands of gold beads around their necks and coral bracelets wrapped around their forearms from wrist to elbow. The bigger the size and quantity of the beads, the older, wiser and more respected the woman was. Maybe she had delivered a lot of babies, healed wounds of the flesh or spirit, or maybe she had just lived a long time. Whatever her experience, the important thing was that she was someone you could trust when things were uncertain. You did whatever she prescribed because you wanted to feel better, even if it broke from convention and scared you breathless—*especially* if it scared you, because that seemed to mean it would work.

I discovered this truth when I sprained my ankle running down the mountainside toward the *casa comunal,* where the one telephone in the community was located. My friend Rachael was there with me. She and our neighbour Rosa rushed to my rescue, helping me hobble home in pain on an already swelling foot. I lay on the bed with my foot elevated while Rachael consulted a popular reference book called *Where There Is No Doctor* and Rosa rushed off to retrieve Nicolasa, the community's wise-woman. Rachael read the instructions aloud, which included icing the joint (we didn't have refrigeration), getting an X-ray (the hospital a bumpy two-hour drive away in the back of a pickup truck), and giving the sprain a month to heal. The underscored advice was this: "Never rub or massage a sprain or broken bone. It does no good and can do more harm."

Soon, Rosa arrived with Nicolasa, who spoke only Quichua. She looked at me, smiled, and then set about examining my injury. Before I could protest, she began an intense and excruciating massage of my ankle. Tears sprang to my eyes and Rachael and I locked fearful glances. *Never rub or massage a sprain or broken bone.* I held back my urge to protest out of politeness and respect. Much to my surprise, by the end of the massage, I felt better. The next morning, the swelling had gone down and the pain had subsided. Nicolasa returned in the afternoon to give me another, slightly less agonizing massage. When that was over, I was up and about as though nothing had happened. Wordlessly, Rachael wedged *Where There Is No Doctor* under one end of an unstable shelf. We'd been looking for something exactly that thickness to balance it. What I gained from the experience was an appreciation for alternative treatments, and an understanding that in times of desperation it's best to have an open mind about the healing process.

Now, years later, I found myself on terrain even more foreign than rural Ecuador, feeling far more desperate to heal than I ever did about that sprained ankle. The aid of medication, other than for sleep, was an option I shelved for the time being. I didn't want to take any drugs for depression or anxiety until I had tried everything else first. I feared they would suppress feelings that would just come back and haunt me later. Sue agreed that there were other ways I could cope with PTSD, and she was committed to helping me.

My next doctor's appointment—in mid-February—took place at my house. Just like Nicolasa, Sue believed in old-fashioned home visits for people who were too sick to go out. There were times when anxiety and fear impaired my ability to get to her office. I could get further ahead in my counselling when surrounded by the comforts of home than I could when I had to walk by the store where the assaults took place or risk encountering people who might scorn me. Sue arrived at my door on a snowy but sunny afternoon. I invited her first into the living room, and then into the room at the back of the house that had been Jason's art studio. Canvases, paints, inks and paper still lay exactly as he had left them. As Sue took it all in, I stood next to her looking almost helplessly overwhelmed by the room.

She turned to me and said matter-of-factly, "I think you should do something with all this stuff."

I began mumbling about donating it to charity or a school. "No, I mean do something for yourself," Sue said.

Do something for myself? I was puzzled. "In two weeks, come to your next appointment with a piece of art you have created using these supplies—something that captures what you've been going through for the last three months since the crimes. Focus on your emotions: What has it all felt like?"

I nodded slowly, but I already felt apprehensive. How could I ever capture the complexity of my experience in a piece of art? I considered myself creative, but not an artist.

"It doesn't have to be beautiful; it just has to be real," Sue said. "Don't think too much, just get those feelings out. You'll feel better."

Everything felt in such a mess that piecing scraps of things together seemed like something that might work for me. I began to gather photos, typed and printed lines of poetry and song lyrics, and chose items that represented something significant: a square of fabric from my wedding dress, a penny for financial strain, a bright red thread that reminded me of my miscarriage. At the end of ten days, I had all the images I needed—many from the film strip in my mind. I began to arrange them on a Masonite board that I spray-painted black and painted over with an image of a dark tornado.

A large, half-moon in the centre of the painting formed a silver bowl. Inside it, I placed a photo from my wedding day: all the guests standing together under the autumn leaves, smiles on their faces. I was in the front row in my wedding dress, Jason behind me with his hand on my shoulder, looking proud and happy—such a long time ago, though just three months had passed. Exploding out of the bowl were sharp pieces of glass, shooting upwards and then falling over the sides. At the top: a photo of Jason as a little boy, a clipping of the newspaper article listing his charges, a large question mark, a cut-out from Frida Kahlo's painting *The Miscarriage,* a photo of the prayer flags Jason and I had hung on our porch last Christmas, and the words: *grasping, time, dangerous, help, sorry* and *years.* Also overflowing the bowl were my house, a figure of a bent-over woman falling, the watercolour Jason did for our wedding invitations, and more words: *dreams, hope, children, relationships* and *privacy.* All of this detritus—as well as a sheaf of film ripped from a camera and a photo of an empty chair—landed in a heap of dry, brown autumn leaves. It looked like the aftermath of an explosion, everything in my life displaced. I named the piece *The Shattering*.

What surprised me were my choices of images that pushed up out of the rubble at the bottom of the work: pictures of a salmon swimming upstream, Canada geese flying north in their V-formation, hands dirty from gardening, a house under construction, a line of lit candles, a statue of the Buddha, and the words *stay, redefine* and *love*. All evidence that I still lived in a world where miracles of new life and peace were everywhere— proof that somewhere inside me I still held the belief that goodness existed.

When I was done, I stared at my work for a long, long time. Creating it had helped. I was able to lift the images out of my mind and put them somewhere I could organize and control them. This was an excellent prescription. I took the piece to my next appointment with Sue. She immediately assigned another piece for homework. We decided I was going to paint and collage my way out of post-traumatic stress disorder.

I displayed my first piece on Jason's easel. As raw and graphic as it was, after looking at it for several minutes I always felt better. It didn't have the same effect on others, though. It was a visual representation of my pain and made some of my friends upset. I realized I should put it away when others came over but hadn't yet found a place for it when my mum arrived one day unexpectedly. I tried to move it, but I wasn't quick enough. She froze in front of it, and then began sobbing uncontrollably. I didn't know how to comfort her; I felt like I was drowning, and a drowning person can't save another drowning person.

What would I do in the future with all the evidence of my life from this time, sometime way down the road when things were better? I lay down on my bed and imagined that one day

I would have a big house with a porch and kids and a husband and a life that was normal. In my house there would be a small room—an attic or a walk-in closet—that would be a shrine to this time. This collage, favourite photos and other artifacts from my old life would line the walls. I'd be able to stare at them for as long as I needed. No one would be allowed in the room unless I said so. My new husband would understand that—he would never ask me to forget my past; it was a part of who I was. When I would come out of the room, he would hug me, and we would go about our lives without missing a beat. He would be a very brave and confident man, and he would fall in love with me because of my huge heart.

CHAPTER EIGHTEEN

THE BLACKNESS

I continued to visit Jason as much as I was allowed, and our bond grew ever stronger. Our visits were too short and the minutes filled with questions and answers. Dialogue was the one path that would lead to peace. I could spend a lifetime wrestling on my own with the questions "Why?" and "What if?" never to arrive at an answer, or I could work with Jason to get as far as possible with the answers to "How?" and then put the rest of my energy into "Now what?" Jason's choices had taken mine away—that's what I understood victimization to mean. I could cling to the label of victim, or I could find a way to move beyond it to become stronger, more loving, more compassionate and more able to stand up against injustice.

For Jason's thirty-sixth birthday—six weeks before the crimes—I had put together a scrapbook of his childhood photos and memorabilia. One thing he had always said about being adopted was that it was hard to look around and not see anyone who looked like him. As we were preparing to marry and start a family, I thought he would enjoy having an album that preserved the past—one he could refer to as his own kids grew up to see their resemblance to him.

Now, as I was clipping newspaper articles about Jason's heinous crimes and filing them with police reports and psychiatric journal articles, I noticed his birthday scrapbook and took it off the shelf. I stopped at a Remembrance Day poem he had won an award for in elementary school. There was a picture of him receiving his plaque in the school gym. He was ten or eleven, with blondish hair, a white suit and an impish grin. Jason and I had laughed together at his imitation of his fifth-grade self, moving in melodramatic rhythm to his ode to poppies, "Swaying, swaying, ever swaying, swaying in the breeze." I snapped back into the present. How did this little boy grow up to be a rapist and a murderer?

That night, Jason called. I listened to the digital operator as her automated voice asked me to accept the charges.

"Hi, Shan."

There was something different in his voice. He sounded hesitant or nervous, as though far away. I pictured him sitting on the floor of his cell, the phone in his lap, and the cord extending out through the slot in the door.

"There's something I want to tell you but I don't know if I'll really be able to say it when I see you, so . . . I thought if I told you ahead of time that I have something to say, then you could make sure I actually do tell you when you come to visit. Does that make sense?"

He was committing to some kind of disclosure.

"Yes, Jason. I understand. Don't worry—I'll hold you to it. Do you want me to combine this week's two visits into one so we have more time?"

"Um, yeah, I think that would probably be good."

"I was planning to come the day after tomorrow. Should I come sooner?"

"No, in two days is fine, but don't come if it's snowy. Don't take any chances, promise me."

"I promise."

The weather was clear two days later as I drove to the jail. I felt nervous as I prepared to hear what Jason was about to tell me. Knowing what he had done to the women, how he did it, and not believing that people are simply "born like that," I was certain that something had happened to Jason when he was small to distort and disturb his sexuality. A guard had said to me once, "You couldn't swing a cat in here without hitting a guy who was abused as a child." All the literature I'd read so far pointed to a common history of neglect and physical, emotional or sexual abuse among sex offenders. I imagined that Jason would tell me that as a child, a man had sexually assaulted him. Nothing prepared me for what I was about to learn.

"Do you remember how I always told you I had just that one clear memory of my dad from when I was four or five—the one where he was standing at the door of the house and was upset about something I did, and I ran away down a little hill and he called after me to come back?"

I nodded.

He took a deep breath. "I never told you what he was upset about. He wasn't really mad at me, though I kind of thought he was at the time. It wasn't something I did, but something I told him about." I watched as the colour drained from Jason's face. "I told him about the stuff Mum was doing to me."

His *mother*? "What was she doing, Jason?"

"It was . . . it was sexual stuff. She was making me touch her."

He could barely get the words out, whispering them into the phone as he looked at me through the glass, his eyes huge pools of tears. He was overwrought. He would start a sentence and then not be able to finish. I just waited.

Jason went on to tell me about different situations in which he had endured physical and sexual violence. There were distinct sets of abuse: sexual abuse by his mother, and by his mother and her boyfriend; and physical abuse by his late grandfather. After Jason's adoptive father died, his mother started what became a long-term on-again, off-again relationship with a man who left the door open while he engaged in violent anal sex with Jason's mom. Jason would be in bed across the hall and could hear and often see everything, able to escape only by drawing on the backs of paper grocery bags. He said he remembered feeling very confused: was his mom being hurt or did she like it? He said he also felt angry and strangely jealous, which he knew was wrong—something to hide and be ashamed of. His mother would frequently leave him at his grandparents' farm, where his grandfather kicked and insulted him. On top of everything, there was a family friend who forced Jason to watch pornographic videos when he was a young boy.

Jason had a particular memory of a trip to Portugal with his mother and her boyfriend when he was ten. While the two of them had sex with the door open in an adjoining hotel room, Jason pretended to read a comic book. It was the only trip they took Jason along on, usually leaving him at his grandparents. I cringed as I recalled placing a cute photograph of Jason from that Portugal trip into the scrapbook I had made for him. Little did I know what memories this picture conjured for him. He never gave any indication, instead thanking me for all my work in putting the album together. He said no one had ever made anything like that for him. Now I wanted to go back in time and undo it, or sit another few minutes on the couch with him until he blurted out the truth of his memories and we phoned our doctor. I would have told him I loved him and there was nothing for him to be ashamed of. He would have gone into therapy and, over time, released all his anguish in a safe place. His hurt would never have hurt anyone else; maybe none of this would have happened.

But it was too late, and I'd committed to steering clear of the whys and what-ifs. I refocused my attention on the present. What was going on inside Jason's mind? Jason described something he called "the Blackness." He said it wasn't like having a voice exactly, but it was a feeling that would come over him every time something went well in his life. The feeling had words and the words formed into phrases that repeated over and over, getting louder as really good things started happening. The Blackness said, "You are disgusting. You don't deserve this. None of this is real. No one knows who you really are. If they did, they would hate you."

The Blackness always wanted him to prove himself worthless, but also encouraged secrecy and superiority—praising Jason for being able to keep secrets to perfection and saying he would one day be rewarded for it. Jason described what was going on in his head the days he videotaped people in our bathroom. He said it was like he had a light-switch in his head that kept flipping on and off: he would commit private, dirty acts one minute, loving acts the next. He would be in the bathroom adjusting the camera for his twisted mission, then he would re-enter the scene of his home life—and attend to something on the stove, cut the grass, put his arms around me. He said that at these times he could detach from seeing the victims as they were—people he knew—seeing them instead as objects. When he came out of the bathroom, they were real people again. His description fit exactly what I had seen with my own eyes, watching that video at the police station: a body vacant of the person that I knew, someone who'd "switched."

I asked Jason how long he had had this "Blackness."

"For as long as I can remember." He explained that he'd gone through long stretches where it wasn't really active. "Like for all the years I spent in prison before—I was completely shut down. No one asked me if anything was wrong and I would have denied it anyway." He said he hated the men around him who "cried abuse" and he kept his distance from them. "I guess the reality was that what they were actually saying was so close to me that it was a huge threat . . . I functioned on control, and all I knew was that the one time I had ever lost control, I had killed someone. Admitting the truth about what happened to me, and how messed up I was, was scarier than having to live the rest of my life in prison. I never told anyone. I thought I could handle it—just stuff it down—and that it would go away. I never thought about the future. I got by how most guys inside do: one day at a time, never thinking back, never looking ahead."

There wasn't enough time in our visit to finish our conversation. Combining the week's two half-hour visits had given us a start, but now I wouldn't be able to return until the next week. The phones clicked off and I mouthed the words, *I'm sorry.*

A few days later I received a letter from Jason. He had gone right back to his cell to write down the rest of his thoughts after our visit. I sat down on the couch in the stillness of my living room to read it. It picked up exactly where our conversation had ended:

"Halfway through my sentence, I realized that they were going to let me out one day, and I started to perk up. I took a few courses and participated in an Alternatives to Violence program—even became a leader, as you know—but I never developed any real dreams or goals. I didn't deserve to, and I didn't know how to. I had fantasies, like that I would save someone's life to redeem my own, but mostly, I just got by. When I came out on work release and met all the folks at Martha's Table, things started to change a bit. I knew that many people in Corrections had helped me get out. I gained purpose and some sense of belonging, and I tried to do what they said—put everything behind me. I wanted to more than anything; I wanted it to all go away, and for long periods of time it did. I didn't look at pornography at all; I started dating nice, smart women and had a real relationship for a couple of years that I learned a lot from. When that broke up, there was a rough patch, but I got through it."

Then, the letter turned to me. What he said left me aching to turn back time.

"You made me feel real, Shan—right from when I first met you. . . . You could reach me and you were everything I ever wanted, that the good part of me ever wanted. You were my ideal. I thought, 'I can do this—I can live up to this opportunity.' But I guess I couldn't. . . . I guess there was still all the other stuff. The stuff with mom and her boyfriend, not to mention the murder in 1988. I couldn't cope with everything good that happened; I was so weak. I knew I wasn't normal, but I never thought I would do what I did. I thought I had all the time in the world to deal with it. Sometimes I got really close to telling you, but then I just shut down or made an excuse. I thought that becoming a father would cure me, so I tried to concentrate on that, but really, I was so afraid. I'm so sorry, Shan—I'm so sorry! What is wrong with me?"

His question hung in the air.

During our visit the following week, I told Jason that he was responsible for all the crimes he had committed—murder, rape, assault, kidnapping and voyeurism—and he was at fault for not asking for help when he had it available to him. But the destruction of his childhood was the fault of the adults who were supposed to protect and nurture him, not abuse and neglect him.

"But other people have gone through worse than I did and they didn't turn out like me."

True, but did his inability to healthily process abuse and get past it make him less valuable as a human being? In the eyes of some, I'm sure it did, but not to me. I looked directly into the eyes of this child, now a grown man, and that changed everything. He wasn't just a name in a newspaper report. He was not equal to the sum of his worst actions. I had the privilege—and the challenge—of a much wider lens on him.

I took a breath, and summoned the words I thought might allow him a chance at recovery. I didn't need to hold him in a victim–offender bond. That wouldn't help either of us on our long roads ahead. "Jason, I know you're sorry for the things you've done. And . . . I forgive you."

He looked at me and was quiet for a moment. "Thank you," he said. But it would take a long time for Jason to truly accept my forgiveness.

—

There are countless factors and variables that lead to the outcome of a life, many of which we can never prove. In a later conversation, I asked Jason if he thought his early life experiences were related to what he did to the women that day. He said he didn't know. He said they were definitely not an excuse. I wanted to go back in time to the point when Jason's birth mother gave him away and adopt him myself. Start things over. But I couldn't do that.

I had no idea what would happen to my relationship with Jason over time except that it would never be the same. As long as I felt right in myself about supporting him and being in touch, I would continue. It was not a sacrifice, nor was it a dependence, though some would make that claim. I continued to visit Jason almost every week for months—breaking the routine only to give my half-hour allotment to a friend or family member who wanted to see him. Many of our conversations involved heart-wrenching disclosures. I always cried for several minutes in the parking lot before I was able to drive home. I made it a habit to pick up a large tea at Tim Hortons before getting on the frozen two-lane highway. Then I had forty minutes to think before I got home, where there would be a pile of mail, phone messages to return, and that merciless to-do list waiting for me. Something that Jason said more than once struck me and I played it over and over in my mind. "Not every kid who has been sexually abused grows up to do what I did."

The only response I could think of was, "Well, thank God." But a new response was forming inside me: Now what are we going to do about those who do?

A letter arrived that gave me an answer—or at least, the chance to discover an answer. The envelope was postmarked from the

United Kingdom and the insignia read "The University of East Anglia." I began shaking as I opened it: an offer of acceptance to the MA program in Development Studies and Education. I was pleased as well as relieved—this was something I could do to point my future in a positive direction—but something about the program I'd chosen no longer felt right. The image of the little boy that Jason had once been came to my mind again, and I looked more deeply into myself. I wanted to work with kids like Jason, and kids like the ones I'd worked with at the shelter: victims and offenders.

I responded to the university's offer by asking if I could be admitted instead to the International Child Welfare program. A week later, I received a second offer of admission, this time with a small scholarship attached from the department of social work. I would have to apply for a student loan and a line of credit to pay the rest of the costs, unless by some miracle I won another scholarship. I could also consider selling my house. There were many uncertainties, but I knew I could figure out a plan somehow. I signed the offer back to the university with the "yes" box checked.

I went about getting used to the idea of living in England. I would gain anonymity and purpose, but I would be without my support people close to me. Would I be lonely? What about Jason's criminal court process? Would I return for his trial or sentencing? I had more than eight months until the school year began to work out the details—surely I would know more then than I did now. The only way I could get from today into the future was one day at a time, one step at a time.

CHAPTER NINETEEN

WHERE DID JASON COME FROM?

During the first week of February, I got a phone call from Barbara, a teacher at my former school. Staff had been told that I was on paid leave, and that I would be returning to work at the beginning of the second semester, but that day had come and gone. Barbara had grown concerned. On the phone I explained what really happened: that I'd been told I would be relocated, that our principal said I represented something terrible, and that I was not to enter the building without permission. Now I was at home on unpaid medical leave, working to recover from PTSD and put a plan in place for the future.

Barbara was dismayed, and she turned her dismay into action. It was clear to her that I needed some kind of voice. At the end of our phone conversation, Barbara asked me if she could talk to some other teachers about what had really happened to me. I gratefully gave her my consent. I needed someone to advocate for me and break the silence. She promised to call back within a few days.

When she did, she called with a plan. Barbara asked if she

could take charge of organizing a healing circle—an opportunity for dialogue that would address our collective need to be connected during tragedy, not separated because of it. It sounded wonderful to me. We set a date for an evening a couple of weeks later.

Barbara looked after everything, from inviting staff, to creating a ceremony that would establish a sense of trust and safety in the group. She arrived first that evening, and we arranged chairs in a circle in my living room. The doorbell began to ring and I answered it each time to find a face of compassion. Some were faces I had predicted I would see—but others surprised me; there were some teachers I barely knew. What I learned that night was that many of my colleagues were not levelling blame at me or assaulting my character, but wanting to express their empathy.

Barbara began the evening with a meditation to focus our energy as light—light that could heal the victims, their families, Jason, me and our whole community. Next she read a poem and then she passed a bowl of stones around the circle and invited each person to choose one. Each stone had a different word written on it—such as *Hope, Fear, Anger, Sadness* and *Guilt*. We were directed to use the word as a starter to help articulate and express feelings we had about what had happened. As people around the circle spoke, I listened with gratitude to their condolences. There was no trace of judgment or condemnation.

Some people shared their frustration and anger about what was going on at school. I learned that the school had received funding to train the staff in restorative justice: a community-centred approach to handling the harm caused by crime. Maybe this would help educate the school community and help people heal, but at the same time, this news was concerning. Programs were being put into place to promote offenders' accountability and rehabilitation, and healing for victims of crime, but still, by virtue of me being Jason's wife, I was left out.

After everyone left, I lay down in bed and tried to hold onto the positive energy of the evening by picturing the soft, pink light of healing that Barbara had described swirling around me. I pictured it embracing Jason in his jail cell. I pictured it encircling the victims, safe within their homes. I pictured it surrounding my family. When I finally fell asleep, for the first night in many, I had a good dream. I dreamt that I was driving on a hilly country road with the windows rolled down and my hair blowing out behind me. I dreamt that I was laughing.

For a while, I was buoyed by the experience with my circle of colleagues, but as winter raged on, stress and strain continued to pile up around me. It had felt good to connect, but no action grew from it. I was still shunned from the school building, left coping with PTSD and trying to move forward through stigma and injustice. Jason's case continued to be remanded week after week with no movement in any direction. No news from his lawyer, no appointment of a Crown attorney, no sign of Jason being transferred out of solitary confinement, no word on my insurance appeal. It was an agonizing limbo.

Then, on March 31, Jason's aunt Joan called to tell me that Jason's mum had died. She had never recovered from her injuries after being struck by a car the previous winter, and finally succumbed to aspiration pneumonia. She didn't know we got married, and she didn't know about Jason's crimes. Now that I knew she had abused Jason, I didn't know how to feel when Joan broke the news.

I had never known how to feel toward Jason's mom. I'd spent time with her on several occasions, but each time she'd been either so heavily medicated or in an extreme bi-polar high or low state, that in some way it was as though I'd never really met her. I put my focus on supporting Jason, and I wanted to tell him about his mom's death myself. I called the jail right away and asked to speak to a chaplain. The chaplain said rules dictated that he had to deliver news of a death to an inmate, but that he would wait until I arrived, and as soon as he told Jason, he would bring him to see me. I called Sue, our doctor, and asked her to come with me. She cleared her schedule and I picked her up an hour later.

I hadn't met this chaplain before, but he greeted us with respect and tenderness, and I knew he would do the same with Jason. He escorted us to a visiting area different from the small room I was used to: a long strip of visiting booths more akin to the kind I'd seen in movies. Then he left us while he went to get Jason. A few minutes later, Jason was on the other side of the glass. His eyes were wide and teary. I picked up the phone receiver.

"Jason, I'm sorry. I'm sorry about your mom."

He nodded. Sue leaned in toward the receiver.

"Jason, we love you," she said.

"I love you too."

Sue went and sat on the other side of the room so that Jason and I could have a little bit of privacy. It was torturous not to be able to touch or hold him. I held my hand up to his against the glass and he began crying softly.

"I don't know how to feel . . . She was the only mom I knew, and she did the best she could."

I didn't necessarily agree, but I listened. She was Jason's mother, not mine—it was his loss. I asked him if he wanted to go to the funeral and he said he would like to, but he was doubtful he would be allowed.

The chaplain had told me that Jason and I should take all the time we needed, that there was no pressure to wrap it all up in the standard half-hour. That was a relief. With the clock closing in on an hour, Jason said he was okay to go back to his cell, and Sue needed to get back to her practice. I told Jason that I would be going to stay with his aunt and uncle for the funeral in a few days. They had been so supportive the last few months, I could now lend a hand to them. And if Jason couldn't be there, I would represent both of us. We said goodbye.

In the hallway, I heaved cathartic sobs into Sue's embrace. After exiting security, we went to see the chaplain. He would do what he could to see if Jason would be allowed to go to the funeral, or at least the visitation.

A phone call later confirmed that Jason would not be granted permission. He'd not had any kind of psychiatric assessment other than the initial defence-appointed hour so he had no risk classification. Without a classification, he could not leave the institution on escort.

The day of the funeral, I went to the florist with his aunt Joan and bought flowers from Jason and me to lay in front of his mother's urn. In the church, I stayed at the back next to Joan to greet the one or two friends we expected.

Suddenly, she gasped. "Oh my God." A group of people was walking toward us. Her face was frozen as she leaned in and whispered, "These are the Staples—Jason's cousins and aunts from his dad's side. We haven't seen them for at least twenty-five years."

Joan introduced me. "This is Jason's wife, Shannon."

I smiled and shook their hands.

One of the aunts said, "We heard that Jason just got married and we're delighted!" Her eyes darted around the church. "Where is Jason?"

With sinking hearts, Joan and I realized that they didn't know. The organ music started as Joan whispered to Jason's extended family, "We'll talk after," and led me to a pew in the front row.

During the service I could not stop crying and neither could Joan. I was mourning Jason's absence, his mother's devastating mental illness, and what she had put other people through. After the funeral, everyone went back to Joan and Dave's house. We told the Staples family about Jason's recent crimes. As I recounted the events, they were naturally distraught, but also compassionate. They offered to get in touch with him, to tell him he still had family. Later, one of his aunts would send me some photos of Jason when he was young and write him a letter saying he was not forgotten—that they cared. A cousin and I would get together and she would tell what she remembered from years ago, how they'd tried to stay in touch with Jason's mom after his dad died. It was difficult because everyone was afraid of her when she was on a bipolar high, or when she was drunk and out of control. All I could think was, *If they were scared as adults, what was it like for Jason as a little boy?*

After the death of Jason's mother, I became interested in learning more about Jason's past—the months before he was adopted. Where had Jason come from? Did anyone in his family suffer from mental illness? His brain chemistry could possibly be another component of his complex personality equation. With his permission, I decided to do a little investigating and see if I could obtain any of his records from the Children's Aid

Society. Maybe one day, in therapy, having this kind of information could help Jason with his identity issues. I made some phone calls and reached a social worker. I explained that my husband wanted access to his adoption records to see if there was any medical history. He couldn't contact them himself.

"Does he have a mental illness?" the social worked asked.

I said yes, even though there was no diagnosis yet.

Next she asked, "Where is he that he can't call himself—is he in prison?"

Yes, again. Maybe my kind of call wasn't so rare.

"May I ask—is he there on charges related to violence?"

A third yes.

"Okay," she said, "I'll see what I can do. Resolving identity issues can be therapeutic. First I need to find out if he was adopted through us. If he was, I will try to locate his social history report. Then you'll need to talk to someone at the Ministry of Community and Social Services—they manage the adoption registry. If he gets on the registry, he can get a copy of the adoption order and also find out if his birth family has registered as looking for him. The only thing is, the registry is closing in five days for a two-year government overhaul. We have to act quickly." She said she would call back as soon as she could and asked for my number. Before hanging up, she said, "You know, there are a lot of adopted people in prison. Adoptees are over-represented in prison populations."

Really? I hadn't heard this before.

With only five days, I knew how slim the chances were that we could get all the necessary papers and forms back and forth through two government offices and a jail. I phoned the chaplain, who rose to the call and helped with faxing documents and getting Jason's signature. With just a few hours to spare,

Jason made it onto the registry. I heaved a sigh of relief and waited for an envelope to arrive that would tell us where Jason had come from. I didn't know what we'd do if his birth family was looking for him. It would be terrible for them to find out what had happened to the child they'd given away.

A few weeks later, the envelope arrived. It contained a copy of Jason's adoption order, which confirmed that he had been legally adopted at the age of three months. Prior to that, he had lived with three foster families and was reported by each to be adorable, a good eater and sleeper, but distressed and tearful when he was not being held. Yet, for whatever reason, none of them had kept him for very long.

The certificate gave his name at birth, and his social history report, dated December of 1969, which said that his birth mother was from Newfoundland. She had become pregnant out of wedlock and moved to Ottawa to live with her brother until the baby was born. She put him into care immediately. Perhaps she had then returned to Newfoundland. Maybe she went on to get married and have a family. Maybe Jason had brothers and sisters. The report indicated that Jason's mother and grandmother had been very artistic and enjoyed drawing and painting.

Reading the report, Jason thought that was interesting, to know that his talents came from somewhere. There was no contact information—no one was looking for him. Jason sighed. "I guess it's for the best."

He said it was okay to share his report with a few people close to him, like his aunt and uncle, my parents, Una and his Martha's Table friends. Everyone wistfully said they just wished they could go back in time and adopt him themselves, like I did. I kept picturing Jason as a little baby with a tiny suitcase going from house to house, wanting only to be held.

PART 3

RUBBLE

CHAPTER TWENTY

ONE DAY THIS WILL BE OVER

The arrival of spring brought the usual signs of hope—ice and snow melting, flowers blooming—but for me it also brought increased feelings of exposure and vulnerability. In the winter I went for long walks to clear my head, hidden by thick winter clothes. Now, warmer temperatures forced me to shed those layers. I found myself avoiding going downtown, but I knew that isolation was a risk to my mental health. I focused on preparing to leave Peterborough and heading to England for the master's program.

The insurance company offered me a settlement that barely covered the debt I had accrued paying my mortgage and living expenses since Jason's crimes. There was nothing left over to extend coverage into the coming months, no future income and a set of post-traumatic stress symptoms that were no better than when I'd first begun my claim. In the College of Teachers magazine I received in the mail each month, I read in the "blue pages" at the back about teachers who were suspended with pay in situations where they had actually been charged with serious offences. I had not broken any laws, yet I didn't deserve pay?

I pointed this out to the insurance company's disability benefits coordinator. She believed I warranted support, but the strict company polices made mental health conditions the hardest for claimants to prove. They had never reviewed a case like mine so they didn't really know what to do with me.

I decided I would rent my house and spend the summer floating between my parents' and friends'. I had a long list of people who had offered to put me up. I advertised my house and began to pack my things into crawl spaces. Wedding presents went into boxes with favourite books and photo albums. As I taped up the cartons, I promised them, "When I open you, it is going to be a better time. I'll be in a better place."

I only had to show the house a few times before I found a nice couple to rent it to. I made sure they knew what had happened in the house, but demand for good housing in Peterborough was so high that they were pleased to have a well-maintained place and its history made no difference to them. I heaved a sigh of relief. One big decision was made, and a bigger decision—selling the house—could be put off until I had more clarity and a longer-term plan.

I got a student line of credit from the bank for ten thousand dollars, and a government student loan for another ten. I would work my annual two-week summer job as a teen counsellor for a music school in Kingston—that would pay for my living expenses over the summer and for my plane ticket to England. I had the one small scholarship from the university, but I still needed at least ten thousand dollars more.

As I tried to think of a solution, I set to work packing Jason's things. There was no word from Corrections about what to do with all of Jason's belongings, only a general rule: whenever he was transferred back to federal custody, I would have thirty days to give him his personal effects. Which items were allowed was a mystery to me so I tried to think like a prison guard and pack everything I thought might be permitted: clothing and shoes, unopened art supplies, photos and paperback books. After that thirty-day period, nothing would ever be permitted into the prison again, except money. No new books or music, no art supplies, no birthday or Christmas gifts, ever. Surely a transfer was imminent—but six months had gone by after I'd been told it would take six weeks. His next biweekly remand was in ten days and I hoped to learn of some progress. It was expected that his case would be transferred to Superior Court, where an experienced Crown attorney could finally be assigned. My chest tightened as I thought about how much I had to do before I moved out of my house and away from Peterborough on the same day, June 1. Time was my newest enemy—it either dragged with excruciating slowness or raced by, leaving me behind.

On Friday, May 26, my mum called. "Did you see the *Toronto Star* today?" Her voice was tinged with urgency. I hadn't seen the paper.

"There's an article about those pills Jason took on the day of the crimes. Listen to the headline: 'Caffeine plus ephedrine a hazard; combination could be fatal.'" My mum continued reading. "Consumers should avoid taking combination products including caffeine and ephedrine or ephedra because they risk serious and possible fatal side effects, Health Canada warns. . . . When used with caffeine and other stimulants, ephedrine has caused everything from dizziness, tremors and headaches to heart-rate irregularities and seizures, psychosis, heart attacks and stroke."

Psychosis. Was it possible that on the day of the crimes, after taking the drugs, Jason had entered a psychotic state? Psychosis might explain his absence of memory about the hours before the attacks, his level of violence and lack of impulse control that day. I recalled our neighbours who had seen Jason in the store earlier that afternoon and described him as "larger than life" and our friends outside the store that evening who said he looked "hyper" and "nervous." I didn't know what impact this could have on his criminal case, but thought it should be investigated. While whatever role the supplements had played wouldn't—and shouldn't—exonerate him, maybe an in-depth assessment would provide us with an answer to at least one piece of a very complex puzzle about what happened on the day Jason committed the assaults.

"We'd better speak to Jason's lawyer and let him know about this," I said to my mum. We hoped an assessment would be ordered by the court when the lawyer received this new information.

By dusk on May 31, I had packed everything I thought I would need over the summer and for a year in England, as well as all of Jason's things, into my mum's minivan. I kept aside my outfit for Jason's court appearance the next morning. He was scheduled to be there in person, rather than via video link from the jail as on previous occasions. It was too early to go to bed, and my mum and I were both anxious about the following day. We needed to calm our nerves. I remembered a sunrise ceremony I had once attended on National Aboriginal Day. An Elder marked the presence of the Creator and our connection to a bigger universe by burning sweetgrass. I had an idea. I opened up a box I had just packed and took out a bundle of sweetgrass given to me by a colleague at the healing circle. It was from a nearby sacred First Nations site. I went back into the living room where my mum was knitting.

"Mum, do you want to go with me to the courthouse and, um . . . pray?"

She looked up. I hadn't prayed since I was a little girl, and she knew it.

"I thought maybe we could burn this sweetgrass or something." I wasn't planning on a return to religion, but trying to connect with "something bigger" might feel good.

Without a moment's hesitation, she agreed. We drove to the courthouse. I pulled the heavily laden minivan into the driveway and parked in the empty lot. We got out and practically tiptoed toward the main doors. We lit the small bundle of sweetgrass near the threshold. We giggled, imagining ourselves caught in the headlights of a police car, like teenagers smoking pot. Laughter undid some of our tension.

The smoke rose in the air. We called for peace to dominate the next day's proceedings. We hoped for common sense and clarity to prevail over every person there, from the judge to the lawyers to the clerks. We prayed for the safe journey of the guards who would transport Jason and other inmates from the jail, and then we prayed for the inmates too. Finally, we asked for protection for the victims and for ourselves. As an offering, I laid the bundle on the pavement in front of the courthouse, and then I crept back to the van with my mum.

That night, my mum slept in my bed upstairs and I slept in the basement. But I felt uneasy as I went downstairs to the room where the victims had been held captive by Jason. It wasn't that the room itself was scary, but more that I knew I wouldn't be able to stop my mind from picturing their terror and pain if I spent time there in silence. As I lay down, I returned to the thought I had had the first day I went home after the police search ended: that this was the place where three lives that could have been lost were saved. I focused on the bravery of the victims who'd brought Jason out of the Blackness and back to reality.

I worked through those painful scenes and then let my thoughts drift further into the past, to the hot summer nights when Jason and I found respite from the heat in the cool of the basement. At times it had been so humid upstairs in our bedroom that we lay next to each other in perfect stillness, knowing any movement would only make us sweat more. We said good night by touching fingertips instead of embracing. Finally, one night we moved our guest room futon down to the basement and slept there for the rest of that summer and the next—it was a little adventure, like camping. Lying in the same place now, it seemed like those moments had happened in another life. I wondered if one day, one day, I would look back on this time and feel its distance; if all the pain would lift and drift away, like the smoke of the sweetgrass.

CHAPTER TWENTY-ONE

A COURTHOUSE ENCOUNTER

Every time I got dressed for court, I had the feeling that I was floating above myself, that someone else was tucking in my blouse and doing up the buttons on my suit jacket. I was dressing for protection in an unfamiliar situation— a suit of armour in respectable navy and pinstripe. This morning was no different.

My mum and I headed back to the courthouse. By now, I had been to court several times, for many of Jason's remands. Though I feared exposure, court was where I hoped to talk to his defence lawyer in person and get a sense of the progress being made toward guilty pleas. But the lawyer usually sent an articling student in his place, someone who was unable to answer my questions. In fact, I hadn't seen the lawyer since I'd met him in his Toronto office six months ago. He'd only been to see Jason once, and had never again sent the psychiatrist he'd hired despite having been approved for a twenty-hour assessment by Legal Aid. Court remand after remand, I was disappointed, seeing no progress at all. A Crown attorney had still not been assigned.

We arrived to the busy and crowded courthouse at about nine o'clock. Traffic court was in the room next to criminal court, so people who were fighting speeding tickets waited in the same area as people involved in much more serious cases. I noticed someone I knew—Greg, who had been on the board of directors of a local charity with me. We hadn't seen each other since everything happened. I assumed he had heard, but I didn't know for sure. Greg was the divorced father of two great kids at my school, one of whom I knew well. Recently, I'd seen his son coming out of a corner store and I'd nodded a quiet hello. I figured Greg was probably in court for a traffic infraction.

There was an awkward pause after he greeted me with a hug. "I'm here for the same reason you are."

I looked at him, confused. Had someone in his family committed a crime?

Then he named the first woman Jason had assaulted. "She is my partner."

I was shocked and started crying, and he pulled me into an embrace. The words spilled from me.

"I'm so sorry, I'm so sorry . . . I have been thinking about you and your family every day but I didn't know who I was thinking about." I asked him how he was. His eyes were full of pain.

"We're, well, we're . . . as you might expect. We've been thinking about you, too, Shannon."

Panic rose. I glanced around frantically. As if Greg could sense what I was thinking, he said, "She's not here today. I came for her; she wasn't up to it."

"I'm so sorry . . . I didn't know . . . I didn't know."

I was saying two things at the same time: I didn't know Jason was dangerous, and I didn't know it was his partner who was the first victim. I didn't even know he had a partner.

"We know you didn't know," Greg said. "We didn't want to tell you it was us because we thought it would be too hard for you and we needed some time first, some privacy. Everyone else on our volunteer board knows, but I asked them not to tell you. I thought it would be better if you found out like this."

His words hit me only on the surface; there was a lot of information to absorb in that short conversation. All I could do was repeat, "I'm so sorry. I'm so sorry." I felt exposed and vulnerable in the busy waiting area as I struggled to regain some composure. My mum was standing behind me and overheard our conversation. She put her arm around me and I heard her introduce herself and express her regrets in a voice that was breaking with emotion.

Suddenly, a loudspeaker announced that proceedings were about to commence in Courtroom Two, so we rushed in and took our seats. My mum and I found two places on a bench in front of Detective Morgan, and Greg sat at the back on the other side of the courtroom. My mum reached over to hold my hand. I took some deep breaths and looked for Jason's lawyer but didn't see him or his articling student. Detective Morgan leaned forward to ask how we were but I didn't know how to respond. I asked him if he had seen Jason's lawyer. We wanted to give him the information about the supplements Jason had taken. Detective Morgan was immediately intrigued and asked to see the article, which we had with us. He read it over.

"You need to show this to the lawyer. This could answer at least one part of what happened—like, how did Jason go from being ten miles an hour out of control for a few months to being a hundred and fifty miles out of control in a few hours."

We all waited in the courtroom while the judge addressed case after case. Some of the accused appeared in person, standing up from the rows right around us, while others appeared via video link from jail. Still others were led by guards into the prisoner's box, dressed in orange, handcuffed, leg-ironed. After more than an hour, Jason's lawyer arrived. I was glad to see him. In the hall, I briefed him on the contents of the Health Canada article as I passed a copy to him. Without looking at it, he put it into his briefcase.

"This won't make any difference; it's not really important," he said. Then he ducked into the lawyers' dressing room and left me standing in the hallway.

I went back into the courtroom and sat down. I was confused. What had happened to the lawyer I met six months ago—the one who promised he would do everything he could? He seemed completely different now.

We waited another hour for Jason's appearance to come up on the docket. At eleven-thirty, court recessed for lunch. As I turned around toward the exit doors, I noticed that Greg had already left.

Jason finally appeared for a minute or two in the mid-afternoon. The case was remanded to the Ontario Superior Court of Justice where a Crown attorney would be assigned. The next court date was set for later in the month. Jason's lawyer left before we could ask him about a psychiatric assessment. The whole day had been a letdown.

As my mum and I drove away from the courthouse and out of Peterborough, I tried to sort through the day's events. The film strip of the assaults reeled through my mind again, only this time, some of the blank faces were filled in. I relived the events of that day and the days after, my body responding with nausea and a new, sharp pain radiating from my shoulder all the way down my arm. The truth of what Greg had told me was also starting to sink in: fellow board members had kept the identity of the victim and her connection to Greg a secret for six months—Greg had asked them to. A couple of them were people who had shown me particular support and I had confided in them about the anxiety I felt over knowing the victims' names but not their identities. They had even written to Jason. I felt my trust begin to fracture.

These people had been put in a very awkward position, and I understood that. But surely they knew that I would find out one day that I had a connection to one of the victims. Did they all agree with Greg that it would be better if I found out in the busy public corridor of a courtroom? Could a compromise not have been considered—one that would have left me less vulnerable? Later, I confronted two of the people, but they were defensive. They'd been asked to keep a secret. I needed to be more understanding and give others time.

My anxiety now hit an all-time high and was coupled with a new and strange sense of betrayal. I understood that I wasn't the only one who hadn't been given a map to navigate this awful experience, but at the same time I felt isolated. I found myself crossing off a few names from my Golden Circle list. More loss. For the very first time, I felt glad that I was leaving town. Glad and devastated.

By the evening, my strongest emotion was anger. I was angry at Greg and his partner for taking control of decisions that affected me. Then I felt guilty—guilty for being angry at people who had been so terribly victimized. Of course he and his partner needed to set some boundaries. Jason had invaded their lives and taken all control away. So, it was all Jason's fault. Anger at him pushed my emotional thermometer right to the top. He was responsible for his crimes and for everything else that happened afterwards—for everything that was hurting me now. But what about the people who had started the cycle of violence in him? Wasn't it their fault too?

All of the anger burst and rained down in confusion, followed by grief. My whole body ached. I lay down in a room in my parents' basement and cried. I was thirty years old; I'd had a husband, a house, a job and maybe a baby on the way. I'd had a full and busy life in my community. Now all of it was gone and I was sleeping in my parents' basement. It felt like I'd been yanked back to childhood, only there was nothing innocent in my world anymore. When was something good going to happen?

NO MORE GLASS

A few days later, something good did happen. I got an e-mail from the Bombardier Internationalist Fellowship Awards committee. I was one of ten recipients of a prestigious ten-thousand-dollar award—exactly the amount I needed to go to England. From the computer in the basement, I whooped with joy. My mum rushed down the stairs, unable to tell if my whoops were joy or terror, but when she saw my face lit up with excitement, she relaxed. She hadn't seen that look on my face since my wedding day.

In the evening, Jason called and I shared the news. "I'm so proud of you. I knew you could do it! You are going to be a great grad student."

For the rest of the summer, I didn't sleep in the same bed for more than five nights in a row. After staying with my parents for a few days, I made a one-week trial trip to England to figure out where I would live, and then I returned home and lived in the university residence in Kingston while working at the music camp. No one at camp knew what had happened with Jason, and being in a professional role with teenagers again was therapeutic. I found respite in being treated by the staff, students and families exactly as I'd been treated the summer before.

When I wasn't working, I visited friends and, in particular, spent quality time with Una. She'd beaten cancer a few years previous, but it had come back. She told me not to worry too much; she wasn't ready to go yet. We had many long conversations about Jason, about life, and about loss. Often we sat in the cool of her stone cottage in silence, drinking tea or just holding hands. I confessed that I felt afraid of going to England—afraid of becoming disconnected with everything that had happened. I was afraid I would never come back, that I would lose my roots. Una gave me a small ivory Buddha that she had been given fifty years earlier by a close friend when she moved from England to Canada. She said it would bring me back home again.

I also went to see a lawyer that Jason and I were interested in hiring to replace the current one, if Legal Aid would allow it. Lack of communication and failure to follow through on many requests for information and action had added enormous stress. Above all, this lawyer really did not seem to understand that Jason *wanted* to plead guilty. He seemed to be pushing for a full trial.

I took some time to search for a certified specialist in criminal law and I found Constance Baran-Gerez, whose expertise included criminal trials and appeals, with an emphasis on sexual offences. I learned that she had also worked as a Crown attorney early in her career, which gave me confidence that she could look at the case from all angles and was equipped to handle the complexity of a defendant who didn't want to defend himself. I met Connie at her office in Kingston and she listened carefully. She was confident, sensitive and intelligent. She kept her practice small on purpose, so she could be accessible to her clients. She said she would take on Jason's case at the Legal Aid rate if the approval to change lawyers came through.

At the end of July, Jason was finally transferred back to federal custody at Kingston Penitentiary, the big and foreboding maximum-security facility surrounded by thick stone walls. I stayed in town to house-sit for friends four blocks away. It was surreal—Jason was so close, yet so far. I was not allowed to see him. In the federal system, one has to apply to be a visitor, a process that normally takes four weeks, but with summer holidays and short-staffing I could expect to wait six weeks or more before I was approved. It was the inmate's responsibility to share information with family and friends and to send out the visitor forms. If the inmate didn't communicate, the visitor was cut off. For some families, this might be a relief—an end to a cycle of family violence—but for others, it might add to their feelings of powerlessness. Fortunately for me, Jason wanted me to visit and did communicate with me.

All of August went by without me seeing him. I heard from him by phone when he was able to call. It was always very noisy in the background. Jason said the range was like a zoo. He was in a temporary unit and would be transferred again, though he didn't know when or to where. Transfer information was usually kept secret from inmates as a security precaution. Who knew if someone's family or gang members might wait for the van out on the highway or in the parking lot of the institution? Finally, in early September, Jason called to say he had been driven that day to the medium-security institution where he'd spent his twenties, an hour outside the city. He hadn't known about the transfer until a guard came to tell him to clean his cell a few hours before he was put in a transfer van.

The window of time before I had to leave for England was closing quickly. When I got word of the transfer, I began making boxes for Jason in accordance with the list of permissible "cell effects" he read me on the phone. This was the only chance I would have to give Jason anything for the rest of his sentence, which might very well mean the rest of his life. I felt like I was packing a kid for camp, only this was a camp for life. Jason's belongings fit into seven cardboard boxes and the boxes went into my parents' van. My visiting application still had not come through, so it was quite possible that I'd have to drive the two hours there to drop off the boxes without being able to see Jason. If I didn't get approved in the next week, I wouldn't be seeing him until I returned from England for the Christmas holidays.

Arriving back at his "mother institution" (a term I found hard to swallow), Jason was greeted warmly but with obvious dismay by many staff and a few inmates who were still there from his previous incarceration. He was ashamed of himself; he had broken their trust and let down all those who had helped him. He was humbled when everyone treated him politely, and in some cases, even with care and concern. His parole officer from the nineties brought him into her office for a long conversation. Jason explained to her how I was about to go to England, and how we were hoping against hope that my visiting application would be approved within the next week so that I could see him before leaving. She asked Jason for my phone number. She called me and faxed me a new form, which I faxed back the same day. A couple of days later, she called again.

"You're in," she said. "When do you want to come?"

It was a Friday afternoon. I was leaving for England in seven days.

"When's the soonest I can come?"

"Tomorrow. We open at 8:30 a.m. and you can stay until 3 p.m. Usually visitors have to book forty-eight hours in advance but these are special circumstances."

I thanked her emphatically. That evening I was filled with anticipation. For the first time since his arrest, I would see Jason in person, not through glass. It had been ten months since we had touched.

I barely slept, and hit the road at six in the morning. That would leave me enough time to drop off all of Jason's boxes at the loading door of the admissions and discharge department before visiting hours. I found the institution without a problem—a concrete campus-style setting similar to the university I was about to attend in the United Kingdom, only this campus was surrounded with high fences and razor wire, in the middle of farmers' fields. After going through a security check and a drug scan, I was let into the visiting room—a big, carpeted space with tables bolted to the floor and four chairs at each. There was a children's play area with a bookshelf and several toys. There were vending machines for drinks and snacks. Windows on one side looked onto the parking lot and the fields in the distance; on the other side, the windows looked onto an outdoor visiting area, where I could see flower gardens, tables with umbrellas and plastic chairs, and a play structure with a slide and sandbox for kids. A wave of sadness hit me as I thought about the children whose fathers were in prison.

At one end of the room, guards at a desk behind a glass wall supervised the visitors and inmates and checked people in and out. I noticed surveillance cameras near the ceiling. Any moment, Jason would walk through the door. The guards told me to have a seat while I waited for him. There weren't any other families there yet, but a few would arrive soon. Saturday is the busiest day, meaning that up to 15 of the 600 inmates in the institution might have a visitor. I found that sad, too, but with the effort it took to get to the prison's remote location, and the difficult road any family would have travelled through crime, arrest, detention and trial, I could understand why so few people made it.

It didn't take long for Jason to make his way down to the visiting room—he had been waiting nervously on the edge of his bed since six. He was security-checked and then the inmate entrance opened and he walked through. It was strange. All of a sudden, after all that waiting, all those visits behind glass, he was right there in front of me. I leapt to my feet and we threw our arms around each other, holding on for several minutes. Jason felt so different than he had the last time I'd hugged him. He'd lost sixty pounds by pacing and doing exercises in his cell using letters bundled in a pillowcase. He often felt too sick with himself to eat. I was different, too, now twenty-five pounds lighter from my stress-and-grief diet.

"You're wasting away," Jason whispered in my ear. "You have to take better care of yourself."

I was self-conscious about being videotaped by the guards, so we went out to the patio area and walked circles, arm-in-arm, around the small gardens. Compared to the grey visiting room at the jail, with its glass wall and phone receiver, this visiting area was paradise. Compared to the life we'd had together, this visiting area was hell. I wondered if it might be the only place I would ever get to spend time with Jason again.

After about an hour, Jason's correctional officer came to meet me. She asked to speak with me privately for a few minutes and we went into one of the little interview rooms normally used by lawyers and their inmate-clients. She wanted to get acquainted and ask me how I was doing. She wanted to know a little bit about Jason from my perspective. She asked about my upcoming time in England, saying she thought it was wonderful that I was going, and said I should try not to worry about Jason—she would be keeping an eye on him. Her tone was kind and sincere, without a trace of judgment. I felt my anxiety level drop. I shook her hand and then returned to the table where Jason was waiting for me.

We began talking about my plans to go to England. I explained each different course I'd be taking, and expressed my worries about living with a stranger and getting to know new people.

"You're great at meeting new people. You'll be surrounded by friends in no time."

"It's just that it's harder now—I don't know what to say about my life and who I am anymore."

Jason's expression saddened. "At least there you'll have a choice about what you say to people and who you let close to you. No one will know anything unless you tell them." He continued. "And speaking of letting people in, I think you should try to go out with people there. I mean, go out with men." I stared at him, motionless. "Date," he clarified. "It could be good for you. You deserve to be in a relationship with someone who can take you places and be there for you—I can't do that. I took all that away from us." His eyes were full of love and sadness.

The thought had crossed my mind a few times recently.

"I don't want to fall in love yet," I responded. "I'm not ready."

"You don't have to," he said. He squeezed my hand. "Just explore, try to have fun. But take care of yourself."

"Do you want me to tell you if something happens?" I asked. "Or would you prefer not to know anything?"

Jason thought for a moment. "I think I would want to know, without any details," he began. "But I don't want you to ever feel like you have to report to me. I'll just need a little time to cope when that reality hits. I have to be careful not to hold onto any fantasies—it's one of the biggest dangers in here, especially for me."

"Will you be okay?" I asked, now picturing all the dangers inside a prison: assault, extortion, drugs, gangs and murder. All through his time at the provincial jail, he'd assured me he was safe. But he'd been in solitary there, whereas here he was part of the general population.

"Don't worry. I can look after myself. Please try to trust me and promise you won't worry about me."

I promised I would try.

Strangely, I felt deeply connected to Jason as we negotiated the emotional terms of our separation. Since finalizing our legal agreement, I hadn't wanted to discuss the prognosis of our marriage any further. We had to wait one year to qualify for a divorce, and I was relieved to put it off until it was absolutely necessary—until I could stomach the word. What I really wanted to do was avoid all decisions and have a nap instead. A long nap—for days and days. I was exhausted to my core.

The rest of our visiting day flew by, and at the end of it I returned to my parents' feeling bolstered by my visit but still highly stressed over the long list of things I needed to do before leaving for England a week later. One of the items on my list was to see Sue in Peterborough for an annual medical exam as well as a last counselling session.

On Monday, I went for my appointment. She found a lump

in my breast and sent me right to the hospital for an ultrasound. The ultrasound technician said she didn't like what she saw. She decided to do a mammogram. I was scared to death.

After the mammogram, a doctor informed me he could not make a diagnosis and that he was concerned. He booked an emergency MRI scan for two days later, the day before I was to fly out. He was very matter-of-fact, and told me that I should prepare myself to stay home from England if it was cancer. *Cancer.* I went numb. I began bargaining with a God I had only recently begun talking to, "Please, no! Not now . . . I will accept cancer at another time in my life but please, not now!"

I drove home to my parents' in a fog of fear. Two days later, the afternoon before I was to leave for England, my mum drove me back to the hospital in Peterborough for the MRI. Lying inside the body-sized scanner I hoped desperately that I was okay. A short time later, a doctor told me the lump was a mass of scar tissue (though I didn't know what from), and therefore benign. I was given a clean bill of health. I cried in relief and gratitude.

That night, my dad drove me to the Toronto airport where, exhausted, I got on a plane and headed toward my new life.

CHAPTER TWENTY-THREE

EXPLODING WITH ANGER

My mum came with me to England for the first two weeks to help me settle in, and to be my companion through Jason's birthday on September 24 and my birthday on the 26th. My dad would come over for a shorter holiday at the beginning of October and stay through my first wedding anniversary on the 8th before he and my mum went home together. By that time, we were certain, I'd be fine on my own, or better yet, I would have made a few friends. My sister planned to come over for a week to cover off the first anniversary of the crimes in November. My brother couldn't get away from work, but would be there when I came home for Christmas—another holiday to get through. My family rallied around me.

The university residence didn't open until our second week, so my mum and I stayed at a bed and breakfast in the centre of Norwich, got our bearings, and then went exploring in London and on a nostalgic trip to Shakespeare's land and the Cotswolds, where we had been on a mother–daughter adventure twenty years earlier. The beauty and history of the area offered moments of distraction and I tried my best to recall them in the long hours of the night when I tossed and turned, still unable to sleep for more than a couple of hours at a time.

As soon as residence opened, I moved into my room and waited nervously for the arrival of my roommate. Two days passed. Finally, on the third evening, I turned my key in the lock and pushed the heavy door—it opened with the extra ease of someone pulling it from the other side, and there she was, Grace Udodong. She opened her arms to hug me and introduced herself as a Nigerian, there to study International Development and Education. She was a teacher just like me.

"A Canadian teach-ah!" she exclaimed in her regal West African accent. "I can't believe it. I had a dream that my room-mate would be a Canadian!" I'd had a vision that my roomate would be from Africa. Grace opened up right away and told me that she was exhausted, jet-lagged and overcome by the grief she felt about leaving her eighteen-month-old daughter at home with her husband while she studied for a master's degree. She had not imagined the separation would be so painful. I tried to comfort her, wanting to say just how much I understood the agony of separation, but I wasn't ready to disclose the details of my own trauma just yet.

It wasn't hard to make new friends within the International Child Welfare program. There were just twelve students in total, and I found an easy connection with two in particular: Ana, from Surrey, England; and Vanessa, from Vancouver. Both had a lot of international experience and I was immediately impressed by the work they and our classmates had done with children all over the world. When classes started, we all hit the library, taking coffee breaks to discuss what we were learning. It was wonderful to have an outside focus, and I was glad a new social life was beginning to take shape for me. After we put away the books, we would chat away about fashion, travel and men.

I acted as though I were a single gal in my thirties, talking about old boyfriends or crushes I'd had before Jason. I didn't mention him. It was good to practise normalcy. We expanded our little trio and had a lot of fun hanging out with a large group of Mexican students. I soon realized that the film strip of violence that had played constantly in my head for close to a year was finally starting to slow down and even pause from time to time.

No one knew anything about me unless I told them, and that was a relief in most ways. I could walk freely around town and felt some release from social anxiety. At the same time, part of me felt suffocated—because I had to live with secrets, and that went against my character. I felt a need to be honest about my life in order to feel whole again, but to do so was always a risk.

One night Ana, Vanessa and I went to a pub, and while gossiping about cute guys we'd seen on campus, Vanessa asked if I was involved with anyone in Canada. I released my rehearsed answer: "I'm actually going through a separation from my husband right now." Vanessa and Ana seemed surprised, but both nodded understandingly without pressing for a single detail. They said I could talk about it whenever I wanted to. It was entirely up to me. That's when I decided to take the risk of trusting them.

A few days later, I chose a quiet spot on a bench down by the lake on campus, and let them know ahead of time that I wanted to tell them a little more about the situation with my husband. I started with how I'd met Jason, about coming to terms with his past, the development of our life together, our wedding day, and then the terrible day of the crimes. I described the limbo of the legal process currently underway. Ana and Vanessa listened intently, eyes turning glassy at several points, and when I finished, they put their arms around me. Vanessa was the first to speak.

"I'm so very sorry. Thank you for telling us."

And then Ana. "I'm so sorry too. It's so sad. You are very brave. We'll be here, and you can talk about this whenever you want."

I thanked them and exhaled deeply.

A little more confident after my experience with Ana and Vanessa, I decided to tell three more people: my roommate, Grace; my academic supervisor (in case I had to go back to Canada suddenly); and a counsellor. The three disclosures went well. People were compassionate and understanding. No one was attached to Jason, the community or the victims, so I didn't have to worry about caring for them.

I now found relief and joy in getting to know my new friends. It was comforting to be around a lot of people my age who were not married with children, and who were also far from home and their families. Most of all, it was good to have fun again. One afternoon, I got up the courage to ask a fellow student out. We walked around the city and then had a drink at a sidewalk café. It was nice to be out with a man just having a beer. We made plans to get together again and said goodbye before I headed into my residence, where I collapsed on my bed and cried. Suddenly, I missed Jason so much. I couldn't believe I had to go through dating again. My emotions were all messy inside.

Grace came into my room and patted my back.

"It's so hard, Grace," I sobbed.

"I can't even imagine, my dear. I can't even imagine."

—

My courses were demanding but I found I still had time to fill. Keeping busy was absolutely necessary for me. My student visa allowed me to work up to twenty hours per week, and having heard that Canadian qualifications were recognized in Britain, I had come prepared with all my teaching documents from home. Getting a job would help fill the time and replenish my dwindling bank account. I had my pick of schools, but the work was not easy—the students were often out of control and the schools rundown. Lesson plans were not provided for substitute teachers. My ace-in-the-hole was my accent, which got the attention of the kids for at least as long as I needed to take attendance. I bought a very cheap guitar to use as a snake-charming device. Singing to my students to calm them had been a failsafe strategy in Canada, and it worked in England too.

Even with new friends and a guitar for company, as well as frequent letters, e-mail messages and phone calls from home, I felt very lonely. I went out on a few more dates with the same guy, but felt no clearer about the experience. I longed for the built-in companionship and intimacy I'd had with Jason to be part of my life again. Not even sex, but intimacy—closeness and touch. Sex had become fearsome and distant to me. The prevailing associations I now had were of rape and violence, even though I had never physically experienced anything remotely similar in my life. I couldn't watch movies or television that involved sex or violence of any kind, save for the necessary parts of my studies related to sexual trauma and recovery. I had frequent, intrusive images of myself being raped and I worried that something was really wrong with me—something abnormal. By researching for my courses, I learned that these visualizations were actually symptomatic of a common post-trauma reaction called "survivor's guilt." I felt better knowing that within the intense abnormality of my situation I was having normal reactions. I was also comforted learning that people with post-traumatic stress can and do heal, as my doctor had said. Therapeutic treatment speeds up the process. Victimhood doesn't have to be a lifetime diagnosis. I assumed that having sex again, with someone I trusted, was probably a vital part of the healing process. I thought about the guy I'd gone out with, whom I'd now seen a few times. I wasn't at that point with him. I'd never slept with anyone with whom I was not in a serious relationship.

Meanwhile, Jason and I talked on the phone every week or ten days, and in our last conversation we had decided to apply for a PFV— a "Private Family Visit"—over the Christmas holidays, which were still two months away. The goal was to have a day to converse without being watched or recorded, and to have more than a few hours together to discuss all we needed to. Sex was not the objective. I could not picture this level of intimacy with Jason after what he'd done, nor did I want anyone to interpret a family-visit request as a commitment to staying married, though I felt a degree of pressure from people in the correctional system to make that decision. On more than one occasion when Jason was in the provincial jail, I had stood in the security line, other visitors within earshot, as guards posed their pointed question: "So, are ya still with him?"

I never dignified the question with an answer. It wasn't any of their business, and the question was ridiculously oversimplified. Sometimes I'd imagine myself replying with an inappropriate retort: "So, are you still with your wife?" Such an outburst would surely have blacklisted me from the visitors' list. I bottled my frustration. Now that Jason was in the federal system, and likely somewhere he would be for years, I hoped that making a private-visit application might open up communication and respectful dialogue with Jason's parole officer. She would be an important figure in his life for the foreseeable future.

On a scheduled weekly phone call at the end of October, Jason told me that our application for a Christmas PFV had been turned down. I was disappointed, but not surprised. I wondered if my desire to have just a one-day visit might not have been apparent in the application. Jason said his institutional parole officer, whom he'd finally met for the first time, had told him that I was welcome to call her if I had any questions. I decided to take her up on the offer.

I called and introduced myself. Then I sat in stunned silence as she launched into a lecture. She demanded that I understand how serious Jason's charges were, though in the same sentence she admitted that she didn't know what they all were herself. My throat growing hot, I kept my voice level as I explained I didn't need to be told how serious the situation was—that I understood more than most. I didn't get very far before I was interrupted. Jason and I wouldn't be allowed a conjugal visit for at least five years, she said. She went on to tell me that it was preposterous to have applied before Jason's court case was even settled. I tried to reassure her that we had not had any expectations and to explain that information and guidelines for visitors were scarce. She interrupted again.

"Well, I don't understand why Jason doesn't just admit his guilt and move this thing along!"

I was incredulous. "Jason called the police himself the night of the crimes and gave a full confession. He has *always* planned to plead guilty. The Crown's office is waiting for disclosure and records from Corrections."

"Oh, well," she huffed. "I haven't had time to look through all of his file."

Making every effort to stay calm, I suggested we could talk again after she had made herself aware of the whole situation. Then I disconnected. I would have loved to slam down the receiver but my cell phone didn't allow for that satisfaction.

I felt rage funnelling through me, filling me from my toes to scalp. I thought I might burst. I wanted to scream but I lived in a dormitory and was sure the police would be called. For the very first time in my life, I felt capable of violence myself. All the groundwork was laid for me to start down a path of destruction: anger, fear, victimization, stigma, humiliation, trauma, voicelessness and loss. I had to find a safe outlet for my rage. If I kept everything bottled up, it could blow at any time, taking over the person I'd always known myself to be. I realized that this was how the cycle of violence began and was perpetuated. I didn't want to become part of that cycle.

I reached for the tubes of paint on my desk. I grabbed black and red—the colours I saw in my mind. I pulled out a piece of white Bristol board and threw it on the floor. I chose a big, fat paintbrush from my jar. I knelt down on the carpet and squeezed paint out of the tube and then messed it about with the brush. It was ugly. It looked angry, but not angry enough. I had some glass from a framing shop under my bed that I'd planned to make into a pretty mosaic. I hauled it out, but I didn't have a hammer so I broke it with my bare hands and arranged the shards over the paint, gluing them down. It was anything but pretty, now.

I was breathless when I stood to look at what I'd created: a portrait of rage. I named it *Exploding with Anger,* then whispered to myself with absolute conviction, "I refuse this violence.

I will not succumb to it. And if there is anything I can do in my life to help other people live non-violently, I will."

That night, still stirred up, I went down to the train station to meet an old friend who was coming to visit me for a week. I instantly noticed the dynamic between us was different, and he confessed to having had feelings for me for years. I'd loved him as my friend, but now I wondered if things could be different. I saw in him a chance to escape. An hour later, we were in bed together. We fantasized about travelling, then buying a farm and settling down to raise a bunch of kids. The thought of having found a way out of the hell I was in swept away reason, clarity and good judgment. Grief gave way to fits of hysterical laughing and, however fleeting the feeling, I was happy and free, alight with the possibility of starting over with someone else.

When my friend left after a week, I felt in a daze. On the phone I told Jason what had happened and his first reaction was a sigh of relief. He said he was glad it was someone we both trusted and whom he believed genuinely cared about me. He said it hurt, but it was also okay.

A few days later, my friend called to say that he'd decided to stay in a relationship he was in previous to our encounter, even though he was unhappy. I was angry with myself for being so impulsive. Another relationship lost and more trust broken.

Before all this happened, I'd never understood the concept of self-forgiveness after victimization, because I could only think, *But it isn't the victim's fault!* Now I was starting to understand why self-forgiveness was so often a component of recovery: it wasn't so much about *fault* as it was about the unavoidable mistakes one made while fumbling for bearings in a world turned upside down. Trauma and victimization destroy the foundation of trust and security in life, and afterwards a person has to relearn how to walk with confidence. I felt like a toddler, falling down frequently and getting bumped and bruised. I was frustrated, and chastised myself for tripping. I could be very hard on myself. I had to learn to accept and care for myself as if I were a child, offering myself encouragement and a helping hand as I stumbled along.

As the holidays drew closer, I threw myself into preparing for my first big presentation at school, one that would be worth a hundred percent of the final mark in my child development course. I had chosen to investigate the effects on children of parent-to-parent homicide, learning that thousands of North American children each year become orphaned in this horrific way—one parent dead and the other in prison for life. I thought of my friend Dawn, whose partner had killed his ex-wife in front of their children. I decided to illustrate trauma theory using *Exploding with Anger* as a central piece and created several more works to exhibit along with it. I practised my presentation in front of Grace. I desperately wanted to succeed. Good marks equalled success. Success led to vindication. Vindication led to freedom. There was a lot riding on the hour I had in front of my professors and classmates.

The presentation went well, and a few days later, I received my mark and comments: the highest grade in that year's class and higher than any grade ever given in any other year. I felt proud of my achievement, relishing the first taste of what it could mean to do something for others in situations similar to mine and to gain my confidence back too. I imagined having a counselling practice one day or running an organization where I would welcome and offer support for people who were coping with the crime of a family member. I would never tell my clients, "Sorry, I can't help you. You don't fit."

Motivated for my next paper, I focused on what can be done to help child victims of crime. I gathered all the research materials I would need to take with me over the Christmas holidays. I had bought a ticket home and was looking forward to time with Jason, family and friends, though I had two papers to write while I was there. A few weeks earlier, Grace had told me that she couldn't be separated from her daughter any longer and that she was going home to Nigeria to get her. Since the university would not allow children in the residence, Grace had to find somewhere else to live and another friend had offered her a room off-campus. Not long ago I'd met a woman named Anne at a community gathering. Recent empty-nesters, she and her husband had a room to offer me. I loved the loft-room in their home and we quickly arranged for me to move my things in before Christmas so that I would be all set up when I returned in the New Year. I packed up all my belongings for a move out of residence.

In my now-empty room on campus, I said goodbye to Grace, and caught the early-morning bus to Gatwick airport where I boarded the plane bound for Toronto. Putting my head back on the seat and closing my bleary eyes, I wished I was on board a time machine and not just a plane. I wanted to go home and find that it had all been a mistake—that my old life still existed.

CHAPTER TWENTY-FOUR

RESTORATIVE JUSTICE

There was no mistake. Everything was the same as I'd left it: Jason was in prison; I didn't live in my house anymore; and enjoyment of the holiday season was nowhere to be found. Christmas had become a hurdle, not a celebration. My first day back, I went to see Jason after three months apart. When the door to the visiting area opened and Jason walked through, his face lit up and his arms opened wide. We held each other for a long time.

"You look good," I said, leaning back with my hands on his shoulders to look at him.

"I've been walking the track at night, so it must be the fresh air and exercise . . . and I'm happy to see you." The transfer to federal incarceration had been an improvement.

"I made it through the first semester, but I have my work cut out for me over the holidays: two papers due the day I get back, and then one more after that. Are you up for more editing?"

"Of course." Jason's correctional officer had suggested that while I was at school, I e-mail my papers to her so she could print them off and give them to Jason to edit. Jason had exceptional talent with language and he'd already helped me enormously with one paper. I asked him once where he'd learned to write. He shrugged and said, "I don't know. I guess I just read a lot." He was the same way with drawing and painting— little formal training but a natural capability for line, form and colour.

We walked over to a table and leaned in to talk while we held hands, both of us starving for contact. We talked about academics, life in England, my new friends, and how things were for Jason at the prison.

"Stable," he said. "There is a routine here, and I'm enjoying my job managing inmate accounts and placing orders in purchasing. It's the same job I had here years ago." His face sobered and his voice fell to a hush. "I can't believe I'm back here."

"Any word from your new lawyer?" Jason's application to change lawyers had been successful.

"There hasn't been any movement in any direction. She's still waiting for disclosure from the first lawyer."

It had been over a year since the crimes. Why was it taking so long?

"My new lawyer told me that a Crown attorney has only just been assigned," Jason explained. Then he asked, "How is everything in your . . . your personal life?"

"Rocky," I said.

Jason's eyes turned glassy. "No matter what happens, I want you to know that I love you." He squeezed my hands tightly in his. "But if it's too hard for you to see me, I will understand. I have to understand."

"I know that," I said. But I was not ready to stop seeing him, and I told him so.

"I don't want to stop seeing you either," he said, "but coming here, probably for years on end—this is no life for you. You have so much to offer the world, and I've taken so much from you. It would kill me if I kept you from having a full life."

I didn't want that for myself either. I just needed time to figure everything out. I felt as though I had to know the verdict, the final outcome of everything, before I could really move forward.

"I promise you, Jason," I said, "as I promise myself, that one day I will have a full and wonderful life."

Jason looked down. "Sometimes I think about that night . . . how the women tried to stop me from killing myself, and how the police came before I could go into the woods . . ." Jason's voice trailed off before picking up again. "And I have to believe that I'm alive for a reason—that maybe my life can still be worth something." He looked up and into my eyes.

"I believe that," I said confidently, "and I'm not the only one who does."

The rest of our visit went by quickly. I promised to return before I went back to England. We made plans to talk on the phone and do our editing that way. Then we hugged goodbye. I watched Jason go back through the doors to the inside world of the prison; then I made my way through security to the out-side world.

I spent the holidays at my parents' house madly writing the two papers that were due the day I got back to England. I was so focused on my work that my mum practically had to force tea and Christmas cookies down my throat and make me take a break. It was good to be looked after a little bit. In addition to my academic papers, I had two other important tasks to handle: an application (through the newly assigned Crown Attorney) for a publication ban on my name and the names of all the other voyeurism victims; and listing my house for sale with a real estate agent. My tenants' lease would run out in the spring and I'd decided I was ready to sell. The little bit of equity from the house could be put toward a place of my own wherever I ended up after finishing the master's program. If it couldn't sell, I would look for new tenants, or even consider living there again myself for a while. The future was cloudy.

When I went to visit Jason just before returning to England, he had something to tell me. "I've never told anybody before." He sounded nervous.

"You can tell me," I said.

"You know the example you gave in your paper of the boy in prison who was . . ." He paused and took a breath and seemed to look for the right words. " . . . attacked sexually by a group of other inmates?"

I nodded, feeling a tight ball forming in my stomach.

"That happened to me, when I was eighteen at the Ottawa detention centre in 1988."

I looked at his face, which had gone quite pale. I lowered my voice and checked to make sure no one was looking our way. "Oh God, Jason—you were gang-raped?"

Now Jason broke into a sweat. He wiped his forehead, then his eyes.

"I'm sorry—I shouldn't have said anything. I kept that secret for so long . . . I already wish I could take it back. It's the only one I had left."

Though horrified, I wasn't surprised at Jason's disclosure. Since I had learned about how he assaulted the first victim, I had held a suspicion that at some point Jason had been assaulted in the same way. I was more surprised in that moment that he wanted to take his secret back.

"Jason, no one should have to live with that kind of secret. I'm so, so sorry that it happened to you. What happened to the men who attacked you?"

"One was released, another was transferred, and the third, well, I guess without his henchmen he never tried anything like that again.

"Were the men charged, or brought to court?" I asked, doubtful.

"No, I never told anyone what happened—the transfer and release of the first two were coincidental. I was terrified, and I also thought that I deserved it—that maybe it was like payback for the life I'd taken."

I put my arm around Jason and tried to comfort him. Images of that awful scene were added to the film reel in my mind and it picked up again. Before this, I hadn't really thought about how our justice system works, or doesn't work, for offenders who become victims once inside the provincial or federal prison systems. This was but one example of the kind of violence perpetrated inside jails. I knew how my own experience of voicelessness, victimization and rejection had set a rage in me that made me feel violent and that I might have acted upon had I not chosen a safe outlet to vent my feelings. I could only imagine how these same emotions would be compounded inside a person who'd already been violent and was locked inside a prison without sufficient access to psychiatric help. The systems were called "correctional services," but did time in detention really reform offenders, or did it just make them even more capable of hurting others?

I returned to England at the beginning of January absolutely exhausted. The marks I received from first semester buoyed me a little and I settled back into life, happier with my new accommodations in a real home. It was also easier to get out to the schools to teach, and I kept very busy. My new friends introduced me to the game of squash, and in it I found a physical outlet for frustration. It felt good to hit the ball.

I returned from classes one day to find a letter from the Crown Attorney waiting for me. I opened it nervously, and then felt disappointment as I read that my request for a publication ban on my name and the names of the voyeurism victims had been denied. The charge of "mischief" under which the offences against us were listed did not warrant that kind of protection. I was asked to understand the public's right to an open administration of justice. I was angry that I didn't qualify and scared that once the case got moving again in the courts, details about what was on the videotapes and identities of the voyeurism victims would be published by the press. I already felt so vulnerable. The publication of my name and my association to Jason would open me to further condemnation, stigma and shame. What else would be taken from me?

I forwarded the letter to Jason's new lawyer, Connie, to ask if there was anything she could do. Though she was hired for the defence, she was the only person I felt I could talk to in the justice system. I had been rejected by police victims' services, and now by the Crown Attorney. The state—by way of the Queen—had a lawyer and the accused had a lawyer, but as a victim in a criminal case, I had no one. Connie said she would see if there was anything she could do, but she could only take instruction from her client and needed to act in his best interests. I told her I understood.

I threw myself into my school work and chose a research topic for my dissertation. I would investigate how a child's attachment to others is affected by witnessing or enduring violence, perpetrating crime, and being incarcerated. "Child" spanned an age range of zero to eighteen, and since the program was internationally focused, I would look at a global range of examples. I reviewed literature in the fields of psychology, social work, criminology and law, as well as numerous United Nations, government and non-government reports. What I read over and over was that there is a negative correlation between incarceration rates and recidivism rates for both children and adults all over the world. Prison does not work as a deterrent to offending or reoffending.

One of the overarching conclusions I drew was that if a society wants to make a pickpocketing boy into a killer and his sister into a prostitute, the best way is to put them in jail at an early age, allow them to be physically and sexually assaulted by bigger children or adults, deny them contact with anyone who might care about them, and take away opportunities for education. Then, once the child is grown, release him or her back to the community with no money, no ability to trust, no skills for getting a job, and no adults he or she can rely on. The same is true for adults.

I combed through government and non-government websites, finding documents containing alarming information. In Canada, despite the fact that our crime rate has declined by close to 20 percent since the late 1990s, incarceration rates have soared to an all-time high—keeping us below the U.S. rate but higher than those of Australia, France, Italy, Germany and Scandinavian countries. Global and local studies consistently show that community-based sentences for non-violent offenders (and sometimes violent offenders) are more successful in reducing recidivism. Yet, Canadian taxpayers now foot almost $2 billion per year to keep prisons operational while social programs—like education and health care, which serve to address the root causes of crime—are cut annually. Recent government proposals to build new and bigger prisons will cost Canadians an extra $100 million in capital expenses alone by 2011. Simultaneously, budgets for rehabilitative programming for inmates have been slashed. The institution where Jason was now incarcerated had at one time hosted some of the most effective treatment programs for sexual offenders in the country. Now that he was back there and in need of them—as were about four hundred other sex offenders—all of the programs had been cut. There was only one psychologist available to treat over six hundred men. Psychiatrists had been removed altogether.

Inside prison, offenders focus on protecting themselves and getting through each day. Without trust, therapeutic relationships, empathy-building education, or meaningful restitution, these convicts return to society with a decreased capability for safe and law-abiding social engagement, as well as a criminal record that closes many doors.

The truth is that most people serving time in Canada are going to get out of prison one day. Who do we want those people to be when they are released into our neighbourhoods? Jason was released the first time without having had any psychological treatment (he underwent assessments only), and though his behaviour over the fifteen years since he had committed a murder convinced all the professionals around him that he was safe, he really wasn't. We spend an average of $100,000 a year to keep one Canadian adult incarcerated, but precious few of those dollars are directed toward treatment programs. In fact, over 50 percent of the people being held in provincial jails have not yet been convicted, and 78 percent of all inmates (both federal and provincial, convicted and in remand) are non-violent, perhaps well-suited to the monitored, supportive housing and social programs provided in community-based sentences. These typically cost a quarter of what it takes to keep someone in lockup. A reallocation of resources—keeping prisons for serious violent offenders and providing meaningful rehabilitative programs for all offenders—would be a step in the right direction. Such an overhaul would also free up resources badly needed for victim support and restitution.

Reading about systems that continually fail both perpetrators and victims of crime was eye-opening but depressing. I wanted to find models that had worked somewhere. A couple of years earlier, in Peterborough, before the crimes, I'd signed up for an introductory workshop on "restorative justice." At the time, I was working mainly with homeless youth, 90 percent of whom were caught up in the criminal justice system. Their lives were characterized by relentless crises and there was scarcely a reliable adult to be found as a role model. I watched as, once they'd been charged with an offence, they moved further away from education and pro-social activities and closer to negative influences, punishment, and cycles of offending. Many of my students reported being victims of crime at one point or another, and I felt that they often hurt others because they'd been hurt themselves. Their lives were marked far more by injustice than justice. I registered for the workshop because I liked the sound of the word *restorative* and was determined to know more about its potential. Now I wanted to deepen my knowledge.

I learned that restorative justice aims to include all people who are affected by crime, and puts the focus on addressing victims' needs, offenders' accountability and empathy-building. In contrast to retributive justice—which focuses on punishment for the offender and tends to use victims' accounts toward conviction and sentencing—restorative justice takes a victim-centred approach that engages all parties in trying to move forward from the harm of crime, righting wrongs when possible, and putting meaningful restitution in place. It attempts to address the needs that harmful behaviour creates for the victims, the community and the offender. Often, after in-depth preparation, victims and offenders come together in a facilitated encounter in which victims have the opportunity to ask the perpetrator the questions to which only he or she has the answers: *Why did you do it? Why me? Are you sorry?* And many more. Participation in such a process is voluntary and can only begin when someone who has offended takes responsibility for his or her actions. There is no possibility for restorative justice where the offender denies causing harm.

Sometimes, once a victim has heard an apology from the perpetrator, that victim offers forgiveness. Though forgiveness is not an expected component of restorative justice, it may occur when the victim is satisfied that the offender fully understands the impact of his or her actions. Though reducing recidivism is not the main goal of restorative justice, statistics from victim–offender programs around the world consistently report significant drops in reoffence rates after participation. Victims report overwhelming satisfaction with their experiences and indicate that after the dialogue process they felt safer, validated, and more at peace. These results were even reported in cases of homicide, in which surviving family members participated in dialogue with the murderer. Nothing could ever be done to reverse such a crime, but some healing could be found in understanding what had happened and gaining some level of reassurance directly from the offender that it would never happen again.

I reflected on the way my ongoing relationship with Jason had taken shape. It was much like a restorative justice process, without any formal facilitation. It was helping me move forward and it was helping Jason be accountable. I wondered if the two assault victims would ever want the same opportunity. I couldn't be certain that they were aware that Jason planned to plead guilty. I hoped that with Connie on the case and with the assignment of a Crown attorney (finally), communication lines would open up.

I began to wonder if things could have been different for Jason if he'd engaged in a restorative justice process with his murder victim's family. Would he have fared better? What if the root causes of his violent behaviour had been uncovered and addressed in such a process—would his early childhood victimization ever have come to light and would his aggressors have been called to accountability?

I decided to do some more research for my thesis, discovering the work of Howard Zehr, an internationally renowned academic and practitioner in restorative justice, and a pioneer in victim–offender conferencing who served on the Victim Advisory Group of the U.S. Sentencing Commission. His writing, based on years of both research and practical work with victims and offenders, explained that whereas conventional justice—criminal justice—sees crime as an assault against the state and a breach of law, restorative justice views crime as an assault on relationships of trust. Therefore, "justice" is an attempt to restore—to recuperate, to recreate, to repair, or in some cases build for the first time—trust and safety within relationships. These relationships might be individual, or they might involve families, neighbours, or entire communities, depending on what harm was caused and who was affected.

Zehr explained that retributive criminal justice systems pose three main questions after crime:

- What law was broken?
- Who did it?
- What punishment does he or she deserve?

These questions place the offender and the state at the centre and relegate the victims to the periphery. That's not to say the questions aren't important—but once guilt is determined, then what? Incarceration only provides victims with the knowledge that the offender won't hurt them again—at least for as long as he or she is in prison. But what about when that person is released?

Zehr went on to describe how a restorative approach poses three different questions:

- Who was hurt?
- What are their needs?
- Whose obligation is it to address those needs?

As I researched in my quiet cubicle at the university library, I felt some hope. These were questions that would make a difference to everyone affected by crime. I thought about how things might be different for me and everyone affected by Jason's crimes (including Jason) if we had another kind of process besides the one barely moving through the court system, holding everyone in limbo.

So, how did restorative justice translate into practice? Was it an alternative to court, or could it run parallel to conventional processes? Was this approach softer or harder on crime? Did it lead to rehabilitation—and, therefore, a safer community for all? Upon further investigation, I learned that restorative justice included a variety of methodologies, such as victim–offender encounters, group conferencing, and circle meetings aimed at offering support and encouraging accountability—many stemming from Aboriginal models. The common feature of all these methods was the voluntary participation of victims and offenders in direct dialogue, nearly always face-to-face, about a specific offence or wrongdoing. The presence of a third party to serve as a facilitator was also integral to the process, as was in-depth advance preparation so that all involved parties knew what to expect. Victims and offenders were usually invited to bring support people to meetings.

The focus of the encounter generally involved naming and describing what happened, identifying its impact, and coming to some common understanding, often reaching agreement about how any resultant harm would be addressed. Application of restorative practices could take place at any point in the justice process, including pre-arrest, pre-court referral, pre-sentencing, post-sentencing and even during incarceration. In all cases where restorative justice was employed, there was an understanding that the harmful act couldn't be undone. In some cases, such as homicide and serious injury, the loss was absolutely irreversible—and so the process was designed to answer questions, to derive the whole truth, to help perpetrators make amends through meaningful restitution, and to help victims and surviving family members of victims move forward with the knowledge that the offender was remorseful and liable.

Plans for rehabilitation and engagement in pro-social living (whether inside an institution or in free society) were then put in place for the offender. Studies in numerous countries, including New Zealand, Australia, Brazil, Colombia, South Africa, Japan, the United States and Canada, showed various results in terms of recidivism, ranging from declining rates of 10 to 50 percent in some cases, and overwhelmingly positive statistics for victim satisfaction, averaging about 90 percent as compared to only 50 to 60 percent satisfied with a non-restorative court process.

Restorative justice has even been used in situations of state-wide harm: for instance, following the 1994 genocide of an estimated 800,000 Tutsis by their Hutu neighbours in Rwanda, justice officials realized that it would take over three hundred years to bring all the perpetrators to justice through a conventional court process, not to mention millions upon millions of dollars in legal fees. Without the time or the resources, the country turned to a restorative approach and offered a chance for freedom to convicts who were willing to own up to their offences. They had to apologize to their living victims and family survivors face-to-face, ask for forgiveness, vow to live peacefully, and then rebuild their victims' homes as restitution. Afterwards, they would be permitted to rebuild their own houses in the same community, the victims accepting them back and allowing them to live side by side. In less than fifteen years, Rwanda transformed itself from one of the most dangerous countries in Africa to one of the safest.

I remembered what Jason had told the police the night he was arrested: "Just put me away. My wife never has to see me again." In so many ways, never being confronted by any of his victims would have been easier. Shutting down and doing time like a robot was the way he'd gotten through his first sentence, and a lot of good that had done. It reminded me of when I was a kid—when I'd done something mean to one of my siblings, and I felt bad. I declared to my parents that I would stay in my room forever. I knew even then that locking myself away was easier than facing the people I'd hurt.

As interested as I was in the subject of restorative justice, I struggled to find and sustain the energy I needed to complete my thesis. Working in isolation was hard. I felt lonely and drained. The English weather reflected my mood. I faced the task of waking up each morning and planning how I would get through the day, blocking out sections of time with different activities to keep me distracted from the reality of my stress and sadness.

I thought a lot about what Howard Zehr and all the restorative justice experts said: *Crime is an assault on trust.* How could I regain trust when the justice system disregarded me as a victim? How could I get back the dignity of my profession? Would I be able to trust a potential partner enough to remarry and have a family? What about friends who had abandoned me? Would there ever be opportunities for restorative justice to help heal my wounds? I decided that once I finished my thesis, I would try to seek them out.

CHAPTER TWENTY-FIVE

THE WHEELS OF JUSTICE

There was no restorative justice to hope for in the immediate future. Instead, after handing in a draft of my dissertation at the end of April 2007, I returned home for Jason's criminal justice proceedings. On May 17, Jason was set to appear in Superior Court for the first time, where he was expected to plead guilty to all charges. I wanted to be close to my loved ones, including Jason, when the gavel came down. I booked a flight home.

Connie, Jason's lawyer, had finally received all of the documents from the first lawyer and was working diligently with the Crown to create an Agreed Statement of Fact, based on the original statements made by the two victims and Jason on the night of the assaults and kidnapping. This was the statement upon which the charges would rest, guilty pleas could be entered and convictions could be ruled. Connie was also working on how to achieve a publication ban that would protect the identities of all voyeurism victims, myself included.

I went to Kingston to see Connie. I wanted to know exactly where things would go from here. She began with the good news: she was almost finished preparing the statement with the Crown attorney. It would be ready by the next court date and it was possible that, if things went smoothly, Jason could be convicted that same day or shortly thereafter. Once convicted, the sentencing process would begin.

"And then what?" I asked.

Slowly and carefully, she gave her response. "You know that a dangerous offender designation means a sentence is indeterminate, and that there is a very good chance that Jason will meet the criteria. The reality is that very few dangerous offenders are ever released. Even if I am able to prove in sentencing hearings that Jason does not fit the D.O. profile, we are talking about incarceration for seventeen years at the absolute minimum. You also have to remember that, with his existing life sentence, there is no guarantee he would get parole after that sentence is served."

Seventeen years at the absolute minimum. Plus, I'd heard from other lawyers that D.O. hearings took months to years. I would be in my fifties, Jason would be almost sixty; many older friends and relatives would be dead. Though I'd heard it before, and in many ways was preparing for this reality, it was still impossible to conceptualize that length of time: decades to forever. There had been so much speculation and such varying opinions from professionals over the last year and a half about the time Jason would serve, some even saying "seven to ten years"—but now I returned to the gut feeling I had had in the hotel room the day the police officer notified me of Jason's crimes: that it was all over for him. Jason had squandered his second chance. There would not be another. When I left Connie's office, I felt as though I'd received a definite terminal prognosis. I spent five days grieving.

Jason called me. He had already spoken to Connie on the phone so he knew the situation.

"I'm sorry, Jason," I said. "She's not very optimistic."

"I know. I was expecting as much." He sounded sad, resigned. There was a brief silence. "I think I'm just going to accept the dangerous offender designation—not fight it. It's probably going to go ahead anyway, so at least I can save the victims the time and drain of a sentencing trial."

I was taken aback. Again, I recalled how he had told police on the night of the crimes, "Just put me away." I knew that Jason was dangerous and I believed in protecting society from anyone dangerous, but all of the Corrections staff I had spoken with told me that if he was declared a dangerous offender, he would find himself perpetually at the bottom of the list for psychiatric care: the category of least hope and lowest priority. He would suffer for years on end, and his family and friends would watch him, helpless.

"What you're telling me is that you want to be labelled a D.O. so they throw away the key. You have to give yourself a chance, and give all of us a chance to see you get help." I was desperate. I wasn't ready to just give up. "The time you spend in jail will be better served if you get to the bottom of what is wrong with you. Please don't throw even more away."

Jason listened but said nothing.

In further conversations, friends and family tried to reason with him. Eventually, he promised to consider what we were saying. In a later conversation with his cousin, a paralegal in a criminal law firm, he found out there would be a parade of expert witnesses and psychiatrists through a dangerous offender hearing. We all wondered if one of them would be someone who said there were treatment possibilities, who could glean some answers from an in-depth analysis, who believed that Jason wasn't a lost cause. Even if he was labelled a dangerous offender, at least he would have gone through a full assessment that might lead to treatment. Thus far, in the year and a half since he'd been incarcerated, he had spent only one hour with an assessing psychiatrist.

I suddenly remembered the caffeine and ephedra supplements that Jason took on the day of the crimes. His first lawyer had expressed little interest in this information, but I wondered if Connie would. She probably knew nothing about it. I wrote her a quick e-mail and she wrote back right away.

"We are going to look into this, Shannon. It's not nothing."

I felt a thin thread of hope. I relayed Jason's wish to waive the full sentencing protocol and not challenge the application for the D.O. label. I told Connie how concerned my family and I were about what this designation would mean in terms of his access to treatment. How could we allow Jason to accept the designation without a full sentencing hearing? We believed in him more than he did and we would help him through. Connie supported us, saying that she couldn't, in all good conscience, let a client take such a drastic measure. If he went through with it, to the best of our knowledge, Jason's admission of guilt and acceptance of the dangerous offender designation of his own volition would be a first in Canadian legal history. The only other case involving a decision not to contest the label—by Paul Bernardo—had happened under quite different circumstances: after months spent in a homicide trial that found him guilty of two counts of first-degree murder and sentenced him to Life-25, Bernardo still made no admission of regret, and his testimony at the trial served only to prove the public perception that he was remorseless—a cold-blooded rapist and killer. Finally, when he ran out of Legal Aid resources, he instructed his lawyer not to challenge the D.O. designation and a concession was signed and put on the table.

After much pleading from those who loved him, Jason reluctantly agreed to go along with our request that he not make such a decision at this time. For now, we would get through next week's hearing. Later, we would reconsider Jason's request.

I tried to distract myself from the looming court date by working on my thesis. I spent some time at my house in Peterborough, having taken it off the market. It had proven too difficult to arrange showings when I was overseas, and it was better to find some new tenants to pay my mortgage until I had a more definitive plan for my future. I was filled with anxiety about what might happen in court, especially about potentially meeting the victims for the first time. They were expected to be there. I tried to find comfort watching my garden make its return after the winter, the pink ballerina tulips rising up along the front walk.

When the court date arrived, my family took its team approach and united inside the courtroom. We sat together in a row: me, my parents, Jason's aunt and uncle, and a few friends. I waited nervously for the two women and their families to arrive, but they never did. As it turned out, nothing that day went as we had thought it would.

The night before, the first victim had submitted a statement to the Crown that made new allegations about the events on the day of Jason's crimes, overriding her original statement. The new information did not alter any of the charges but added details about the assaults (important later in sentencing) and revealed discrepancies between her version of events, Jason's and the second victim's. Jason did not admit to the new allegations, so the statement put together by Connie and the Crown was no longer agreed to. The process could not move forward and was adjourned until June 29.

Memory changes over time, especially when trauma is involved. I felt no blame or anger toward the victim for changing her account of the crime against her. But I was frustrated with the slow-moving legal process and how it seemed to be prolonging the situation for everyone. Jason had admitted his guilt and taken responsibility the very night of the crimes, yet there was still no resolution eighteen months later.

The only good news came at the end of that day. At Jason's request, Connie asked to have his mischief charge elevated to voyeurism, and it was. On that upgraded charge, my request for a publication ban on the names and identities of all the victims was granted by the judge. Connie had discovered that just one week after the crimes, the laws covering Jason's type of videotaping had changed. The offence now fit the category of sex crimes, giving it ban eligibility. Jason didn't care about any effect upgraded charges would have on him—he wanted to help protect me and the other victims he had videotaped. The reality was that all his other charges were so serious, a change in the most minor offence would barely affect the final sentence. I was still frustrated by the fact that I had to apply for a publication ban at all, wanting again to ask what value there was for anyone in releasing victims' identities to the press. Surely, an open justice process could still take place with this privacy ensured. Further, it was upsetting to see that there was a ranking system for who deserved protection by virtue of what crime had been committed. The universal experience of vulnerability seemed disregarded. And there was nothing to protect me from being identified as Jason's wife; my only protection came as a result

of being a victim of one of his offences. I still feared exposure—
I'd endured enough.

On June 29, the case was adjourned again. Then, on July 12,
Connie succeeded in convincing the court that a full psychiatric
assessment should be carried out to examine if Jason had had
a psychotic reaction to the supplements he took. He was
remanded as a patient-in-custody to the Mental Health Centre
in Penetanguishene (about 130 kilometres from Toronto) for
sixty days beginning in August, where he would undergo a bat-
tery of tests, including—as we understood it—those that would
examine his sensitivity to the caffeine-ephedra combo. What
confused me was that the assessment was called an "NCR" (Not
Criminally Responsible). In other words, Jason was being
assessed not first and foremost to determine what impact, if any,
the drugs may have had on his mental state the day of his crimes,
but to rule as to whether the impact of those drugs made him
not guilty. Neither Jason nor any of us close to him were looking for him to be exonerated, nor did we think he should be
even if the drugs *were* found to have had some influence on his
behaviour that day. Despite our concerns, there was nothing we
could do but trust the legal procedure that was unfolding and
hope that it would result in answers for the good of everyone.

That same day, the judge also ordered a "Gardiner Hearing,"
a "mini-trial" that involved testimony under oath given by the
two victims and Jason. After the testimony, the judge would
decide—beyond reasonable doubt—which details were indisputable facts and would comprise a Judge's Finding of Fact.
Dates for the hearing were set for six months down the road,
December 21 and 22. Jason asked Connie if it was an option
just to go along with the new details the victim had provided

so that the Gardiner Hearing wouldn't be necessary, but she said it was not possible. First, if Jason wanted to acknowledge in court things he told her hadn't happened, she could not be his lawyer anymore. Second, the statement of the second victim was still the same, so even if Jason changed his own statement, only two statements would match, not three. Third, if Jason admitted to a version of events that he didn't believe was true, he would have to maintain those lies through his whole sentence and any treatment he would ever have—and more secrets was the last thing Jason needed.

CHAPTER TWENTY-SIX

DANGEROUS OFFENDER

I went back to England one last time to meet with my professors, hand in my dissertation, and say goodbye to my friends. I returned from England for good at the beginning of September 2007, having earned my master's degree with distinction. Back in Canada, I faced a barrage of decisions: Where would I live? What would I do? How would I support myself? Before tackling any of these, I wanted to know about Jason's assessment, and I wanted to see him. I drove straight to Penetanguishene— about two hours north of my parents' home in Burlington—to visit him at the mental health care centre where he had been under assessment for over a month. I felt waves of disbelief as I drove in the laneway. How had life brought me to such a place?

The hospital looked like a prison, in that there was a security check and a big metal gate, but the guards at least seemed less intimidating. They asked which patient I was there to visit, not which inmate. I wasn't made to feel like a criminal or that there was something wrong with me for visiting one. The visiting room was welcoming and smelled like coffee. A radio was playing music. I hadn't heard any music in the same room with Jason for almost two years. When Jason came in, we sat down on one of the couches side by side. It was such a change from the bolted-down tables at the prison that for the first time in ages, I felt I could actually relax. We talked about England, about his mental state and about his assessment, which seemed to be moving fairly slowly. His living quarters weren't nearly as peaceful as the visiting area. He spent his time in a cell-like room, all white with bars instead of a door, on a ward where screaming and outbursts of mania constantly broke the brittle peace.

The following week, I went to stay at my mum's cousin's cottage—a ten-minute drive away—and visited Jason every day. During that second week, Jason and I attended a patient–visitor social, which felt completely surreal: it was the kind of event that we had so often been the ones to organize—me at schools and him at Martha's Table—but this time we were the clients. Someone approached us, mistaking us for staff. During the event, I watched other patients out of the corner of my eye, saddened to think so many of them would spend the rest of their lives in this setting. Everyone that I could see showed very obvious signs of severe mental illness and delusions; Jason didn't seem to "fit." Whatever was wrong with him, however severe, was not immediately visible.

I considered what people who didn't know Jason might think of him: he was a calculating and cunning predator who had fooled everyone around him until, thinking himself invincible, he had finally turned a twisted fantasy of rape and violence into reality. I'd heard this type of assessment drawn before, and I didn't like that it put anyone who knew and loved Jason into the category of fools. Neither did I like that this perspective ignored all the good contributions he had made and his efforts to make something of himself. His companionship in our relationship had been wonderful—he was thoughtful and kind, so much fun to be around, and a mule for household work of any kind. He made me gifts and recreated meals we had at restaurants, enjoying a feeling of success when he got just the right combination of spices. He designed logos and completed paintings for charity auctions. This part of him didn't fit the profile of a criminal mind. My view of Jason as more complex was not mine alone. It was shared by friends who had known him for a long time, and even professionals like Detective Morgan, his Peterborough parole officer, and several people at the federal institution where he'd spent the year (the same one in which he served his first sentence, during the nineties). Would his psychological assessment include only the negative? Would the assessing psychiatrist see all parts of him, not just the disturbed ones? He told me he had met with the lead psychiatrist only twice and he'd been at the facility for five weeks. There had been no mention of testing him for sensitivities to the drugs he'd taken on the day of the crimes. The psychiatrist simply had told him that it wasn't possible for the drugs he'd taken to cause an effect of violent psychosis.

As we waited for next steps, we enjoyed the hospital setting—such as it was—and the relative luxuries it brought: visiting hours from nine in the morning until nine at night, and the ability to bring in photos, books, clothing, food and art supplies. Our visits became a regular stream of show-and-tell. I relished the quiet time I found at the cottage, walking along the beach of Georgian Bay in the early mornings and late evenings. One day, Jason asked one of the social workers to buy a cake with his petty cash and had the baker write *Congratulations, Shanny* on it so we could celebrate the completion of my master's degree. A staff photographer took pictures.

Near the end of Jason's sixty-day remand, he was given a copy of the doctor's report. He brought it to the visiting room and we read it over together. There, in neat, black type, were three diagnoses: Sexual Sadism, Voyeurism, and a Personality Disorder Not Otherwise Specified (With Narcissistic Features). I felt my chest constrict.

"What does that mean: 'Personality Disorder Not Otherwise Specified'?" I asked. "Isn't that like saying, 'There is something wrong with you but we don't know what'?" We continued reading. The doctor's notes underscored Jason's lack of predictability, extreme behaviour, and sadistic sexual preferences as high-risk factors for reoffence. This made sense—it's what made him dangerous. He had exploded twice in his life—with devastating consequences each time. It had to be assumed that he was capable of hurting someone again if left to his own devices. He could not live in society as long as he posed this risk. Jason was looking down at the papers in his hands. The beautiful, healthy-looking man in front of me had just been diagnosed with devastating mental illnesses. He'd committed devastating violence. This cruel irony—that someone could look one way and still be so dangerous—was hard to grasp, but it couldn't be denied. I would never deny it. His put-together presentation was part of what made him such a high risk, as the doctor stated in the report.

What I wanted to know now was this: What plan would be put in place to treat these disorders? Even if Jason could never be released from prison, he could possibly have a healthier life inside. He could understand himself, and be released from the prison of mental illness by learning how to change his thought-patterns and cope with his many demons. Maybe something could be learned from him as a case study that could help others. In turn, that could save lives—lives of would-have-been victims and lives that would otherwise have been wasted in prison.

I remembered how the Toronto psychiatrist specializing in sexual deviance had said that many patients respond to a combination of psychotherapy and medication. I thought of how other doctors I'd spoken to were optimistic that Jason would be diagnosed with dissociative identity disorder (DID) and be a good candidate for treatments like cognitive behavioural therapy. He was smart, had support, and was a willing participant—three key factors affecting response to treatment. I turned back to the report to see what this doctor recommended.

"Mr. Staples should proceed through the justice system. Should any consideration be made for future release into the community, the only known potentially risk-reducing intervention is sex-drive-reducing medication (such as leuprolide acetate [Lupron]) for chemical castration."

Jason put his hand to his forehead. I quietly asked him if that meant what I thought it did. He nodded, fear in his eyes. He would be given mammoth doses of anti-androgen drugs designed to reduce sex drive, compulsive sexual fantasies, and capacity for sexual arousal. Unlike surgical castration, which removes the testes through an incision in the scrotum, chemical castration does not physically castrate and is generally considered reversible when treatment is discontinued—that is, if it doesn't kill the patient first. Side effects include loss of body hair, muscle mass, bone density; increase in body fat; the growth of mammary glands; high cholesterol; cardiovascular disease and osteoporosis. This was the doctor's only recommendation. It would do nothing to get at the psychological and emotional factors that led to his crimes. And what about the personality disorder:

where was the plan for addressing that? What about the caffeine and ephedra? What about a second opinion? The report ended with the declaration of Jason as Criminally Responsible. The doctor supported the Crown's application to have Jason labelled a dangerous offender.

I felt an instant rush of emotion: confusion, frustration and anger at a diagnosis that still seemed inconclusive but which came with a precise (and potentially lethal) prescription to treat just one aspect of the illness. I asked to speak with the psychiatrist, and with intervention on the part of a social worker, a meeting was reluctantly agreed to. My objective was to ask questions about Jason's diagnosis, treatment and prognosis, and to advocate for further assessment. Instead I was the one who was questioned by the psychiatrist—almost interrogated—not about Jason, but about me. What did I understand about addiction? Why did I think that a range of treatment that included therapy would be effective? Did I know how serious this was? I turned to look at the social worker, who was obviously horrified at how this was going. I felt like a criminal on trial in a case of mistaken identity.

I struggled yet again to find an outlet for my anger and helplessness. Connie was upset with the assessment and the recommendations, but the court would not approve a second assessment with another psychiatrist, even though I'd found someone who was world-renowned for his research and successful treatment of sex offenders and he had offered to assess Jason. Jason had already seen him once years ago and mentioned in recent laments that if only he'd been able to admit then that there was so much wrong with him, maybe everything would have turned out differently. Now it seemed it was too late.

CHAPTER TWENTY-SEVEN

FULL-TIME SELF-CARE

I was living in a landscape of broken dreams. As I tried to construct new ones, I found myself holding back with uncertainty. Now that I had my master's, I wanted to work in trauma recovery or restorative justice, but I was overwhelmed by the thought of having to market myself to potential employers. I had so many needs myself that I didn't know how I would work for someone else, yet my needs included an income and something meaningful to do, so I *had* to get a job. I also had to find another place to live. I had lived at four temporary addresses in the last year. I craved permanence but it was somewhere far in the distance.

While staying at my parents' house, I plugged in my laptop and browsed the Internet for jobs. I applied for a position at a children's mental health centre in Toronto, and was soon called for an interview. Driving into the city, I pictured myself living there. Before everything happened, I'd never thought of myself as a big-city dweller, but now the anonymity that living among a few million people offered was appealing. The position was in a treatment program for children ages six to twelve who had committed crimes (not criminally responsible because of their age, but on a trajectory for serious reoffending into adolescence if not provided substantial help). I was interviewed and offered the position. I wished I'd felt excited, but instead I was daunted. Taking it seemed like something I *should* do. I would figure out how to ask for days off for Jason's trial and for doctor's appointments later, and what I would say to protect my privacy. I accepted the job.

I viewed some apartments in different regions of the city but they all felt lonely. I narrowed my search to keep me close to my friend Lisa and her husband Peter, and to my siblings. I found a lovely unit in a 1930s walk-up with leaded glass windows, hardwood floors and a big bay window. I moved in and fought off melancholy as I unpacked my boxes. This was the "better time" I'd hoped for when I'd packed these things away, I told myself. But I still had a long way to go.

At my new job, I went through the motions—pretending to be my old self, but not feeling that way. I found it hard to get to know colleagues and maintain my privacy at the same time. My motto became "Fake it till you make it." Faking it worked for a while. I spent long hours at the office doing administrative work instead of the direct client work I'd been promised. My training period required me to spend several hours each week in a dark observation room watching through mirrored glass as clinicians worked with children and families. I felt isolated and out of place. After all the time I'd spent looking at Jason through glass I could not stand the experience of doing the same in this new job.

Looking for something that might engage me more than my new job, I found a training course called Strategies for Trauma Awareness and Resilience (STAR)—which included a unit on restorative justice—at the school where Howard Zehr taught, Eastern Mennonite University in Virginia. Six weeks later I launched into the program. Our group was small, with only six students. We established trust, safety and confidentiality through ice-breakers and activities that required incremental risk-taking. The first three days centred on trauma theory and recovery and we were taught in a participatory, experiential way. In bits and pieces, I started to disclose for the first time in a group setting what had happened in my life. It was hard, but it felt good, safe and meaningful. It was validating to be heard, and when others shared their stories, I found it a privilege to be listening. In my tent at a campground near the campus, I slept peacefully for the first time in two years.

One day at lunch, I sat with Kathy, a nurse and bereavement counsellor from Alaska. Recognizing much of my journey as being similar to that of a widow's, she asked me if I'd ever considered attending a bereavement group. The thought had indeed occurred to me, but I had always been quick to dismiss the idea, presuming I would be turned away: after all, the person I was grieving wasn't dead. I shared my thoughts with Kathy, also explaining the many times I'd been told (in one way or another) that I "didn't fit." She encouraged me to try to find a group anyway. She said that if I came to her as a bereavement counsellor and told her my story, she would never turn me away. She believed there were others in the field like her—I just had to find the right professionals.

During the last two days of the course, the focus shifted from trauma to restorative justice and the potential for healing it brought. We viewed a documentary that followed the journey of a victim–offender encounter. I watched as a young woman faced the man who had killed her mother, and as her grandmother faced the man who had killed her daughter. I recognized their questions as the same ones I had asked Jason: What happened? How could you do it? And, what do you feel now? I watched as the man cried and said he was sorry. I watched as the two women put their arms around him in the prison, and finally got the answers to questions they'd held for years. I watched as seeds of peace and healing were planted. The images and emotions hit so close to home that I could not stop crying for some time after it was over.

I recognized something in this experience of reconciliation, and I longed for it to occur in other relationships affected by Jason's crimes—ones that had been broken by anger, judgment and fear. Would it ever be possible for Jason and the two women he'd assaulted to one day come together in a facilitated victim–offender encounter? Would the women Jason had assaulted ever want to address him directly? I hoped someone supporting them now would let them know it was an option, if and when they were ready. I'd heard that there were victim–offender encounter programs in Canada they could access, and I knew Jason would enter into one if invited.

I still had a lot of my own wounds to address. Within the context of a small and trusting group, I came to understand that the problems I was facing in my new job were coming from the unresolved trauma of having my position as a guidance counsellor taken away, and having all those relationships with staff, students, parents and the community severed. I still sought answers and justice about this loss, and I wondered if I could engage in some kind of restorative process with my former principal and superintendent. I wanted to be able to trust and connect again. I wanted them to understand the negative impact their actions had had on me. On a broader level,

I wanted to stop that kind of treatment from happening to anyone else.

After the workshop, I met Howard Zehr in his office where I immediately understood why he is often referred to as "the grandfather of restorative justice." He was kind and approachable, as well as generous with his time. He listened for over an hour while I told him about everything that had happened to me. At the end, I asked him if he thought restorative justice would fit for me and if he knew where I could go for help in Canada. He gave me the name and contact information of one of his former grad students—Judah Oudshoorn—now working as a facilitator with Community Justice Initiatives (CJI) in Kitchener, an hour west of Toronto. I thanked him and made a motion to leave.

"Before you go, can I ask you something?" Howard said.

I was curious about what he wanted to know.

"Have you thought of writing a book about your experience? It's an important story to tell, and it would have meaning for many people—not just people in restorative justice."

Write a book? A wave of preemptive exhaustion flooded me. I was nowhere near emotionally ready for such a thing; I didn't have the time, and the thought of reliving the pain of the last two years as I put it all down on paper frightened me. On top of that, how could I write a book when I had no idea what the ending would be? The road ahead was still long and bleak. I shook my head.

"Well, maybe one day," Howard said, standing up. "I'll see you before too long, I'm sure." He smiled.

"I hope so," I said, smiling back.

That night, before leaving for home the next morning, I opened up the little notebook I had brought to the course—the

same one I had filled with my lists from the early days. "To Do
When I Get Back," I wrote. I put two items on the list:

- contact CJI about a restorative justice process with school
  board/principal
- find a bereavement group

I took a deep breath and added one more item:

- quit my new job?

CHAPTER TWENTY-EIGHT

"'MONSTER' APPEARS IN COURT"

A week later, I resigned. I went in at nine on a Monday morning to give two weeks' notice, but left at ten-thirty and never went back. There was nothing more for me to do there. Driving home, I felt a weight lift off my shoulders. At my apartment, I made coffee and got right to work organizing an office space. Then I started working full-time again— for myself.

I set up an appointment for early in the new year with Judah Oudshoorn and his co-worker, Jennifer Davies, at Community Justice Initiatives in Kitchener. Then I filled out an application to join a bereavement group. A couple of weeks later, I was interviewed by the group facilitators and we discussed the uniqueness of my situation. They decided that I was welcome to join a group that was starting in January, and they hoped that all the participants would be understanding. With some trepidation, I looked forward to the experience and the chance to explore and cope with the loss of my spouse as I also listened to others.

These two plans for the new year in place, I had to get ready for the next stage of Jason's court process: the Gardiner Hearing. It was almost December. At the hearing, the victims would be called to the stand to testify as to the events that had occurred two years earlier and most likely Jason would have to take the stand as well. All three would be cross-examined, a concept that filled me with dread. I hated the thought of the victims having to recount their hours of terror and then be questioned about them. I worried that it would harm them further. Connie assured me that she would go as easy as she could on them; indeed she did not relish the thought of pressing their painful memories for inaccuracies or inconsistencies, though it was her job.

All of us who planned to be there were also anxious about how Jason would react. With us he was honest, real and connected; in psychiatric, correctional and police reports he was frequently described as robotic and detached. If this was the only part of him that would show in court, how would anyone know that while guilty of horrible crimes, he wasn't a monster? The closer the dates got, the more tension I felt. The night before the hearing, I was restless and jumpy. I decided to bake muffins. Silly, but what else could I do? Dr. Sue had offered her art studio as a quiet place that my Golden Circle and I could retreat to during the midday recess, so I got some drinks ready and ordered some sandwiches to be delivered. Then I made a lunch for Connie too. She usually stayed with Jason in or near his courthouse cell during recesses and there was no food for her there. Jason was usually given a bagel from Tim Hortons.

Before I went to bed, I lit a candle, smouldered some sage in a bowl, and sat down on my bedroom floor. Since the night my mum and I had burned the sweetgrass in front of the courthouse, this had become my calming ritual. I thought about the victims and what they might be going through. I concentrated on sending them positive energy. I didn't know what it would feel like to see them for the first time after thinking about them every single day for two years. Would they or their families talk to me? Did they hate me and my family? Would they think we were on Jason's side? I hadn't seen Greg, the first victim's partner, since I'd run into him at court eighteen months ago. I reached my arms out to gather the smoky air and bring it toward me, rinsing it over my head, face and chest. *May I be at peace, may I be safe, may I know I am loved. May Jason, my family, my friends, the victims, their families, everyone in the courthouse . . . be at peace, be safe and know they are loved.*

I lay on the floor and looked up at the ceiling. Finally I moved to my bed where I closed my eyes and waited for sleep. It never came.

At six o'clock, my alarm sounded but I was already awake. I had a shower, drank a cup of coffee and put on my suit. A small bowl of yogourt calmed my churning stomach. At seven o'clock my parents picked me up and we drove to the courthouse in Peterborough with my brother and sister following us. Jason's aunt and uncle and some of our friends would meet us there. It would be the first time any of Jason's proceedings would be held in Superior Court, on a hill overlooking my old school. As we approached, I worried that members of the press or public would be waiting—for us or for others—but was relieved to find both the parking lot and the courthouse empty, save for one newspaper reporter. The courtroom itself was still locked, so a clerk showed us to a small waiting room next door. Opposite was what looked like another identical waiting room. Suddenly, that door opened and the victims' services counsellor who had declined to help me brushed past. My stomach clenched. In that room, the victims were probably waiting. I turned and went into our waiting room with the rest of my group. No one said much. We were all too tense.

A few minutes later, an official unlocked the courtroom doors and we all filed in. The courtroom was beautiful, a prime example of mid-nineteenth-century architecture, the space adorned with intricately carved, dark wooden seats for the jury, tables for the lawyers, and a raised table and throne-like bench for the judge. A gated railing led out from each side of the prisoner's box, which was in the centre of the room, separating the gallery from the stage of justice. Even the prisoner's box was decorated with thick, polished woodwork. The whole place oozed solemnity. I would have loved to see the court on a historic walking tour or a class field trip, but not as I was seeing it today.

We sat in the second row of the raised gallery in the middle section, about ten feet behind the prisoner's box, where Jason would sit. He would have his back to us; everyone would face the judge. The courtroom was huge, and we were far away from the lawyers and clerks, who occupied the space in the middle. The witness stand, below and to the judge's immediate left, looked small in the distance. The atmosphere for us up in the gallery was strained, but on the courtroom floor the professionals—lawyers, clerks and guards—seemed relaxed, even joking around with each other like one would in a normal workplace. It was surreal—like we were about to watch a tragic play—but the scenes about to unfold were very real.

People trickled into the courtroom. My senses were on high alert for the arrival of the victims. Connie arrived through a side door that led directly to the stage area. I got up and walked to the edge of the railing to greet her. When I was returning to my seat, I saw Greg, my former colleague, enter the courtroom. He came over and hugged me like he had in the lower courthouse eighteen months ago, but neither of us said anything. Then we took our seats on opposite sides of the gallery.

Several minutes later, more people—including two women—sat down where Greg was, across the aisle. I instantly knew they were the victims; they were the right ages, and their hair matched the descriptions I'd heard. I wanted to give them some kind of sign that would express my sympathy, but I couldn't think of an appropriate way to do that. Seeing them sparked an onslaught of emotion. On the one hand, it was a relief to know I could now recognize them if I ever saw them in town, but on the other hand, it was painful to attach faces to the abuse they'd experienced in Jason's hands. The film strip of violence began to reel through my mind again, but for the first time the cloudy shapes of two anonymous victims were replaced with exact identities: faces, hair, eyes, hands and mouths. They were regular women, just like me, with families who could have been mine. I felt sick to my stomach.

Moments later, Jason was led in by two Correctional Service guards. He was wearing a suit I'd delivered to the prison with the rest of the personal effects he'd been allowed to receive during the first thirty days after his transfer from provincial detention. The last time I'd seen him wearing that suit was at a post-wedding party my parents hosted for us three weeks before the crimes. He shuffled across the room in leg irons, his hands cuffed in front of him, his shoulders and head down. As he stepped into the prisoner's box, he looked up at us—his friends and family. We made eye contact and he gave a short, sombre nod. The guards positioned themselves on either side of Jason, just outside the wooden half-walls of the box.

Suddenly, there was shuffling at the front of the court as a clerk stood up and called, "Oyez, Oyez, Oyez! Anyone having business before the Queen's Justice of the Superior Court of Justice, attend now and you shall be heard. Long live the Queen." We stood up quickly, and then the judge strode in to take his place at the head of the court. The old-fashioned language made me feel as though I were in a historical re-enactment, only this was real, and I was very much in the present.

The proceedings began with the Crown bringing forward a request to expand the publication ban to include Jason's name, explaining to the judge that because I was widely known in Peterborough, the publication of Jason's name (even though it was different from mine) and the fact that I was married to him, could expose me to further stigma. He also asked that the ban include the exact address of my home, though by this time the street name had already been published numerous times as had a photo of my house on the first day. It was strange to hear the Crown speak on my behalf when he had never spoken to me before. The judge listened and then ruled that the publication ban be applied. I breathed a small sigh of relief, the last one I would breathe for the rest of the day. There was a newspaper reporter present in the courtroom who didn't seem very pleased with the ban.

Next, the charges were read and Jason pleaded guilty to them. I was confused by the procedure. It seemed out of order that the pleas came before the testimony—but there was no chance to ask for explanation.

The testimony of the victims began next. For the next few hours, I listened to their descriptions of the horror they had endured. Some of what they recounted happened in a different way than I'd originally been told by the police, and I tried to fit the new details together as best I could. I cried a lot and other times I just went numb. Hearing them describe Jason's assaults in their own voices lifted their typed names on reports into reality. Abstract memories I had from the time I went back to my house after the crimes were coming together with who the women were as individuals. Words I had read now had voices, intonation and emotion. I learned the exact source of a dark stain I had scrubbed out of my basement carpet after the crimes: dirt from the cellar of the store where the sexual assaults had taken place, ground into my floor as the women struggled to free themselves from the duct-tape bonds Jason had wrapped around them. While Jason was outside waiting for the rental van company, the first victim tried to make contact with the second by inching her tightly bound body toward where she'd heard him lay another body down. She wanted the woman to know that she wasn't alone, if she was still alive.

I had overwhelming feelings of wanting to comfort the victims, but I could not. I was frozen in my seat. I looked at Jason, who did not move at all during the women's testimony. He was staring straight ahead. As the women repeated the offensive and degrading things he'd said throughout the ordeal, my ears tried to put his voice to the words, but it was virtually impossible. I had rarely even heard Jason swear. I felt extremely angry with him then. I wanted to shake him, to jump out of my seat, take him by the shoulders and scream, *How could you? How could you say that? How could you do this? Who are you?* Fear of being thrown out of court was all that held me back.

Listening to the cross-examination angered me further. As she had promised, Connie did her best to go easy on the women, but her job was to point out discrepancies to the judge, who would later have to rule on what was fact and what wasn't. In strictly academic and legal terms, I could understand the purpose of the procedure, but on a moral and human level it looked not like justice but further victimization. By the end of the day's testimony, we were all drained and exhausted, but we still had another day to get through: a day that would include Jason's testimony.

After a second sleepless night, my family, friends and I returned to court in the morning. The women and their families did not attend that day, and when I saw what happened, I was glad for their sake they weren't present.

When Jason entered the courtroom, I could already tell he had detached and was absent from his body. He wore the same expression as on the voyeuristic videos he had taken and at his arraignment the day after the assaults. Order was called immediately so I couldn't approach him. It was just as we feared: on the stand, Jason was robotic and dissociated. He told the court that he was "a monster" and that he had "always been this way." When Connie asked him if anything had ever happened to him that might have contributed to his rage or deviancy, he said in a defensive and cocky tone, "We all have things in our childhood that affect how we are as adults." Connie was caught off guard. She made another attempt to urge him to present a broader and more complex picture of himself, asking him outright if he had suffered any abuse in his childhood or teenage years. Jason flat-out said no, he hadn't. I was enraged but I couldn't move. I wanted to yank him back, snap him out of whatever trance he seemed to be in. Later, I wished I had tried. Even if it had gotten me thrown out of the courtroom, it would have been worth it. It might have freed him from whatever power had taken hold in the moment.

Suddenly I understood why Jason had wanted to accept the dangerous offender designation without a sentencing trial: on some level, he must have known what he would be like in court. The newspaper reporter didn't have to stretch the facts too much to get a sensational headline for that evening's article. He just quoted Jason directly, writing "'Monster' Appears in Court." The purpose of the hearing had been to ascertain the facts. Though Jason had pleaded guilty, he wasn't yet convicted so there was no outcome to print yet. The judge had ordered a return to court in February, at which time he would rule on what was indisputable.

When I got back home that night, I was thankful for the sanctity and privacy of my apartment. It surprised me that it was still standing, since I barely was. The few Christmas decorations I had put up—glass ornaments hanging on dogwood branches in a vase—reflected the light from the streetlamps outside my window. I placed the stack of holiday greeting cards from my mailbox on the coffee table with my keys, took off my coat and lay down on the floor. I tried to still my mind but the film strip wouldn't stop. All the graphic testimony provided new images to illustrate my nightmares. My heart raced as I reviewed the horror of it all. Other images intertwined—the faces of the women, how they looked so small yet so brave up on the stand in that huge courtroom; how it felt when Greg hugged me and then we sat down on different sides of the gallery; how the judge looked at me so frequently and sternly, making me feel as though I were on trial too.

Jason called the next morning and I let him have it.

"How could you have acted like that!" I yelled into the phone. "How could you *lie* like that? After everything we've been through—after all the support you've been shown, how could you get up there and say you were a monster?"

There was silence on the other end. Then slowly and quietly Jason said, "I'm not sure what you mean."

"What?" I exclaimed. "You were cold, detached, and even cocky. I barely recognized you."

"I'm sorry . . . I don't really remember anything after I went into the room. I felt everyone staring at me and I . . . I felt panicked, and threatened. After that, it's all a blur. I don't remember what I said up on the stand, though I do remember being there."

I was flabbergasted. Was he telling the truth? I recalled him describing the day of the crimes and not being able to remember anything from the time before the first victim walked into the store, when he described feeling the same thing: panic and a sense of danger. I thought of his empty eyes in the voyeuristic videos he took, and his seemingly vacant body at the arraignment hearing the morning after the assaults. Were these reactions evidence of a true dissociative disorder—an ability to slip into worlds and personalities so separate that he couldn't remember them? Or was he making a conscious choice to avoid responsibility for his behaviour? I didn't know. I couldn't tell. I felt like giving up.

I remembered my choice to forgive Jason. Did it still stand? I was realizing that forgiveness was a decision I would have to revisit over and over. It was turning out to be a process, not a single act. Forgiveness neither erased nor diminished the magnitude of Jason's violence and its continuing ripple-effect. It didn't take away the anger, frustration or loss I felt about what he'd done, and it couldn't bring back the life I'd had with him. What forgiveness did do was remind me that there was a human being behind the violence, and that his heinous acts did not represent the sum of who he was. Forgiveness gave me the permission to see and know both aspects of Jason, to be enormously angry and pained by his violent acts, but also to let go of that anguish before it took complete control over my mind and heart. Forgiveness stopped rage from becoming resentment, and it released me from having every aspect of my character and the life I still had ahead from being bound to Jason's violence. Forgiveness put my life back into my own hands.

I decided to recommit to my choice, not so much for Jason, but for me.

Christmas Eve and Christmas Day were a solemn and sad blur, and by Christmas night I had begun to write a long e-mail, describing the past two days. I needed to record what had happened in court. I needed to clear my head, to "dump the harddrive." I needed to reach out to my friends, as well as to report to those who'd wanted to be in court but couldn't. I felt trapped by the legal process, but at the same time wasn't sure that if I stopped attending I would feel any better. I feared Jason being alone, too, in all this, if only because if the shoe were on the other foot, I wouldn't want to be left alone. I also felt that as a victim of an offence I needed to be remembered in the process, though having a voice in it seemed less and less probable. For all those reasons, I decided to continue through the court process until the sentencing.

I kept telling myself, "No way out but through," and I tried to envision some new happiness, some existence of joy, some profound sense of peace that would come in the future, some goodness as unimaginable to me as this horror and trauma had been. As sad as I felt, I had also heard myself laugh and even sing from time to time in the last two years. I had held new babies and seen flowers bloom through the snow. Examples of human compassion appeared with amazing consistency. I was making it through. Somehow, I was making it through.

CHAPTER TWENTY-NINE

HEALING JUSTICE

People, places, routines and rituals: this mantra of trauma recovery came back to me as I faced the start of another new year: 2008. My four cornerstones had been blown into a thousand pieces and I was still gathering the fragments. I needed to work hard to reconstruct the foundation for my life and keep it stable. My bereavement group began in mid-January and I found enormous comfort meeting weekly with others who accepted my loss as I accepted theirs. I finally had the time and space to grieve the loss of my husband and a way to meet my emotional needs. I also began to meet with Jenn and Judah, the restorative justice facilitators at CJI. They provided the opportunity for me to find an alternative track toward justice that could address the wider effect of Jason's crimes, including how my position at the school had been taken away. They agreed to help me see if I could meet with my former principal in restorative dialogue after some preparation. I wanted to start a conversation with her first, before including the superintendent, because we'd worked together on a daily basis. This addressed my need to right what I felt was a wrong

THE STRANGER INSIDE   287

done to me and peel back the suffocating blanket of stigma.

Next, to develop a meaningful daily routine, I got a short-term contract with Canadian Families and Corrections Network. My project was to research and make recommendations to the Correctional Service of Canada's new victims' services department on how to better and more fairly address the needs of all victims of crimes, including the families of offenders. I wrote a booklet designed to help these families directly. It was something I wished I'd been given.

To help make financial ends meet, I got a second job as a high school supply teacher. It fit my need for flexibility and I loved being around teenagers again, though I struggled to feel confident in a school environment. I could be a substitute teacher in England without inviting questions about my career. Now, back in Ontario, I didn't have answers to those questions. I'd resigned at the end of my leave from the Peterborough board because I could never work for them again having been treated as I was, and because I no longer felt safe living in Peterborough or one of the small outlying communities. I needed the anonymity a big city like Toronto offered. This choice left me to start my career in education over from the beginning, with no status or seniority. Staff I met at each different school I supplied at seemed to assume I was either an inexperienced new teacher, or that I was unable to get a "real" teaching position. I tried to just hold my head high—there was no shame in the work I was doing—but inside I was hurt, angry and frustrated. A voice inside me kept repeating, "You shouldn't be going through this." I struggled to keep resentment at bay.

Though I'd made a lot of positive changes and pushed open doors toward healing, I still felt heavy with sadness, worry and loss, and my muscles constantly ached. I feared the toll that

PTSD was taking on my body. I registered for salsa dancing lessons. I had to do something for my physical health—something that would give my mind a break from thinking, my muscles a chance to move, and an opportunity to practise having fun again. I dated occasionally, and even had a short-term relationship. I still felt mixed up, but I needed to start somewhere if I was to one day fulfill my dreams of having a partner and family.

On February 8, 2008, I returned to the courtroom with my family, Jason's aunt, uncle and cousin, and some supportive friends. Jason was brought in after us and placed in the prisoner's box. He acknowledged us. Then he sat down facing the judge, just like he had at the Gardiner Hearing in December. On the phone the night before, I had begged him to stay "real" and not slip into detachment. I suggested he try to make eye contact with us or with Connie if he felt panic or threat rising. He was not expected to take the stand for any purpose, which alleviated some of my anxiety. There was no sign of his two assault victims or their families. The gallery was empty save for us and the same newspaper reporter.

Unbeknownst to me, the first order of the day was to address the publication ban yet again. The reporter had come to present his arguments to the judge for having the publication ban narrowed, arguing that a ban on Jason's name was unfair to the public's right to observe an open legal process. I immediately felt scared and vulnerable. I sat voiceless in the gallery as the young reporter spoke up about my life, my privacy, and the privacy of all other victims. I heard the judge, the lawyers and the reporter discuss "the wife of the accused" as if I weren't there at all. I wanted to wave my arms and say, "HEY!

I'm right here! I'm the one you're talking about! Why don't you ask *me*?"

Sitting there in court, I didn't know how to fix the problems I was seeing, how to ensure a fair and equal trial for accused persons, and to recognize and address the harm caused to all victims. It was complicated and the philosophical questions overwhelmed me: Why did the state and the accused have lawyers assigned automatically but victims didn't? Why was the system focused so much on the offender often at the exclusion of those affected? I didn't think victims should be given the responsibility of punishing an offender—a system used in feudal times—but why weren't they at least asked about their own needs and what would help them recover?

The judge ruled that Jason's name could once again be published, but the ban on the names and identifying features of any victims, as well as my street address, would still be protected.

After the ruling, I listened nervously for three hours as the lawyers reviewed all the details from the Gardiner Hearing testimony and entered their submissions to the judge for his consideration on what would be deemed indisputable, resulting in a Judge's Finding of Fact. Jason sat in the prisoner's box, unmoving. I heard someone start to cry behind me on the other side of the gallery. When I turned around, I saw that it was the first victim. She was all alone. It was awful. She had to hear everything again and then listen to the defence attempt to prove that she was "unreliable" as a witness, because some of her account no longer matched her original statement. I thought about what to do. Should I go over to her? What could I say? Would contact from me make her feel threatened or more vulnerable? Would she see me as her enemy? I didn't know, but I decided to take the chance.

A few minutes later, a recess was called. I stood up and walked over to where she sat, pausing at the end of the row. She looked up at me and I mouthed the words *Is it okay?* and motioned to ask if I could approach. We held each other's gaze for a moment. Her eyes seemed to speak so many emotions: fear, anxiety, sadness and surprise. I waited at the end of the row for another moment until she nodded, through tears. I walked slowly toward her and sat on the edge of a seat, leaving one space between us.

"Please," I said. "Can I do anything for you? Would you like some water?" It was all I could think of.

"No, thank you." She sniffed and blotted her eyes with a tissue, shaking her head and looking back at me.

Then I said it. I said what I had been holding inside for two long and painful years. "I want to tell you that we are all extremely sorry for what happened." I motioned to where my family was sitting and looking at us with anticipation. Her eyes took it all in and then returned to meet mine. "We think you are very brave." She nodded, and began weeping again. I paused for a moment, unsure as to whether I could or should say more. She brushed her hair off her forehead, still looking at me. I trusted that meant it would be okay for me to continue.

"We want you to know that we are here for you too, and, well . . ." I struggled to find the right words. "I know it might seem strange, but if you don't want to be alone, you can come and sit with us."

She nodded again and said, "Thank you. I'll . . . I'll be okay. It's okay."

I stood up slowly and walked back to the end of the row, turning left and heading out through the courtroom doors instead of back toward my family. I rushed down the big oak staircase to the bathrooms on the main floor where I began to sob. A minute later, my sister pushed open the door and reached out to put her arms around me. There was nothing to say. After a few minutes, I splashed some cold water on my face and we walked back up to the courtroom. The woman had left, and she did not come back. I was very worried about her, but there was nothing I could do but hope I had done the right thing.

The proceedings continued until lunch, and then again afterwards until about four o'clock. At the end, the judge ruled, on all but one detail, in favour of the victims' combined accounts. Jason was convicted on all the charges. It was the pronouncement we'd been expecting for over two years, and it brought relief. I hoped his conviction would give the victims some sense of justice, though I worried about what lay ahead for them in sentencing hearings. Would they have to testify again in front of expert panels? A return court date was set for two weeks later. At that time, the Crown would formally begin the process of applying to have Jason labelled a dangerous offender, for which he would first have to seek the approval of the Attorney General. One phase of the legal process was finished, and another was about to begin.

On my long drive back to Toronto, I thought not so much about the conviction or the next stage of sentencing, but about my encounter with the victim. There was no way that I could be certain my words had the effect on her that I had hoped they would: to assure her that our support of Jason as a human being was not at the exclusion of our concern for her and the other victim.

I wondered if the two women and I would ever have the chance to talk—if we might even help each other—under the right circumstances. I had recently met a man named Bud Welch at a conference Howard Zehr had invited me to attend. Bud's twenty-one-year-old daughter was killed in the Oklahoma City bombing and he had found a healing opportunity in meeting the father of Timothy McVeigh, the bomber who received the death penalty for his crimes. Bud said when he met the senior Mr. McVeigh and realized that he was also a father who had lost his child, there was no separation between them. They were bound by their grief and they cried together. To them, the death penalty had only brought more loss, not justice. Connection and compassion were what healed.

Purple shamrocks were sitting on the sill of my bedroom window, and as I opened my eyes the morning after the trial, I saw the blossoms had unfurled. Little pink flowers had bloomed the day before while we were all in court, while Jason was being convicted. Life went on, no matter what.

The phone rang and I rushed to answer. It was Jason. He said, "I want to accept the dangerous offender designation. I'm sure of it. Please let me." He believed that fighting the dangerous offender designation would make it appear that he was not taking full responsibility for his crimes, as if he were denying or minimizing what he had done. Jason knew that he was dangerous and he didn't ever want to be released until he could be safe. Despite my fears about what this would mean for his psychiatric health, I couldn't argue with his decision: it was the right thing to do on a moral level and one of the only ways that Jason had the opportunity to do the right thing after so many wrongs. I had to accept that what would happen to him thereafter was completely out of my control, as was my ability to reverse his actions or to have prevented them in the first place. The best I could do was uncurl my fingers, release my grip. It was the hardest thing for me to do; I was the closest to him and my grip was the tightest.

Connie also had to understand Jason's point of view on the matter and come to terms with the idea of allowing her client to accept the country's highest sentence without a fight. She had seen him in court and knew first-hand how he became hostile to his own defence; her chances of beating the dangerous offender designation were slim. "Success" took on a different meaning in this case: it would come by carving out a path for dignity and responsibility and not through achievement of a lesser sentence. There would be a different kind of justice in that. Connie understood this. Expanding the usual role of a defence attorney and listening to the needs of her client's family, she arranged a time when a few of us (Jason, his aunt and uncle, my mum and me) could meet with her at the prison and discuss the best way to proceed into the sentencing process—"best" meaning what we could all live with.

Prison rules did not normally allow an inmate to visit with family and professionals at the same time, but with Connie advocating, someone decided to make an exception. We met in the afternoon on the day before Jason's next court date (at which a date would be set for the sentencing hearing to begin) and sat in a tight circle around one of the small, square tables bolted to the floor in the prison visiting room. Mercy was upon us and no other visitors were there, though there were guards in the glassed-in observation area at the other end of the room.

Connie talked us through the papers she had prepared at Jason's request. She said she didn't know if the judge would accept them—there was no exact precedent for an offender not to contest a D.O. application, only the Bernardo example. We were solemn as we looked over the papers, but also surprised to learn that Jason, like all dangerous offenders, would have the right to go before the Parole Board of Canada seven years after the date he became incarcerated and then every two years after that. We had never heard this before. While we knew that less than one percent of dangerous offenders ever achieved parole—and we never wanted Jason to be paroled as long as he posed a threat—we still found a shred of hope in at least knowing that Jason's progress would be evaluated at intervals. Perhaps upcoming parole hearings would give him an opportunity to ask for treatment. Jason insisted that no matter what happened, he would work hard to get to the bottom of what was wrong with him. He promised us that he would not simply "shut down" while in prison. We held his hands, and one another's. His aunt Joan broke down beside him and he put his arm around her. Then he loosened his other hand from mine and reached forward for Connie's pen. He signed the papers instructing her not to fight the Crown's application for him to be labelled a dangerous offender.

Connie submitted the papers in court the following week, where a date was set for Jason's sentencing: May 15, 2008. I had two and a half months to prepare myself.

CHAPTER THIRTY

VICTIM IMPACT

I've heard it said that "Justice and power must be brought together, so that whatever is just may be powerful, and whatever is powerful may be just." It was with this in mind that in the early spring, I decided, after many preparation meetings, that I was finally ready to try to meet with my former principal in restorative dialogue. I had recently read an article about her in the Ontario College of Teachers' magazine where she was hailed as a leader in school-based restorative justice, so I was optimistic she would accept an invitation to dialogue. I was soon disappointed. My request, made via the facilitators, was turned down. My principal told them she didn't see any need for restorative justice in this situation. I wrote her a letter to explain my position and again asked her to meet with me.

My focus then shifted back to the criminal justice process and the ominous date of Jason's sentencing. Barring something unforeseeable, Jason would be declared a dangerous offender on May 15.

Detective Morgan asked me if I planned to give a Victim Impact Statement. "What you went through needs to be known and this could be your only chance to tell your story." My restorative justice facilitators said the same thing. I took their thoughts into careful consideration and discussed it with my family. It had hurt me so much to be voiceless, to be rejected and stigmatized over crimes I had nothing to do with, to be misunderstood and judged, to be betrayed by my husband and then abandoned by the systems that had once encouraged our union. I decided I would make a statement. I had the right to make a statement by virtue of the fact that I was a victim of voyeurism, but that offence was only one aspect of how I'd been victimized. I could use the opportunity to also give voice to my experience as the wife of an offender.

I honed in on the word *impact* and set to work writing a statement that would explain the multitude of ways Jason's crimes, and the fallout from them, had affected me. I would express how much my family and I were concerned about the victims. I would explain to the Crown attorney and the victims' services counsellor how it felt to be ignored and polarized, and I would let the press know what it felt like to be at their mercy. I would explain to the judge that my employers' treatment of me, and their decision to remove me from the school, made me feel I was guilty by association and I hoped that he or someone in the justice system would do something to right the wrong. I wanted to go on record saying that I rejected Jason's actions but that I did not reject him as a human being, and that it was my hope that he would be supported during his time in prison so that he could be held meaningfully accountable for what he did. I would argue that it wasn't fair to those who loved him to let him rot. He owed a debt to society but that payback was useless if it was time served idly. Though I had said all of this to Jason before, it was important that he hear it in a court of law. I would stand up for the kind of justice that was important to me.

Writing my statement was incredibly difficult. I was over-whelmed almost to the point of panic. It was stressful to be articulate in such a formal way and also to try to describe every-thing that had taken place in the aftermath of Jason's crimes. There were many pages. I sent my statement to Detective Morgan, who encouraged me to keep going and not hold back. When I finished, I called the Crown attorney to let him know I would be exercising my right to make a statement. It was through his office that victim impact statements were vetted. As another victim of voyeurism, my mum had decided that she would make a statement as well in the same vein as mine.

I wanted to meet with the Crown attorney before the hear-ings, so we set a time for the late afternoon on the day before sentencing. My goal was to make sure he explained to Jason's assault victims that in order to tell my story honestly, my state-ment began with a description of Jason in the way that I knew him before he'd committed these crimes. I wanted them to know that in no way was sharing my experience meant to discount theirs, nor was it meant to suggest that Jason's crimes were anything short of heinous. I wanted the victims to have the chance to decide for themselves if they wanted to be in the room when Mum and I read our statements. I asked Detective Morgan to join our meeting.

We met at the Crown's office in Peterborough. The Crown attorney was dressed in a regular business suit instead of robes and was sitting down behind a desk instead of towering at the front of the courtroom. I instantly felt less intimidated. Though I wouldn't say he was particularly warm, he did devote himself to listening to me and my mum for close to an hour. I felt able to explain myself and was assured that the victims would be prepared for our statements.

"I must say," the Crown said, "it is surprising to hear most of this. I assumed that you must not understand the gravity of the offences to be so supportive of Jason, and I did not realize that he had ever expressed the remorse that you just described. I've never talked to him myself, other than during the cross-examination at the Gardiner Hearing. I had no idea that Jason wanted to plead guilty until about six or eight months ago."

We were simply astonished. How could the Crown not know that Jason had *always* intended to plead guilty? I glanced over at Detective Morgan, who looked as baffled as we were. I recalled that at least a year passed before the Crown had even been assigned. I imagined he had a heavy workload. I wondered if there was a systemic problem that would explain the communication breakdown.

Soon after, we stood up to leave and the Crown attorney put his hand out to shake mine. Then he moved toward the door, reaching in front of me to open it. The next time I saw him would be in court the next morning. After that, I would probably never see him again. I had one more thing I wanted to say.

"All those times we saw you in court, you never talked to us or even looked at us. Except for the letter turning down the publication ban request, we never heard from your office, even though we were victims on your list."

"You know, you could have approached me at any time," he replied.

I looked up at him, way up. The courtroom was his domain, not mine. I mustered my courage. "Sir, I'm afraid you're wrong," I said. "It is you who should have approached us."

He looked down at me. He paused, and then said, "You're right, and I'm sorry."

They were powerful words—words I never thought I would hear from him. He was taking responsibility for his mistaken conclusions and for ignoring me—and by extension my family, Jason's family, and our friends. In that moment, I felt respect and a temporary release from the confines of false assumptions. I hoped his change in attitude wasn't too late to affect what was left of the court process.

"Thank you for that," I said. "We'll see you tomorrow."

CHAPTER THIRTY-ONE

THE SENTENCING

On May 15, 2008, I woke up and didn't know where I was. My sleep had been plagued with nightmares and now my pyjamas were soaked through with sweat. I tried to orient myself. I saw my mum stirring in the bed next to mine and I remembered we were in a hotel close to the courtroom, the same hotel where out-of-town guests had stayed during my wedding two and a half years earlier. I got out of bed and showered. My fingers felt numb a short while later as I buttoned the jacket of my suit and put the pages of my statement in a folder. How would I feel at the end of this day?

At eight-thirty, my mum and I drove the short distance to the courthouse where we were met in the parking lot by my dad, my brother and sister, Jason's aunt Joan and uncle Dave, his cousin, and our friend Brian from Kingston. We saw the Correctional Service van pull in, and we solemnly waved to Jason though we could see only a dim outline of him through the tinted windows. How would he act in court today? We'd spoken about this day, and initially, Jason said he didn't want to make a statement at all. He said he didn't deserve to take up any more of anyone's time, but I impressed upon him that making a statement wasn't about him receiving anything—it was about offering to others. It was the least that he could do.

Jason worried that whatever he said, whatever kind of apology he could offer, would sound trite or cliché. I responded that it was a chance he would have to take and that if his remorse and pain were authentic, they would be felt. He decided to go through with it. He worked on his statement for weeks. I hoped that he'd have the courage to read it today and that it might serve some good to the victims. Maybe, too, whatever newspaper article was written would finally tell the public of his remorse. To this point, it had still never even been reported by the media that Jason had called the police himself on the night of the crimes—a fact that might have helped an onlooker understand why I or anyone else would even consider communicating with him.

I watched the tinted windows of the van and saw Jason raise both his hands, cuffed together, and give a little wave back. The van stopped and the officers helped him out while we stood at a distance. He looked over at us and nodded, mouthing the words, *Thank you. Thank you.* I was relieved. So far, he was still the Jason I knew.

We made our way through the courthouse and up the big oak-railed staircase to the criminal courtroom on the second floor. As we took our place in the gallery behind the prisoner's box, a few more friends joined us. The newspaper reporter sat just a few seats away from us. Shortly thereafter, the two victims arrived with several family members and support people. They sat on the other side of the aisle. Altogether, there were about twenty-five people in the expansive gallery.

The atmosphere was tense. I tried to breathe as deeply as I

could. I looked out the courtroom window—I could see the trees in the park, the fountain where, as a Trent student, and later as a teacher, I had met with other women for our annual "Take Back the Night" march, and the rooftop of the high school where I'd worked. Not far away was the venue where Jason and I had had our wedding reception and the store where the crimes took place. Just two kilometres east was my house. This had once been my community, my home.

Jason was brought in by guards and he shuffled to the prisoner's box in his leg irons. He looked up at us briefly, then sat facing the judge, his back to us. I glanced over to where the victims sat with their families and friends and noticed a young man who appeared to be the boyfriend of the second victim. His clenched fists and jaw, and the way he stared at Jason, showed enormous—and understandable—anger. I saw that the guards were watching him. I averted my eyes and looked for my former colleague Greg. I couldn't see him anywhere. The lawyers came in wearing their black robes and white collars: Connie took her place at a table to the front and left of the prisoner's box, and the Crown attorney took his place at a table to the front-right. He nodded at me and I nodded back, our first courtroom salutation. Detective Morgan sat at a table inside the gated area next to the Crown. Everything felt solemn and theatrical like it had at the Gardiner Hearing.

The judge's clerk rose and called the court to order. We rose. The judge entered and sat down, facing Jason and all of us behind him in the gallery. It was hard to see the judge, and as we sat down and the lawyers began speaking, I had to strain to hear because they were facing him and therefore had their backs to us. Even when the judge spoke, it was hard to hear. The microphones barely made a difference in the huge courtroom.

I was the first to be called to read my victim impact statement. I walked up to the stand, took my oath and sat down in the witness box. Now the judge was behind me, over my right shoulder. It felt awkward to read my statement to him with my back turned. At least I was facing in the direction of everyone else I hoped to address. I could see Jason fairly well, and the lawyers, but everyone in the gallery—my family and friends, the victims and their supporters—seemed far away.

The registrar asked me to begin by stating and spelling my name for the record. "Shannon Moroney," I said, and spelled it out.

The registrar thanked me.

"Is it Ms. or Mrs. Moroney?" the Crown asked, standing up and taking a few strides toward me.

"Ms.," I said.

"Ms. Staples?"

What? I was confused. He knew I hadn't taken Jason's name. I had just spelled my name out. What was he trying to do? What had happened to the understanding we'd come to yesterday afternoon? It felt like I was about to be cross-examined rather than give a victim impact statement.

"It's Ms. *Moroney*," I repeated as clearly as I could. I was getting more nervous.

The Crown asked me to begin reading. My voice sounded small in the huge courtroom. Not long into my statement, as I talked about the wonderful life I had had with Jason, the first victim left the courtroom in tears. Had the Crown prepared her as I had asked him to? I paused, but the Crown nodded for me to keep going. As I began to describe the events of November 8, 2005, and how a police officer arrived at my hotel room door to inform me my husband had committed assaults the afternoon before, I could hear several people crying. I swallowed hard. I had to get through this.

About two-thirds of the way through my statement, the judge interrupted me and announced we would be taking a recess. Had I said something wrong? Why was I being cut off? The Crown attorney ushered me off the stand, back through the wooden gate toward the gallery. Out of the corner of my eye, I saw the second victim stand and push her way through the row where she sat with her family, out to the aisle, and then rush toward me. I felt a flash of fear until I saw her tears and a look of deep concern in her eyes. There was no trace of anger or animosity. Reaching me, she opened her arms and I stepped into an embrace that was one of the most meaningful of my life. We held each other for a moment there in the middle of the courtroom. Then we let our arms drop so we could step back and look one another in the eye, still grasping each other at the elbows. We both began talking at once.

She said, "It makes me so angry to hear how you have been treated. I want you to know I have never thought you were responsible for any of this."

I could barely hold back my tears. I looked at this woman— this could-have-been sister or friend. I had thought about her every day for two and a half years. I told her so, asking how she was and if there was anything I could do.

"I want you to know that I don't hate Jason," she said firmly.

With the truth of my whole heart, I responded, "It's okay with me if you do—you can hate him."

I had no expectations for her to react a certain way toward Jason. I knew what it felt like for people to demand a response. She explained how hard it was to feel pressure to hate when it wasn't what she felt. I knew this feeling too. We continued talking for several minutes right there in the courtroom aisle. I was only vaguely aware of people watching. Later, my mum told me the guards had turned around, alert to her approach, but when they saw us embrace they became still, perhaps in disbelief. The rest of my family and friends watched in hope and fear. Jason later told me he saw our embrace while being led from the prisoner's box to the exit for the duration of the recess. He described getting back to the holding cell, putting his head in his hands, and weeping. He was ashamed that his violence and trauma had caused our lives to intersect. He hoped the encounter taking place was a positive one.

When I left the courtroom, my chest felt as though it was going to burst. I went to the bathroom and cried alone in a stall, tears of relief falling onto the marble floor. When I came out to splash some water on my face, my sister, mum and friends were there to check that I was all right. I was. They each hugged me and then we went back upstairs to the courtroom—the recess would soon be over. I made sure my statement papers were in order and waited to be called back to the stand.

We were all surprised when court was called to order and a different judge breezed into the room, robes flowing behind him. He took his place. He looked just like our previous judge, only he had a thick moustache. My brother whispered, "Wow, that was a really long recess!" It was the only moment in the long day that offered any levity.

As it turned out, an entirely different case was about to be heard. It was supposed to be over quickly, at which point Jason's case would continue. Instead, for close to half an hour we listened to the proceedings as an emotional young woman pleaded guilty to a host of offences related to her involvement in an accident that killed her father. It was hard to listen to her testimony but we were trapped. Connie turned to us and mouthed, *I'm sorry! I didn't know.* I tried to tune out what I was hearing. There's no way I would have chosen to sit through that case if I'd had advance notice.

Finally the judges switched back and I was called to resume my statement. This time, I could see that the second victim was looking at me with encouragement. She nodded vigorously when I described how painful it was to endure the press coverage and the bad treatment I'd been shown by the victims' services counsellor. I felt a sense of solidarity with this woman in the gallery, a woman I'd thought about so often, and I was deeply grateful for her tacit support. Her strength bolstered mine. The other victim was also present and the people close to her whispered and shook their heads. I feared that they were not pleased with what I had to say.

Close to the end of my statement, I showed the judge the collage I had made so many months before at my doctor's suggestion—the one I called *The Shattering.* I stood up in the witness box and turned to face the judge. The bailiff held the heavy frame up next to me and the judge turned his chair so he could face it directly. He studied it intently for what seemed like several minutes, as though trying to read and understand every symbol. When he finished, he entered a colour photocopy of the piece, which I had provided, into evidence as a numbered exhibit, and the bailiff put the original down to rest against the witness box. I sat back down and concluded my statement.

I put everything I had into my statement—all thirty months of suffering, and every hope, every plea for some way forward. I wasn't prepared for the emptiness that ensued, the utter silence that followed until the Crown said a clinical "Thank you" and told me I could step down. I don't know what I had expected, but I hadn't expected *nothing*. The air felt cold. I walked back to my seat in the gallery, where I broke down in tears. For what reason had I just made this enormous effort and exposed myself?

My mum took the stand next. There she was, my beautiful mother describing the horrific experiences she had endured—reading aloud in almost the same voice she used to read stories to kindergarten students. This shouldn't have happened to her. It shouldn't have happened to anyone. What my parents faced resembled what I had: some friendships sustained the impact of what happened while others came to a painful end. Instead of knitting baby booties for an expected grandchild, my mum found herself in courtrooms, prisons and police stations. She described the day she and my dad accompanied me to the police station when we were first informed of the assaults: "I couldn't believe what we were hearing—the sickening and unspeakable details of crimes that Jason, *our Jason*, had committed. . . . This couldn't be happening to me, to us, to our family, to my dear daughter. Her husband couldn't have done these terrible things to not one, but two innocent women. . . . In court, I am desperate to comfort my daughter who is, I can see, tortured with pain. But my own pain is so severe that I can do nothing but wipe our tears." At the end of her statement, my mum bravely denounced Jason's actions and then declared her love and support for him, saying she would always consider him her "son-in-love." Her statement was entered into the court record and a lunch break was called.

When court resumed, the second victim was summoned to read her statement. Her voice was strong and clear, and she looked at Jason directly several times as she described how her life had been impacted by his crimes against her. She said she still didn't feel safe in many circumstances. She spoke about how hard it had been on her family, and how difficult it was to face the expectation to hate Jason when instead her overwhelming feelings were of sadness and loss of trust. She said her experience had at times isolated her from her friends. She felt pressure to do something extraordinary with her life or to be very accomplished since she had survived a near-death experience, but she wasn't able to focus on anything and didn't know her life's meaning. She described the moment before she lost consciousness as Jason was choking her, saying that was when her heart broke. She said she just could not believe that someone would want to hurt her. "Whether I lived or died was literally in his hands."

Next it was time to hear the first victim's statement. She outlined much of her physical pain and ongoing problems related to the assaults. Because of the way in which Jason had assaulted her, she'd had to take anti-AIDS and STI (Sexually Transmitted Infection) medication until his tests came back negative. The side-effects made her sick. She was tested several times herself and for months was constantly afraid for her health, even for her life. She endured significant financial loss and was not yet able to work full-time. She said she was afraid to be alone with male clients at work and that she had not taken any new ones since this happened. She said she never felt safe, not even in her own home. While recovering from her assault, her brother and mother had died. She described feeling robbed of the time she would have had with them. She described how she felt that the chance for an intimate relationship, which she would welcome at this point in her life, had been destroyed. I concluded that her relationship with my former colleague, Greg, had ended. During her statement, she did not look at Jason. I cried the whole time she spoke, and when she finished, the court was silent except for the sound of sobbing. Like all the other statements, hers hung in the air until the Crown thanked her and the judge told her to step down.

Next the Crown attorney made his submissions of support for the dangerous offender designation. I found much of what he said to be almost impossible to follow since it was so heavily laden with legal terminology and references to precedent.

The Crown read from Jason's psychiatric assessments. Jason was described as deviant, sadistic, controlling, narcissistic, charming (in a cunning way), and someone who "takes pride in fooling others." There were some graphic details about Jason's sexual "paraphilias." He said, with respect to my statement and my mum's, that Jason had people in his life with whom he shared significant connection and who should have known him the best, yet the depth of our shock indicated that Jason was still unable to disclose his private demons—even to the people he trusted most. It was hard to hear—I wasn't sure if he was blaming us for not having drawn out those demons or if he was blaming Jason. After the judgment and scrutiny I'd endured over the last two and a half years, I was very sensitive to any allegations that we should have known he was a danger.

When he finished his submissions, the Crown surprised us with his final words on the matter: "If there is any hope in this present situation, it is Mr. Staples' expressed willingness to say, 'I can't trust myself. I want to plead guilty, and I want to try and shorten the length of time these victims have to deal with the situation' and that is very much to Mr. Staples' credit. . . . There are bright spots with respect to Mr. Staples and it's about time he started to focus on those and realize he is an intelligent individual, he is capable of relating to others in a socially appropriate manner. His biggest prison is that within his head. He thinks he's essentially evil. He thinks he's essentially a monster, and he has committed monstrous crimes. . . . And as long as he continues to think that he is not intelligent enough or resourceful enough to actually open up and sincerely want to change—that means indicating that all of his offences are motivated by exactly what they're motivated for; discussing his problems in a sincere fashion with those that may be able to help him in the correctional system. Until he's able to do that and deal with those issues in his life, he's not likely to be able to realize that his essential essence may be good as opposed to bad, that he may be able to control his behaviour. At this point in time, Your Honour, he can't. . . . Mr. Staples is very resourceful and it's my fervent wish that he apply those resources while incarcerated in a socially appropriate manner."

I was completely blown away by the Crown's closing words. It was the kind of fair and just statement that I'd hoped to hear from my justice system, never expecting to hear it from someone who up until now had seemed an antagonist. I was extremely grateful for the conversation we'd had the previous afternoon. Without it, maybe he would have presented a portrait of an offender who was nothing more than the monster he had once described himself to be in that very courtroom.

Next Connie entered her submissions, which included a booklet of eighteen letters of support written by me, my family, Jason's family, and several friends and former co-workers. The letters attested to the fact that Jason was not a one-dimensional person, not a monster, and that he was loved whether he could believe it or not. All of the letters expressed extreme regret over Jason's heinous acts. The other submissions were several samples of Jason's artwork, as well as a couple of photos of him as a child and some more recent photos of him. We wanted the judge to know that he was a human being—there was no attempt to appeal for anything beyond that. We wanted this evidence in Jason's file for when he would one day—we desperately hoped—meet with a psychologist or psychiatrist in a treatment program. Then Connie submitted Jason's request not to contest the dangerous offender designation.

The last submission would be Jason's statement.

When Jason was called, he stood up and tried to turn around to face us and the victims, but he was told to face the judge. I was filled with anxiety, fearful that he would be overcome by the Blackness, incapable of showing his authentic remorse. He began to read. He struggled to get out his words, pausing frequently as he addressed the victims first: "I am so sorry for the pain I caused you. I can't expect you to believe me, let alone forgive me; but I still hope you will hear me when I tell you how filled I am with shame and remorse for what I did to you. It sickens me to remember the brutality of my actions that day. You were both very brave. I, on the other hand, was a demented coward who failed to see you as human beings until it was too late, until I had already put you through hell. Despite what I did, you both showed not only courage, but compassion as well. After assaulting you physically and sexually, after kidnapping and terrorizing you, and after putting you both in fear for your lives, you still showed incredible humanity in trying to convince me not to take my own."

I wondered how the women and their families were reacting to this. It would have invaded their privacy if I'd turned to look at them, so I didn't.

Then Jason surprised everyone by speaking about his first crime, the murder he'd committed at the age of eighteen, describing his shame at not addressing the victim's sisters at the time, and how he hated himself, shutting down emotionally while in prison for all those years. I could hear soft sobbing in the courtroom, and noticed one of the police officers wipe his eyes. I felt deep sadness, and also some relief. This was the Jason that I knew.

He continued. "In 1998, when I began [my] return to the community in earnest, I was amazed at the opportunities which presented themselves. I began to meet many good people and they welcomed me into their lives. I was introduced into strong and caring communities, first in the city of Kingston and then here in Peterborough. Some of the work I was fortunate to become involved in seemed to make a real difference in people's lives, and as I became more and more a part of it, I began to feel my own sense of worth and purpose increase and wash over old perceptions. The love that entered my life seemed to keep pace with this new way of seeing myself, and in 2003, I met Shannon. She opened up a window for me to the kind of values, family and friendships I had either long since forgotten or had only dreamt of or idealized. Because Shannon was never a closed person, or comfortable with secrets, and because she felt it was the right thing to do, over time I revealed my history to her family and many of her friends. At first, I was very anxious about such exposure, but I wanted to live up to Shannon's trust by placing my own in her and those she cared about. As all of these people came to accept me, despite what I had done, I felt some of my fears and reservations begin to lift away, replaced by a deep desire to be a part of something more special than I had ever known. It was a sense that seemed to grow with each passing day.

"Yet, as all of this was happening, as my life became increasingly surrounded by warmth and acceptance, I also began to pull away from it. In secrecy and in time away from Shannon or the responsibilities of work I would engage in twisted fantasy—separations from healthy reality which I further fuelled with video games, pornography, even sites showcasing the most brutal horrors of crime, war and gruesome violence. Eventually, and as a last escalation and disconnection before attacking [the victims], I crossed the line to secretly capturing the private moments of people known and even dear to me for my own sick gratification." He continued for several more minutes, describing his deviant behaviour and self-disgust in detail.

As he neared the end of his statement, he said, "As I try to come to terms with who I am and the pain I have caused, I struggle to both take responsibility and understand how I could be this way. Since Shannon and many of our family and friends first visited me after my arrest, I have begun to reveal the harmful things I experienced from a very early age. These are memories that I have struggled with in the aftermath for my entire life. However, I am at all times conscious of the fact that many people in the world have suffered in similar ways themselves and do *not* take their pain out on others. This leaves me with a keen awareness that I have no possible excuse or justification for what I've done. The only reason I have revealed the things I have is because I believe I owe it to those who want or need to understand and because maybe one day I'll be able to comprehend as well. I cannot and will not shut down as I did before."

The judge and all the court officials stared intently at him—perhaps they had not heard such a statement from an offender before. The sobbing around me seemed to subside as everyone strained to hear each word. Every muscle in my body was frozen with tension as my eyes fixed on the sliver of Jason's profile I could see. Scribbling notes at his table, the Crown attorney was the only person who didn't look at him as he spoke, but he was the one who passed Jason some tissues. Trying to hold his papers with his hands cuffed together, he awkwardly tried to wipe his eyes. Then he finished his statement.

"Even after what I took from Shannon—her husband, the dreams of family and a shared future, her good work in the community, a life of promise, not stigma and judgment—even after all this and more, she hasn't abandoned me, nor have my in-laws, my aunt and uncle, cousins and friends, some of whom are here today. These people continue to offer me guidance and support, and I am constantly amazed at their love and more grateful than I could ever express that it could be mine after what I've done."

In closing, Jason explained his reason for accepting the dangerous offender designation. "I never wanted to prolong this process for [the victims], their families, their friends, and my own. I can only hope that in accepting the designation of dangerous offender, I can offer some small amount of peace to the people I've harmed. By fully accepting my responsibility for these terrible offences, I hope and pray for all possible peace and safety to return to those I so cruelly took these precious rights from."

As the judge thanked him, gave his statement a number for the court record, and called a recess, I heard the sobbing around me resume and soon realized some of the sounds were coming from me. Jason was taken back to a cell, and in the gallery, my family, my friends and I clung to one another. I wanted to embrace Jason, just to hold onto him for a moment. I was proud of him for being authentic and responsible, but I was also completely devastated. We all were. It felt like a funeral, but the person we were mourning was still alive.

About forty-five minutes later, Jason was brought back in. We composed ourselves and rose as order was called. The judge entered and took his place. He reviewed the facts and then made a statement about the strength of the victims. He noted the incredible compassion and humanity they showed as they tried to convince Jason not to take his own life that night, even as their lives were in his hands. He said the case was "remarkable" in this way, and also in the support shown to Jason by his wife, family and friends. He said that Jason was talented and intelligent, but that he had a great capacity to fool people, to enact violence, to lack empathy and to be unpredictable. He declared Jason a dangerous offender, sentencing him to an "indeterminate period in a penitentiary" for the offences that qualified for the designation and suspended sentences for the lesser crimes of mischief, voyeurism and threatening death. He also applied a lifetime firearms prohibition, an order to surrender a DNA sample to the national databank, and a lifetime order on the sexual offenders' registry.

Jason bowed his head.

There was no gavel. The judge finished his statement and then the clerk said, "All rise!" We stood and the clerk declared that the Queen's court was adjourned.

The guards moved to take Jason out, but I rushed to the front and asked one of them if we could have a moment with him while he was still in the prisoner's box. Our families had followed me down from the gallery. They stood right behind me. The guard paused, looked at us, and then said, "All right—but just a minute."

Jason turned around in his handcuffs and leg chains and looked at all of us with tears in his eyes. We said, "Jason, we love you. We are proud of you." He told us he loved us too.

We could not hug him and he could not hug us. Then the guards took him away.

There was nothing to do then but go home. As I turned toward the doors, I noticed that the victims had already left. I wondered what they were feeling. I wondered if I would ever see them again.

It was almost six o'clock. We were all exhausted, drained and sad as we made our way to the parking lot where we stood in a semicircle, debriefing the proceedings for a few minutes. Connie arrived, towing big boxes of Jason's files on a little cart behind her. I hugged her and thanked her. She was truly amazing. I sensed it had been an emotional journey for her too.

Some friends and family said goodbye and got into their cars. My mum, dad, brother, sister and I were the last in the parking lot, along with Detective Morgan. We made small talk, but I was distracted. Standing in the lingering daylight, I felt as though we were still waiting for something . . . or for someone.

A few minutes later, Jason was led out of the courthouse by the two courtroom guards and escorted to a van in the parking lot. As he passed us, he raised his shackled hands and gave a little wave. We waved back. Then we watched as he got into the van and was driven away to prison. The words of one of Jason's friends ran through my mind as I watched the van disappear: *What a waste. What a waste of a life.*

CHAPTER THIRTY-TWO

LETTING GO

J ason was taken back to the institution where the sentencing papers would be processed and some kind of plan
would be made for his incarceration. At some point, he
would be sent to Kingston Penitentiary for security classification, and then his final destination would be determined.
We had no idea if that process would begin right away, or in
typical prison time—weeks to months. Jason's correctional
officer had already said she would do her best to keep him
where he was, in his medium-security "mother institution."
There, at least, were a few people who cared about him. With
their advocacy, maybe he wouldn't get lost in the system.

Jason called the next morning and we spoke to each other
softly, the way one would to someone who's just been told they
have a terminal illness. But because we were facing prison, and
not a hospice centre, there were no "comfort measures" to
request. In fact, things could still get worse: Jason could be sent
to maximum security, or somewhere even farther away. He
asked me about my encounter with the second victim, and I
told him how positive it had been. I could hear the relief in his

317

voice as he said, "Thank God for that, at least." He asked how everyone else was, saying he would try to check in with each person who'd been there in court. I asked how he was and he said he didn't know—he felt numb. I did too. Before I hung up, I said I'd be up to visit on the weekend. Jason said, "Only if it's right for you." Then we said goodbye. I looked at the blossoms on the tree outside my window and felt something inside me fall away.

Everyone around me seemed to expect that I would feel relieved that the court process was over, but instead, I felt drained and empty. The survival adrenaline that kept me going through so much of the turmoil had run out. The sentencing hearings had revealed so much pain and loss. Yet, at the end of two and a half years, it didn't feel to me like justice was served. Instead, it seemed like all that happened was one person was sent to prison for the rest of his life and everyone else was just sent home.

I heard back from my principal via the human resources department at my former school board. She had forwarded them my second request for her to engage in a restorative justice process. The HR letter—sent to my restorative justice facilitators at CJI—said it was not in my former principal's best interest to participate due to the supervisory nature of her position. Any future contact I wished to make should be directed to them. I was angry and frustrated—rejected again.

I supply taught until the school year ended in June, and then I sank into my most feared of all states: depression. I felt lethargic, listless and lost—as though I were approaching the edge of a cliff and about to fall off it. Going to visit Jason at the prison now involved facing the hard fact that this was really his life now, and it would be my life too, if I didn't try harder to loosen the bond that had held us close throughout the whole legal process. Though our relationship had undergone some drastic changes, the truth was that in some ways I still loved Jason like my husband. How does one transform love from romantic to platonic? How could I dissolve the bond I held? I was sure it would involve going through with a divorce. With this looming finality on my mind, many nights I lay in bed too sad to sleep. Realizing this only made me sadder. I hadn't fully come to terms with the definiteness of Jason's sentence, or the absolute end of our marriage. I still needed more time.

Meanwhile, life kept piling on more stress. My mum had emergency eye surgery and needed caring for at the same time as my rapidly aging grandparents needed help moving. Then my grandmother died. Then Una stopped responding to cancer treatment and was given "days to weeks." I'd brought her to see Jason before his sentencing, the radiation in her body causing the alarms to go off at the security check, but she would not be well enough to see him again for a goodbye. He would not be allowed to go and see her. Instead he painted a portrait of her, which I delivered. I took a picture of her with the portrait and sent it to Jason. They said goodbye on the phone. She went into hospice just a few days later. I tried my best to support her family and Jason as we prepared for her death, but my own sadness was crippling. I drove back and forth between Toronto, Kingston and the prison as much as I could, but the high fuel prices that summer only added to my worries. I felt stretched in every aspect of my life, and I feared I would finally snap. The odometer on my car told me that I had driven thirty-five thousand kilometres in the ten months since I'd bought it after returning from England. Where had I driven to? Prisons, hospitals, courthouses, and lawyer's offices. I just drove and drove and drove, but where was I really going?

I just wanted someone to look after me for a change. Someone to make me lunch, pay some of the bills, do something with. Someone with whom I could do nothing at all. I felt annoyed at books and media messages prompting me to enjoy solitude. When alone, my heart hurt so much I was surprised it kept beating. I couldn't see a positive future for myself, and nothing comforted me, except my visits with friends. I would wait out the hours of the day, slowly and mechanically completing mundane tasks, breaking from them to lie down on the floor and cry. I tried positive self-talk: *You'll feel better tomorrow, or the day after. You felt better two Mondays ago, and for a few days in April.* Often, the only thing that worked was looking at my recovery as a math equation, counting good days to convince myself that things were getting better. But there were a lot of dark days.

Una died at the beginning of August after being in a coma for three days. Before she lost consciousness, she held my hand in hers, told me she loved me, and gave me one last piece of sage advice: "You must try not to take on other people's burdens so much. You need to look after yourself and try to find happiness again. You are a young woman with so much ahead of you."

She was right. I had to get started. It was up to me.

PART 4

REBUILDING

CHAPTER THIRTY-THREE

FINDING MY VOICE

One of my friends believes there are no accidents in life—that seemingly chance encounters at "just the right time" are really blessings that lead us to our life's purpose. Other people believe "everything happens for a reason," which to me seems too cruel. I think some things are just absolutely senseless—like Jason's violence. Life didn't have to lead him there, but it did.

Summer was drawing to a close and so was my tolerance of my depression. Now, I needed to draw something good from the senselessness. At the end of August, just before I was set to begin another school year as a supply teacher, I was invited to present my master's thesis at a conference called "Restorative Justice: Humanizing the Criminal Justice Process" in Oaxaca, Mexico. There were experts from all over the world attending—but it didn't seem that anyone would be speaking directly from personal experience as the family of an offender and a victim of crime. This didn't surprise me: in close to three years I had failed to find support services directly related to someone like me. There were millions of people incarcerated in the world, but where were their family members? How were they coping? Who was helping them face the shame, the stigma and the loss? Before this happened to me, I didn't know what went on in the aftermath of crime for the family of an offender. Now I knew. I knew the pain and anguish, and I also knew something about hope, forgiveness, compassion and love. What if instead of presenting an academic paper, I asked to tell my own story? What impact would that have on humanizing the criminal justice process?

I shared my story with the conference organizer and she immediately scheduled me into the program to speak from personal experience. I had two and a half weeks to prepare. I wrote my speech, and then chose ten of my paintings and collages to help illustrate my journey. I arranged some pictures of Jason and me and our families on poster board because I thought it would help people to put faces to names. I asked my mum if she would accompany me to Mexico and she was enthusiastic; my dad had to work but sent messages of support via email. My talk had been scheduled for the morning of September 25, the day between Jason's birthday and mine, the day we'd called the "unbirthday." This year the date was going to take on new meaning: it was going to be my re-birthday.

In a room filled with almost a hundred restorative justice professionals, as well as judges, lawyers, victims and students, I started at the beginning, explaining how I met Jason, and I told my whole story up to the present. When I finished, I was amazed to see there was barely a dry eye in the audience, and a loud applause filled the room. The translator rushed from her booth at the back and threw her arms around me, sobbing. I straightened up to face the audience, standing taller than I had for ages. I answered questions for close to an hour. One was from a judge, who asked me what she could do in her

courtroom to make things easier on the families of the defend-
ants presented to her. Afterward, many more people came forward to tell me their stories. Some were victims of offences;
some were family members of people in prison; some were like
me: both. They knew exactly what I was talking about. I wasn't
alone. The mothers in the group talked to my mother. The reaction of the audience reassured me that what I had believed for
so long was true: that we, as human beings, have a profound
longing to be connected to one another through our experiences
of love and loss, and that there are many, many people who
feel that justice, as it plays out in courtrooms around the world,
rarely fosters healing for anyone touched by crime. It is this
connection that can bring about triumph over tragedy.

The next day, I turned thirty-three. I was surrounded by new
friends as the conference drew to a close. When I returned to
Canada, doors to a new chapter of my life began to fly open.
I received invitations to speak to inmates, family members, victims and law enforcement officials; to address university students and faculty at several universities in North America; and
to speak to a large audience that included many Correctional
Service professionals at Canada's national restorative justice
conference. Each time I told my story, I was rewarded with the
experience of having been heard. Audience members often
approached me to share their stories too. Somehow, standing
up and saying "this is what happened to me" made it okay for
others to express their own struggles and losses. I received letters from inmates who said hearing my story helped them realize what they'd put their families through. I received e-mails
from relatives of offenders asking for advice, resources, or
simply if they could tell me their own story. I was buoyed by
the responses of police officers, lawyers, judges and victims'

services workers who said they planned to examine the way they worked with offenders' families. I was inspired to hear about programs that resulted in sharp decreases in youth violence in New Zealand, Brazil and Colombia, and about communities engaging in restorative dialogues in Canada. I was honoured and humbled to meet some of the leaders of the truth and reconciliation commissions in South Africa and Rwanda. The positive synergy was infectious.

When I returned from Mexico, Jason congratulated me on my accomplishment and all it was leading to. "I'm proud of you," he said. "You're going to be fine—more than fine. I think this is only the beginning." Before I told my story again, I needed to consult him. I could only make a meaningful contribution by sharing openly, and that meant exposing him. His identity had only briefly been protected under a publication ban, but I still needed to know how he felt.

"Is all this okay with you?" I asked.

"It has to be," he said. "For one thing, I don't deserve to be protected after what I put you and everyone through, but more importantly, if I support the work you're doing, then maybe in some small way I'm making a contribution."

I was thankful for his attitude.

Then he changed the subject. "Have you thought any more about the divorce?" He'd mentioned it a few times over the summer, but I'd been too busy or too tired to do anything about it.

"I guess it's time," I said.

I downloaded the standard forms from the Internet, but before I could arrange for Jason to sign them, he was transferred to Millhaven maximum-security prison for an assessment to determine in which penitentiary he would serve his sentence.

He was told he'd be placed within a couple of weeks—the divorce forms would have to wait.

When he first transferred to Millhaven, west of Kingston, I wanted to visit, but Jason protested. "I don't want you to see this place." It was infamous for poor conditions, fights and riots. He was allowed out for a walk around the track every few days, but that was about the only positive. "Besides," he said, "I won't be here long."

I had to admit, the better way for me to spend my time was building my life in Toronto.

At the end of his first week at Millhaven, Jason called and asked me if I could get in touch with his home institution—he wanted his correctional officer there to call Millhaven to make sure they knew he was there in holding. He had been without a shower or change of clothes for seven days, and he feared that only the officers who had driven him over and the ones who had checked him in knew where he was. There was no word as to when a meeting with a psychiatrist or psychologist would take place. I could hear distress in Jason's voice, but when I asked him how he was he told me, like always, not to worry about him, that he'd manage. He just wanted me to make that one call, which I did.

I remembered Una's advice from her deathbed: *Try not to take on other people's burdens.* And so there I was: I could fret and worry about Jason, or I could try to trust that he could look after himself.

CHAPTER THIRTY-FOUR

SMOKE, ASH, FLOWERS AND GLASS

Prison time moves at a pace far slower than that of the outside world. Jason's two weeks at Millhaven soon became two months with no sign of a transfer anytime soon. I kept busy teaching and preparing for more presentations at conferences. I went out a few times with a lawyer I'd met, and found myself subjected to the same ups and downs of dating as any other single person. It wasn't easy. In early November of 2008, a police officer called from Peterborough to let me know that since the investigation was now officially over, they could return evidence to me. They had several bags of items from my home. I could no longer remember what was missing from my house, other than the computer, which had long ago been returned and given away. This was a chance to tie up some loose ends; to literally clean up the mess after the disaster. I didn't tell anyone else about the call. Facing that evidence was something I needed to do on my own, and I didn't want anyone to try to talk me out of it.

And so, on November 7, 2008—three years to the date that the crimes occurred—I found myself back in Peterborough at the police station. The weather was beautiful, unlike three years earlier. I was welcomed by an officer who led me to the very room where I had sat with my parents and the sergeant the day I heard the news of Jason's crimes. The officer brought in three large boxes filled with paper and plastic bags. Each one had a tag and a number. He explained that I could look in each bag and if I wanted what was inside it, I would sign the tag and take that bag home. If I didn't want the contents, I could just leave them and they would be disposed of.

"What do you do with the discarded items?" I asked.

"We incinerate them at a facility near the nuclear power station."

Perfect. The idea of burning evidence—especially the video-tapes of the voyeurism—was relieving. It was what I had thought I would do with them, only I didn't have a fireplace, let alone an incinerator. These reminders would all disappear forever.

The officer took the first bag out of the box and put it on the table in front of me. I couldn't yet see inside. As I gingerly reached for the bag, he said, "Shannon, I just want to say, before we start, that while I've never met you, I know a lot about you—from the reports, from other officers, and from Detective Morgan—and for what it's worth, I think you deserve an award for what you've been through and how you handled it. A lot of people around here feel that way."

I was astonished. That officer probably never knew just how much his words meant to me, though I tried to convey my appreciation. I told him how much judgment and alienation I'd endured, and explained what had happened to me when I'd asked for help from the victims' services counsellor.

He shook his head. "Have you ever spoken to anyone about that?"

I explained it had been in my victim impact statement, but that nothing came of that disclosure.

"There is a lot we can all learn from this situation, a lot we can improve upon. Would you consider speaking to our officers sometime?" Just a few hours earlier, I believed I was on my way to the police station for the last time. But what if I came back in a different context? I would not be in one of these little interview rooms as a "victim" or "the wife of the accused," but instead as a partner in improving justice for all. I told the officer that I would be honoured to speak to him and any of his colleagues, any time. I also decided I would finally register with the sergeant a formal complaint about the victims' services counsellor.

Then I went back to the task at hand. I opened each bag and examined the contents. Some of the bags, like the ones containing scissors and duct tape covered with the victims' hair, I closed immediately and passed back to the officer. I concentrated on imagining the smoke rising from the fires that would burn them away and turn them to ash. I went on to the next bag and the next, until I'd looked through all of them.

I left the police station with only two items: a jacket of Jason's that he had already assured me he had not been wearing during the crimes, and the bottles of leftover caffeine and ephedra pills he had taken that day. The latter items I kept in case a doctor assessing or treating Jason in the future would want them for analysis. The jacket I kept because it was almost new and would make a good coat for someone in need.

I also left with something I hadn't predicted: a sense of vindication. The officer's words and attitude had made me feel pretty good. But as I drove to Toronto, I thought things through and imagined how things could have been, and my good feelings turned bittersweet. What if someone at the station had reached out to me earlier? What if I had been referred to someone who would have listened and advocated for me, giving me information and reassurance? What if victims' services had been able to see that families of offenders are victims too?

That night, back at home, I got out a new canvas. I painted it a very soft, washed-out blue, blending a pale yellow into the top-left corner. The sun was coming out. I glued a mosaic of clear glass to form a bumpy landscape along the bottom of the painting—sharp ground, but solid enough to walk on. Then from a photo I'd taken of the front garden of my former home, I clipped out the pink ballerina tulips and placed them on the canvas, growing out of the broken glass landscape. Hope personified in flowers. Last, I found a small photo of a burned house—one quite similar to my house in Peterborough—and glued it in the bottom-left corner. It represented what I understood "loss of innocence" to mean: the undeniable fact that what happened would always be with me. I could never go back to "before." I called the painting *Three Years Later*.

Winter came and went in a fury of snowstorms. Jason was finally classified and returned to the prison where he'd now spent almost half his life. Though he was deemed high risk to society, he was low risk to himself and others in an institution, so medium-security was where assessors decided he fit. He was put on a waiting list for an intensive sexual offender's treatment program and was told it would be three to five years before a space opened up. Knowing what I knew about Correctional Service time, I had to think it would be closer to eight or ten years, but at least he was on a list. In the meantime, he would work some kind of job, play board games, read books and write letters. Sometimes friends or family would visit—we would try to keep him connected. He would fight his own demons or deny them as he had before—the choice was his alone. At some point, he would come before the Parole Board, where hopefully he could request some counselling. There was still only one psychologist for over six hundred inmates at the prison, the biggest federal institution in the country.

Once Jason was transferred back, we were finally able to proceed with filing the divorce application. The completed forms now lay on my desk in a folder, signed by Jason, stamped by a commissioner of oaths, and reviewed by a lawyer over the course of the winter. All I had left to do was take them to the courthouse in downtown Toronto, swear an oath, and sign them myself. But every time I thought about that possibility, I got a big, fat, throbbing lump in my throat.

Finally, on the one-year anniversary of Jason's sentencing, in May 2009, I put the folder in my bag and headed downtown to the courthouse. I'd decided it would be best to lump two sad anniversaries together—sentencing and divorce—rather than tarnish another day on the calendar. A few hours later, I had stamped and signed documents in hand. As I left the courthouse, I noticed the winds had strengthened considerably from earlier in the day. I watched as people struggled against the gusts, dashing from their office buildings into subway stations or taxis. The world seemed as chaotic and messy as I felt inside. I now had the legal right to marry again, but it was still hard for me to imagine I'd be ready to exercise that right.

The next time Jason called, I gave him an update.

"It's done, over. We're divorced."

"I'm so sorry to have put you through all this," he said.

"I know." I was consoling myself as much as him. "I hope that we will find a way to be friends. I don't want to lose you from my life completely."

"I don't want that either. But I want to see you move ahead—to find someone else. Maybe now you can do that."

"I promise I'll try," I said, but wasn't sure how I'd keep my word.

At least now I could say I was actually divorced, though I still hated the word. I understood from other single friends that dating was a vulnerable experience at the best of times. I had the added complication of disclosing the fact that I'd been married, what had happened, and where things were at now. It was a lot for someone else to take in, but it was even more for me to share. Small talk ran its course pretty quickly when someone was trying to get to know me, but at least I could tell fairly early on what someone's character was made of by how they reacted to my story.

CHAPTER THIRTY-FIVE

THE FUTURE IN MY HANDS

On a hot July day I went to a family social at the prison, an annual event that gave inmates and visitors a break from the hard lines of the regular visiting room and a chance to be outside. Guests were given gifts, photographs were taken, and piles of food were served by inmate volunteers. It seemed the one day a year when visitors weren't treated as a nuisance. I was giddy from playing basketball and running around the court with Jason under the open summer sky. I felt a bizarre sense of freedom—this is what I had wanted for so long—to have one more chance to laugh with Jason, to be my old self, to run free instead of being trapped at a table bolted to the floor or separated by glass, every word and movement filmed and recorded. I had made it to this moment.

I smiled at the man in front of me: my friend, Jason. I looked past his tall silhouette, out beyond the basketball court to the football field, the inmate gardens, the cell ranges, the overseers' towers and the fences. Freedom lay beyond it all. I deserved a whole lot more than a life closed in with fences. I was standing in a prison, and I didn't have to be. There was nothing and no one holding me there but me. The future was in my hands.

I didn't see or talk to Jason for a long time after that. A riot at the prison the following week kept him in lockdown for months, and my speaking engagements frequently took me away. When home, I taught full-time at a new school with a principal who believed in me and the work I was doing. In and out of the school, he thought I was a good role model for young people. My students energized me during the week, and I used weekends to do what Howard Zehr, and by now many more people, had suggested: write my story.

I began volunteering as a restorative justice circle-keeper with Peacebuilders International. Making space for victims to tell their stories and have their needs addressed felt amazing. Helping young people understand the impact of their actions, what had led to their choices and mistakes, and creating restitution agreements felt very gratifying. Listening to judges rule that young people follow those agreements and therapy orders instead of going to jail was hopeful. Over several years, not one youth who had been in a Peacebuilders program had reoffended.

I also became involved with an inspiring youth organization called LOVE—Leave Out ViolencE. My new friend Katy Hutchison—a family victim of homicide and Canadian advocate for restorative justice—and I developed a workshop on forgiveness, which we called "The F-Word." Later, I was invited to become a member of the Forgiveness Project, an organization that explores forgiveness, reconciliation and conflict resolution through telling the stories of people affected by crime and violence around the world. Now, instead of feeling stigmatized, I felt solidarity.

Preparing to publish my story for the Forgiveness Project, I realized that though I had taken every precaution outlined in the publication bans to protect all the victims, I would be breaking the ban on my own name if I shared that I had been a victim of voyeurism. The last thing I wanted was to be in violation of a court order, but neither did I want to adopt a pseudonym. I had pushed my way beyond blame and shame and I had nothing to conceal anymore. The only thing to do was to return to court and try to have the publication ban on my name overturned—to win back my right to tell my own story, as myself. My mum also wanted the ban lifted off her name, so that I could speak to her experience as a victim. With the ban in place, the newspaper reporter referred to us in the article after Jason's sentencing as "character witnesses" rather than victims, which misled the readers, making it look like we were there to blindly support him, or even that we denied his guilt.

It took weeks to track down the documents I needed to take to the lawyer I'd hired—a woman known as the best victims' advocate in the country. As soon as I met her, I could tell she was dedicated, smart and an excellent listener, but when she told me her fees for arguing to reverse the ban, I was stunned.

"You mean to tell me that as a victim of the offence for which I sought the ban in the first place I will now have to pay almost five thousand dollars to tell my story?"

"I'm sorry," she said. "I know it doesn't seem right. If I could let you argue your own case, I would, but I'm not even sure there is precedent here. It will be better—and faster—if I help you." Looking at me with sympathy, she then offered to slash her rate by a third. Next, I set up a meeting at the Office for Victims of Crime (an advisory body to the Attorney General of Ontario) to find out if there was any financial aid I could apply for, since the bill would still be significant—even at a reduced rate. The chair of the OVC explained the organization's desperate need for funding. She explained that many victims approached her when they realized that the Crown was not their lawyer—that, in fact, if they wanted a lawyer to represent them as individuals, they would have to hire their own. "We don't have the resources to help," she said. "It's a big problem in our system." Indeed, I had made that very mistake: thinking that, as a victim, the Crown was my lawyer, when really I'd had no one. This was a problem I one day hoped to address. For now, I had to concentrate on my immediate needs. My mum offered to split the lawyer's fees with me and I was grateful.

A few weeks later, I returned to the courthouse in Peterborough and the very same judge who had sentenced Jason altered the order. It was done. I could be me, freely.

With all these challenges and activities, I hardly had time to feel lonely, and for the first time in four years, I stopped dreading the weekends and holidays. I still had trouble sleeping and the odd nightmare or panic attack, but overall, my PTSD symptoms were vastly improved, as were my depressive symptoms. I found myself looking forward to things again and accepted every invitation to a party I got. Months went by, then a year. Soon it was 2010. I'd made the 5-year mark I'd been given by my colleague in the beginning.

My new friend Angie invited me to a Valentine's Day party. Although it wasn't a singles' party, she said that there was a guy she wanted me to meet. I laughed, but promptly forgot about her matchmaking idea and instead made plans to attend the party with a female friend.

We got to the party and I was immediately drawn to an attractive man who arrived at the same time. I fell into easy small talk with him as we removed our coats and boots, and continued chatting over at the buffet table, quickly discovering we had many things in common: cycling, travel, food, music and other things we both loved.

Half an hour later, Angie spotted us, came over and said, "Great! I see you two have already met! Shannon, this is Mike—a fabulous guy, works in banking, loves art—and Mike, this is one of my favourite people, Shannon. She's a speaker, an advocate, an artist, and she's writing a book."

Oh boy. Here it comes, I thought.

"What's your book about?" Mike asked, on cue.

I could have said something vague like "restorative justice," and then changed the subject, but I didn't want to hide anymore. I was proud of my journey and of my work. My friends were proud of me, as was my whole family. I looked into Mike's eyes, took a deep breath and said, "It's the story of how I was happily married until my husband committed violent sexual assaults on two strangers while I was out of town five years ago."

Over the course of the next hour, I told him about the aftermath—the betrayal, the loss, the stigma, the press, the criminal trial, Jason's sentencing, and the divorce. As I described my journey over the past four years, Mike listened intently, stopping me occasionally to ask a perceptive question or to express empathy. He was respectful and seemed able to just take everything in. I felt so at ease with him, and scarcely noticed anyone else at the party.

As I finished, Mike took a deep breath and said, "You must be very brave. For someone who's been through so much, you seem so . . . normal."

"Thanks!"

"Another glass of wine?" he asked.

"Absolutely."

We continued to talk and laugh easily throughout the evening, and as the party came to an end, Mike offered to drive me home. When he dropped me off, I went upstairs to my cozy apartment, feeling happy but a little confused by the fact that he hadn't asked for my phone number or e-mail address. It didn't matter; I'd had a lovely evening with him.

The next afternoon I received an e-mail from Mike. I learned later that he'd simply Googled "Shannon restorative justice" and found my website. I read his message:

> It was great to meet you at last night's party. I thoroughly enjoyed our time together. I'm looking forward to hearing you try to convince me—over dinner, hopefully—that you hadn't planned all along to leave something behind in my car just to see me again. Call me and we'll find a suitable venue to reunite you with your gloves.

I smiled as I realized that I hadn't even noticed that my gloves were missing. Then I called him.

We made plans for dinner the following evening, and had a wonderful time. Our second date lasted all weekend, and our third date stretched out over a month as we quickly grew closer. In the spring, Mike accompanied me to Colorado for one of my speaking engagements. He sat in the audience next to my friend Rachael, telling her he had never met anyone with a heart like mine.

On the May long weekend that year, Mike took me to New York and, at the top of Belvedere Castle in Central Park, asked me to marry him. Joyfully, and with every fibre of my being, I said, "Yes!" I laughed and cried at the same time, overwhelmed with happiness and the promise of a new beginning.

Mike and I leave our New Year's Eve wedding in the early
hours of 2011.

Newton's third law of physics says, "To every action there is always an equal and opposite reaction." This came into my mind right after Jason's crimes and I held onto it, trusting that both scientific and spiritual forces would make it so. I had to believe that just as the most horrific, unimaginable situation had come about, so would a situation so beautiful and filled with joy one day—the equal and opposite reaction to violence and loss; something just as unimaginable. Not only is it possible, I told myself, but it is mathematically probable.

On my 36th birthday in September of 2011, Mike and I learned that we were expecting a baby. Two weeks later—on the day of my Canadian book launch, between media interviews—we went for an ultrasound. Holding my hand and watching the screen very closely for a heartbeat, Mike exclaimed, "There are two. I see two heartbeats!" The technician smiled and confirmed: we were expecting twins. We looked at each other, faces full of love, joy and amazement. Two perfect little lives were coming to us—the privilege of parenting was ours to embrace. Newton's law was proven again.

I'm often asked, "How's your new husband with all this?" The question usually comes in a caring, curious whisper and could be directed at many different aspects of my life: my book, my work, my forgiveness for Jason, and probably Jason himself. I never want to put words in his mouth, so I asked Mike what I should say. He told me he'd like a button that says, "I'm Mike and I'm fine with everything." I smiled, because that is truly how he is: loving, supportive, proud, understanding and *definitely* fine with everything.

The day after the launch, I began my official Canadian book tour which took us from coast to coast in eight days, though thirty media interviews, and to meet hundreds of readers from all walks of life. It was both exhausting and exhilarating, draining and energizing. Thankfully, Mike, my mum and dad came with me for different legs of my travel. I needed someone to be there just for me, so I could be there for others. My email inbox had already begun to fill up with messages from readers and from people who heard, saw or read the media interviews. I was overwhelmed by how many letters began with, "something like what happened to you, happened to me". I heard from the mothers, fathers, grandparents, sisters, brothers, neighbours and friends of people who had committed crimes and were serving time. They had lived with the same shame and loss that I knew; the same utter disappointment, confusion, sadness and stigma. I heard from victims who related to the healing journey, who had chosen a path of forgiveness, or who hoped they might choose that path one day. Judges, lawyers and legal professionals wrote to say they had never before considered the family of the offender, while others said they always tried to do what they could within the confines of the system. Victims' services groups asked me to come and speak or bought the book for training purposes—one agency said they were revisiting their definition of 'victim' and looking at ways to reach out to the family of an accused person. The response from across the country humbled me greatly at the same time as it assured me that what I had gone through wasn't for nothing, and my choice to write about it could make a difference. There was something good that could come out of everything bad.

Of course I had my critics, too—though they mainly posted their comments on the webpages of newspapers under pseudonyms, never writing to me directly. The harshest critiques came from those who could not get past the fact that I had married Jason knowing about his past, and were convinced that I should have known—somehow seeming to view my trust as a crime, one that should exempt me from having a voice or deserving help. Opening myself up to renewed judgment and criticism was (at times) a high price to pay for all the good that came with my book's publication, and I worked hard not to let it get me down. I cringed at many of the headlines given to articles about me or my book—they were the expected: lurid and sensational—but there was little I could do about them. The double flood of hormones that comes with a twin pregnancy made me extra-sensitive, and I did my best to keep my focus on responding to the great compassion of so many Canadians, to thanking the many thoughtful journalists who gave me a voice with integrity, and to the healthy growth of the delicate lives inside me. I reminded myself of what my mum always says, "Your story is your story. You can't change it to please other people." She is right.

My little twin embryos proved to be very good travellers and together we continued touring the country over the following few months, even making it as far north as Whitehorse in Yukon Territory. From each of my trips, I came home with the intangible gifts of important memories and the feeling that attitudes toward families of offenders could change. Sometimes I came home with tangible gifts: in Whitehorse, I was given a handmade dreamcatcher for my babies' room made by a woman inmate at the jail where I spoke; in Winnipeg, a "lifer" who read my book and helped organize my talk at the prison made me a beautiful leather bag. These gifts remind me that none of us is one-dimensional—that people who do terrible things can also be the creators of beauty. We don't live in a black-and-white world; issues of crime and justice are never simple. We don't have labels on our foreheads that say, "good" or "evil". It might be easier if we did, but we don't. I will never condone the violent or harmful acts of Jason or anyone, but nor can I plaster a simple term like "monster" on an individual. Knowing what I know, I don't have that luxury.

I haven't seen Jason for quite a long time. I just hate going to the prison itself; I never know how I'm going to be treated, whether there is going to be some kind of problem or delay getting in, or how I'm going to feel during and after my visit. After my last visit, I felt like I had an emotional hangover for a day and a half. There were so many reminders of everything that happened, and talking to Jason somehow felt more like an awkward conversation with an acquaintance than a heart-to-heart with someone I once shared a life with. I guess a lot of people whose marriages break apart feel like that—you don't need prison walls between you to make you strangers to one another. Months later, after learning from my mum that I was pregnant, Jason called to offer his congratulations. He sounded much more like the old Jason I'd known, and truly happy for Mike and me. It was a nice conversation. I think on some level it helps him to see me fulfill the life dreams he took away; maybe the alleviation of some part of his massive guilt will make him more capable of one day getting to the root of his offending behaviour, of his "dark side". I'll never advocate for his release from prison, but I do hope that he can make the most of his time inside and that more answers can be found as to why he did what he did.

As time goes on and new memories are created, the old memories have begun their retreat into the shadows. Anger at Jason does resurface when I speak or think of his disgusting violence and remember all the details or picture it happening. Other times, the sadness and trauma of what happened gets triggered and I have to work through it, fighting against resentment. Over the years, I've had to train my mind to let these painful memories and images enter my thoughts and then leave again, or I risk damaging the new health and happiness I've found. Forgiveness has turned out to be a decision I have to revisit and remake over and over. Though some people say that forgiveness is weak, or that it lets someone off the hook, I know differently. Choosing forgiveness over and over again has been one of the hardest things I've ever had to do, but what it does is let *me* off the hook; it releases *me* from a lifetime bond to the violence and betrayal that I hate so much, and makes trust and love possible again.

Somewhere in the middle of my book tour Mike and I managed to sell our condo and buy a family home in a tree-lined Toronto neighbourhood. We settled in as quickly as we could and set up the nursery. After all my travelling, I was happy to declare myself on maternity leave and trade in my daily vocabulary of "crime, violence and prison" for "diapers, sleepers and lullabies". Our daughters made their arrival in early May, making our family complete and bringing with them the sweetness and innocence that only new life can. How I love to hold them in my arms!

June 2012

ACKNOWLEDGEMENTS

It is with a grateful and humble heart that I extend my appreciation to the following people, without whom this story would be absent of hope and healing:

To my mum, Pat—a velvet rock whose love knows no bounds—and my dad, Pete, a gardener of more than just flowers—for modelling resilience, commitment and compassion. To my brother, Kevin, for steadfast love, and for the one moment of levity in this book. To Trang, for her joyful spirit and helping hands. To my dear sister, for her quiet conviction, her efforts to comfort me, and her companionship through so many holidays and hard days.

To Jason, for working with me to transform our love into a supportive friendship, for being brave enough to let me share my story, and most of all, for being accountable. To Joan, Dave and Danielle, for comfort and togetherness in crisis.

To my husband, Mike, whose love, support, confidence and energy make everything easier, for giving me back built-in fun and laughter on a daily basis, and for embracing the work I do with overwhelming pride. To his family for welcoming me.

To my extended family of grandparents, aunts, uncles, cousins, and "long-armed cousins," particularly Paul and Sue, for their outreach and support. To my great-aunt, the late Sister Helena McCarthy, who told me when I was young to "err on the side of trust," and who exemplified strength during suffering.

To my Kingston family—Susan Gilger, Brian Yealland, Shirley Hornbeck, Dan Fraikin, and Una Beer—who enveloped me in their love and whose strength of conviction buoyed me when my reserves were low. To my teaching colleagues and members of the Martha's Table community who reached out.

To my friends, especially Rachael Pritchard, for her bravery and compassion. To Lisa McDonald, Peter Stevens and their beautiful blue-eyed buddhas for Friday-night dinners, comforting companionship and a key to their house. To Stephanie Howie for reminding me that I was a normal person in abnormal circumstances. To Jill Goodreau for listening and a place to write. To Jorge Nef for contagious energy. To B & E for inspiration and many late-night conversations. To Georgina and Mark for their example of community. To Colleen for sisterly companionship and understanding. To Sandra Fuller for solidarity. To Daniel Shipp, Trent Parmiter and Ramsey Hart for their open hearts. To Justine Dawson for the meditation. To Pam Hart for a steady stream of cards and phone messages. To Fay Laderoute for warmth and spunk. To David Francey for the gift of music and old-fashioned letters. To Katy Hutchison for openly sharing insight and experiences from her own journey through the fire.

To Dr. Sue Gleeson for her dedication, insight and the healing prescription of art therapy.

To defence attorney Connie Baran-Gerez for making every effort to humanize the justice system, and for listening.

To Cathy Belanger, Beryl Orok, Randy Dyer, and all those who extended compassionate support from inside the walls.

To my circle formed in England, especially Ana Vacas, Anne Dismorr and Nigel Brimms, Vanessa Currie, Cristina Read, Grace Udodong, Susana Armenta, Citlalli Berecil, "Rafa-Uno" Guerrero Rodriguez, "Rafa-Dos" Calderon Contreras and Ann Lewis.

To my circle that remains in Peterborough, especially my neighbours and colleagues who reached out.

To Rosa, Bea and the community of Angla, Ecuador, for friendship and love across miles.

To Community Justice Initiatives of Kitchener-Waterloo, Bereaved Families of Ontario (Toronto Chapter), and Canadian Families and Corrections Network, and the dedicated staff, volunteers and donors who keep them going. To my restorative justice facilitators Jennifer Davies and Judah Outshoorn for restoring me, and to Mark Yantzi for pioneering and connecting.

To my wonderful students at Oakville Trafalgar High School—*Muchísimas gracias*. To the supportive staff, especially Pam Calvert, Terry Ruf, Peter Stevens, Kathleen Carroll and Julie Hunt-Gibbons.

To the many, many more people who became part of my Golden Circle through their acts of kindness and compassion. I cannot name each of you here, but your names are forever etched on the pages of my heart.

—

For helping my story become a book, I offer heartfelt thanks: to my agent, Beverley Slopen, for embracing me and my story and teaching me that "structure is everything". To Terry Fallis and Meredith Lee for creating synergetic connections.

To my extraordinary editor at Doubleday Canada, Nita Pronovost, for her gentleness, tenacity, discernment, and for placing herself in my shoes.

To the rest of my Doubleday team: Nicola Makoway, Amy Black, Susan Burns, Bhavna Chauhan, Kristin Cochrane, Val Gow, Lynn Henry, Martha Leonard, Brad Martin, Scott Richardson, Tim Rostron and the many others working behind the scenes, for your support and encouragement. Special thanks to Brian Rogers for legal advice and copy editor Allyson Latta for thoughtful and meticulous parsing.

To my team at Simon & Schuster UK for their enthusiasm and

expertise, especially Kerri Sharp (Editor), Matt Johnson (Designer) and Emma Harrow (Publicist).

To Howard Zehr for encouraging me to write and for his revolutionary work in restorative justice. To writing coach Diana Claire-Douglas for helping me get organized.

To my many readers who patiently and delicately sifted through drafts, particularly Pat Moroney, Jason Staples, Ingrid Phaneuf, Pat Weber, Rachael Pritchard, Connie Baran-Gerez, Cathy Belanger, Lisa McDonald, Erin McCarthy, Detective Jeff Morgan, and my husband, Mike. Special appreciation to those for whom reading meant reliving.

To lawyer Jill Arthur at the Attorney General's Office for help deciphering documents and court records. To the staff at the courthouse in Peterborough for the same effort and for their transcription work. To lawyer Tony Bryant for a great conversation. To Dr. John Bradford at the Royal Ottawa Hospital for his generous time and lifelong dedication to advancing the understanding, diagnosis and treatment of his patients. To the many more professionals in the justice and mental health care systems who are not named herein, but whose guidance, expertise and support is nonetheless appreciated.

Finally, to the many people who have given me a voice by organizing, hosting and promoting speaking events, and to the audience members who offer insight and share their own stories. To The Forgiveness Project, the inspiring youth, staff and volunteers of Leave Out ViolencE (LOVE) and Peacebuilders International for allowing me to work with you to transform the power of violence into the power of peace.

RESOURCES AND RECOMMENDED READING

MEMOIRS

Hutchsion, Katy. *Walking After Midnight: One Woman's Journey Through Murder, Justice and Forgiveness*. Vancouver: Raincoast Books, 2006. Also visit www.katyhutchisonpresents.com.

Morris, Debbie (with Gregg Lewis). *Forgiving the Dead Man Walking*. Grand Rapids, Michigan: Zondervan Publishing House, 1998.

Prejean, Helen C.S.J. *Dead Man Walking: An Eyewitness Account of the Death Penalty in the United States*. New York: Random House, 1993.

Schwartz, Sunny (with David Bloodell). *Dreams from the Monster Factory: A Tale of Prison, Redemption, and One Woman's Fight to Restore Justice to All*. New York: Scribner, 2009. Also visit www.sunnyschwartz.com.

Virk, Manjit. *Reena: A Father's Story*. Victoria, BC: Heritage House Publishing, 2008.

REFERENCE

Black, D., J. Harris-Hendricks and T. Kaplan. *When Father Kills Mother: Guiding Children Through Trauma and Grief*. London: Routledge, 1993 (2nd ed. 2000).

Chödrön, Pema. *The Places That Scare You: A Guide to Fearlessness in Difficult Times*. Boston: Shambhala Publications, Inc., 1997.

Chödrön, Pema. *When Things Fall Apart: Heart Advice for Difficult Times*. Boston: Shambhala Publications, Inc., 2002.

Dussich, John P.J. and Jill Schellenberg, editors. *The Promise of Restorative Justice: New Hope for Criminal Justice and Beyond*. Boulder, Colorado: Lynne Reinner Publishers, 2010.

Fine, Carla. *No Time to Say Goodbye: Surviving the Suicide of a Loved One*. New York: Broadway Books, 1997.

Garbarino, James. *Lost Boys: Why Our Sons Turn Violent and How We Can Save Them*. New York: Random House, Inc., 1999.

Hannem, Stacey. *Marked by Association: Stigma, marginalisation, gender and the families of male prisoners in Canada*. PhD Dissertation. Ottawa: Carleton University, 2008. Available via: http://gradworks. umi.com/NR/47/NR47466.html

James, John W. and Russell Friedman. *The Grief Recovery Handbook: An Action Program for Moving Beyond Death, Divorce and Other Losses*. New York: Harper Collins Publishers, 1998.

Levine, Peter A. with Ann Frederick. *Waking the Tiger: Healing Trauma*. Berkeley, California: North Atlantic Books, 1997.

Nhat Hanh, Thich. *Peace Is Every Step: The Path of Mindfulness in Everyday Life*. New York: Bantam Books, 1991.

Pranis, Kaye, Barry Stuart and Mark Wedge. *Peacemaking Circles*. St. Paul, Minnesota: Living Justice Press, 2003.

Ross, Rupert. *Return to the Teachings: Exploring Aboriginal Justice*. Toronto: Penguin Canada, 1996.

Towes, Barb. *The Little Book of Restorative Justice for People in Prison: Rebuilding the Web of Relationships*. Intercourse, Pennsylvania: Good Books, 2006.

Withers, Lloyd. *Time Together: a survival guide for families and friends visiting in Canadian federal prisons*. Kingston, Ontario: CFCN (Canadian Families and Corrections Network), 2000.

Yantzi, Mark. *Sexual Offending and Restoration*. Waterloo: Herald Press, 1998.

Yoder, Carolyn. *The Little Book of Trauma Healing: When Violence Strikes and Community Security Is Threatened*. Intercourse, Pennsylvania: Good Books, 2005.

Zehr, Howard. *Changing Lenses: A New Focus for Crime and Justice*. Scottsdale, Pennsylvania: Herald Press, 2005.

Zehr, Howard. *Doing Life: Reflections of Men and Women Serving Life Sentences* (A book of portraits and interviews). Intercourse, Pennsylvania: Good Books, 1996.

Zehr, Howard. *The Little Book of Restorative Justice*. Intercourse, Pennsylvania: Good Books, 2002.

Zehr, Howard. *Transcending: Reflections of Crime Victims* (A book of portraits and interviews). Intercourse, Pennsylvania: Good Books, 2001.

ORGANIZATIONS AND SERVICE PROVIDERS

The Forgiveness Project works to help build a future free of conflict and violence, and empowers people to explore the nature of forgiveness and alternatives to revenge. **www.theforgivenessproject.com**

The International Institute for Restorative Practices (IIRP) is dedicated to the advanced education of professionals at the graduate level and to the conduct of research that can develop the growing field of restorative practices. They also offer training courses for schools and agencies. Based in Pennsylvania. **www.iirp.edu**

Prison Fellowship International (Centre for Justice and Reconciliation) provides information, statistics and resources on world prison populations, children living in prisons or with parents in prison, victim needs and restorative justice. **www.pfi.org/cjr**

European Forum for Restorative Justice aims to establish and develop victim-offender mediation and other restorative justice practices throughout Europe. **http://www.euforumrj.org/**

Restorative Justice Online is a clearing house of information including research tools, bibliographies, training, tutorials and expert articles. **www.restorativejustice.org**

Restorative Practices International offers training, resources and international conferences:
www.restorativepracticesinternational.org

Restorative Justice Council UK is the national voice for restorative practice, advocating for the development of restorative practice with Government and providing information to the public through its website and media work. **http://www.restorativejustice.org.uk/**

Restorative Solutions is a not-for-profit Community Interest Company committed to enabling the use of innovative restorative approaches as a practical and cost-effective intervention for reducing harm or conflict. **http://www.restorativesolutions.org.uk/**

Victim Support is a national charity giving free and confidential help to victims of crime, witnesses, their family, friends and anyone else affected across England and Wales. It also speaks out as a national voice for victims and witnesses and campaigns for change.
http://www.victimsupport.org/

Action for Prisoners' Families is a membership organization for those interested in the wellbeing of prisoners' and offenders' families. It provides advice, information, guidance and training to its members. Membership is free. **http://www.prisonersfamilies.org.uk/**

Offenders' Families Helpline UK: (toll free) 0808 808 2003 or **http://www.offendersfamilieshelpline.org/**

Partners of Prisoners and Families Support Group offers services developed and delivered by families, for families, to tackle the stigma, distress and practical issues that arise when supporting a relative in the Criminal Justice System. **http://partnersofprisoners.co.uk/**

For new additions to this list of resources, please visit
www.shannonmoroney.com